Supermarket Vegan

Supermarket
Vegan

225 Meat-Free, Egg-Free, Dairy-Free Recipes for Real People in the Real World

Donna Klein

A PERIGEE BOOK

A PERIGEE BOOK
Published by the Penguin Group
Penguin Group (USA) Inc.
375 Hudson Street, New York, New York 10014, USA
Penguin Group (Canada), 90 Eglinton Avenue East, Suite 700, Toronto, Ontario M4P 2Y3, Canada
(a division of Pearson Penguin Canada Inc.)
Penguin Books Ltd., 80 Strand, London WC2R 0RL, England
Penguin Group Ireland, 25 St. Stephen's Green, Dublin 2, Ireland (a division of Penguin Books Ltd.)
Penguin Group (Australia), 250 Camberwell Road, Camberwell, Victoria 3124, Australia
(a division of Pearson Australia Group Pty. Ltd.)
Penguin Books India Pvt. Ltd., 11 Community Centre, Panchsheel Park, New Delhi—110 017, India
Penguin Group (NZ), 67 Apollo Drive, Rosedale, North Shore 0632, New Zealand
(a division of Pearson New Zealand Ltd.)
Penguin Books (South Africa) (Pty.) Ltd., 24 Sturdee Avenue, Rosebank, Johannesburg 2196,
South Africa

Penguin Books Ltd., Registered Offices: 80 Strand, London WC2R 0RL, England

While the author has made every effort to provide accurate telephone numbers and Internet addresses at the time of publication, neither the publisher nor the author assumes any responsibility for errors, or for changes that occur after publication. Further, the publisher does not have any control over and does not assume any responsibility for author or third-party websites or their content.

First edition: January 2010

Library of Congress Cataloging-in-Publication Data

Klein, Donna (Donna M.)
  Supermarket vegan : 225 meat-free, egg-free, dairy-free recipes for real people in the real world / Donna Klein.
    p. cm.
  Includes index.
  ISBN 978-0-399-53561-1
  1. Vegan cookery. I. Title.
  TX837.K5476 2010
  641.5'636—dc22   2009028030

PRINTED IN THE UNITED STATES OF AMERICA

10 9 8 7 6 5 4 3 2 1

The recipes contained in this book are to be followed exactly as written. The publisher is not responsible for your specific health or allergy needs that may require medical supervision. The publisher is not responsible for any adverse reactions to the recipes contained in this book.

For Emma and Sarah,
my real-life heroes

Contents

Acknowledgments

Tremendous thanks to my literary agent, Linda Konner, and the staff and crew at Perigee, namely John Duff and Jeanette Egan, for making my sixth cookbook possible—wow!

Sincere thanks to the vegetarian and vegan communities for their continuing support and encouragement.

Special thanks to my canine hero, Trevor, for holding down the fort and keeping us real.

Introduction

Life's fast pace can leave anyone with no time to cook, let alone time to shop for all the ingredients. For vegans, the challenge is typically compounded by the extra weekly trek (or two) to the health food store, along with the daily grind of prepping countless fruits, vegetables, grains, and legumes. With the help of *Supermarket Vegan*, followers of a plant-based diet will never again have to compromise health and nutrition when they're on the run. This cookbook offers healthful dishes free of meat, eggs, and dairy, using simple, straightforward ingredients that require a minimal amount of preparation, all with just a quick trip to your local grocery store—no specialty items from the health food store, co-op, or whole foods market necessary.

Indeed, as more and more people are turning toward a healthier diet and lifestyle, an increasing number of conventional supermarkets are stocking a treasure trove of vegan-friendly convenience items, such as precut and washed fresh fruits and vegetables; bagged salads and slaws; exotic frozen fruits and vegetables, such as mango and edamame beans; whole wheat pastas and Asian noodles, such as cellophane, rice, soba, and somen noodles; quick-cooking grains, such as bulgur, couscous, polenta, and quinoa; whole wheat pitas, wraps, and pizza crusts; a wide assortment of canned beans and lentils; prepared salsas and hummus; and an extensive array of international sauces, chutneys, olives, and other condiments. By finding new and innovative ways to use these products, this book presents you with many memorable recipes, from appetizers to desserts, all made with real food. No meat analogs, such as seitan, tempeh, and textured vegetable protein (TVP), or egg and dairy substitutes are needed. Moreover, most recipes are ready in forty-five minutes (or less), require ten ingredients (or less), and are easy on the budget to boot.

Healthy eating is more important than ever when you're trying to keep up with a hectic schedule. When real-life people become overwhelmed and overly busy, it's all too easy to slip into poor eating habits. As a result, we feel depleted and run down, bereft of the precious time and vital energy we need to pursue our everyday activities and ultimate purpose in life. Find some time to incorporate a few of *Supermarket Vegan*'s real-deal recipes into your daily cooking routine, and find more time for the rest of your life.

GLOSSARY OF INGREDIENTS

Barley A hardy, ancient grain used in soups, stews, cereals, breads, and beer. The most common variety found in conventional supermarkets is pearl barley, which has had the bran removed and has been steamed and polished. Though less nutritious than husked or whole-grain barley, pearl barley is still a good source of soluble fiber and is available in regular and quick-cooking forms.

Black bean sauce An Asian sauce or condiment typically made of fermented black soybeans, sugar, flour, garlic, and soy sauce.

Bulgur A cracked wheat made from the whole kernel that has been cooked and dried. It is most commonly used in Middle Eastern tabbouleh salad.

Cajun seasoning A boldly flavored dry seasoning blend from Louisiana, typically containing garlic, chilies, onion, black pepper, mustard, and celery.

Capers The unopened flower buds of a shrub native to the Mediterranean region. After curing in salted white vinegar, the buds develop a sharp, salty-sour flavor and are used as a flavoring and condiment.

Chinese chili paste A fiery Asian blend of hot chili peppers, garlic, oil, and salt; also known as Chinese chili sauce.

Chinese hot chili oil A fiery condiment typically made from soybean oil that has been infused with dried chili peppers; also known as hot oil, red oil, hot sauce, hot pepper oil, or chili oil.

Chipotle chilies in adobo sauce Chipotle chilies in adobo sauce are smoked jalapeño chilies canned in a flavorful red sauce that typically contains tomato puree, onion, vinegar, garlic, oregano, and cumin. Because the seeds are included, the chilies and sauce can be quite hot. This product should not be confused with commercial brands of chipotle sauce, a spicy, smoky-sweet condiment with a mild to moderate degree of heat.

Chipotle powder The dried, whole, smoked jalapeño chili, ground up into a fine powder. It has a spicy, smoky flavor and is not to be confused with chili powder, which is a milder blend of ground chilies and other spices. It can usually be found in the spice aisle, next to the standard chili powder, in most large supermarkets.

Chutney An East Indian relish consisting of fruits, generally raisins and mangoes, spices, herbs, sugar, and vinegar or lemon juice.

Couscous A granular semolina pasta of North African origin, typically available in conventional supermarkets in quick-cooking, precooked form.

Edamame The Japanese name for fresh soybeans, edamame beans are jade green and plump, with a creamy texture and nutlike flavor. Edamame beans are sold in or out of the pod, fresh or frozen, and must be eaten cooked, with the pods discarded. All the recipes in this book call for frozen shelled edamame.

Fennel Often mislabeled "anise," which is an annual herb, fennel is an aromatic plant with a bulbous base, celery-like stems, and bright green, feathery fronds; both the base and stems can be eaten raw or cooked, while the fronds are used for garnish. The licorice-flavored seeds are available whole and ground and are used in both sweet and savory foods. Fresh fennel is available from fall through spring. Choose clean, crisp bulbs with no sign of browning and bright green fronds with no sign of shriveling. Refrigerate, wrapped in plastic, three to five days.

Five-spice powder A pungent Chinese blend of five ground spices, typically consisting of equal parts cinnamon, cloves, fennel seed, star anise, and Szechuan peppercorns.

Ginger A tropical root plant with a tan skin and gnarled, bumpy appearance, fresh ginger is a mainstay in Asian, Indian, and Caribbean cuisines. The flavor is peppery and slightly sweet, while the aroma is pungent and spicy. The mature ginger found in most conventional supermarkets has a tough skin, which must be peeled.

When purchasing mature ginger, look for plump roots with smooth, unwrinkled skins and a fresh, spicy fragrance. Fresh unpeeled ginger, wrapped in plastic, can be refrigerated for up to three weeks.

Gnocchi Italian for "dumplings," gnocchi (pronounced NYOH-kee) can be made from potatoes, wheat flour, or farina. Sometimes eggs or cheese can be added to the dough, so check the label carefully. Frozen and vacuum-packed gnocchi (usually found near the dried pasta or jarred pasta sauces) are available in many conventional supermarkets.

Hoisin sauce A sweet and spicy Asian condiment, also called Chinese barbecue sauce, hoisin is a thick and dark sauce made from a combination of fermented soybeans, garlic, vinegar, sugar, chilies, and other spices.

Hominy Dried white or yellow corn kernels from which the hull and germ have been removed either mechanically or chemically by soaking the corn in slaked lime or lye. Canned hominy can be found in most conventional supermarkets, either near the canned corn or in the international food aisle among the Hispanic foods.

Jerk seasoning A spicy and dry Caribbean seasoning blend, generally consisting of a combination of chilies, garlic, onions, thyme, and other spices, such as cinnamon, ginger, allspice, and cloves; also known as Jamaican jerk seasoning.

Jicama Often referred to as the Mexican potato, jicama (pronounced HEE-kah-mah) is a large, bulbous root vegetable that has a thin, brown skin; white, crunchy flesh; and a sweet, nutty flavor. It is eaten both raw and cooked, and the skin should be peeled just before using. Available from November through May in most large supermarkets, jicama can be stored in the refrigerator in a plastic bag up to two weeks.

Kalamata olives Large, black, highly prized Greek olives with a fleshy, succulent texture, kalamata olives are pickled in wine vinegar, which produces a pronounced flavor of salt and vinegar.

Liquid smoke Made from water that has captured the flavor of smoke, liquid smoke adds smoky barbecue flavor to food without using a grill. Because the flavor is highly concentrated, liquid smoke should be used sparingly. It can be located near the barbecue sauces in most major supermarkets.

Masa harina A dry corn flour made from a special lime-processed dough derived from wet hominy. It can be found in the international aisle of many well-stocked supermarkets.

Mesclun A French term for a mix of assorted small, young salad greens, sometimes called spring mixes or spring blends. The mix generally includes arugula (rocket),

Swiss chard, mustard greens, endive, dandelion, frisée, mizuna, oak leaf, mâche, radicchio, sorrel, and/or other leafy vegetables. Bagged salads labeled "mixed spring greens" can be used interchangeably with mesclun.

Mirin Also known as rice wine, mirin is a low-alcohol, sweet, golden wine made from glutinous rice. Essential to Japanese cuisine, it adds sweetness and flavor to a variety of dishes, sauces, and glazes.

Mushrooms *Cremini mushrooms* are cultivated brown mushrooms with a rich and pronounced flavor that strongly mimics the flavor of wild mushrooms. Also known as "baby bellas," creminis are actually immature portobello mushrooms. Store cremini mushrooms in the refrigerator in their original container, or wrap tightly in plastic wrap, and use within 24 hours of purchasing. *Portobello mushrooms* are extremely large, dark brown mushrooms that are the fully mature form of cremini mushrooms. Valued for their dense, succulent, and meaty texture, portobellos are typically eaten grilled, broiled, or baked in their whole form, or sautéed in their sliced form. Store portobello mushrooms in the refrigerator in their original container, or wrap tightly in plastic wrap, and use within 24 hours of purchasing.

Noodles *Cellophane noodles* are thin, transparent Asian noodles typically made from mung bean starch; also known as bean threads or glass noodles. *Rice noodles* are flat (stir-fry or linguine style) or thin (rice vermicelli) long Asian noodles made from rice flour and water, which are used in soups, spring rolls, cold salads, stir-fries, or are deep-fried until crispy. Generally sold in bundle form, they can be located in most major supermarkets in the Asian foods section of the international aisle. *Soba noodles* are Japanese noodles made from buckwheat and wheat flour, with a dark, brownish-gray color. *Somen noodles* are thin, white Japanese noodles made from wheat flour. Soba and somen noodles can be found in most large supermarkets in the Asian foods section of the international aisle.

Orzo pasta A tiny pasta shaped like grains of rice that is frequently used in soups and pasta salads. It can be found among the dried pastas in most supermarkets.

Panko breadcrumbs Lightly toasted, unseasoned Japanese-style breadcrumbs characterized by big, light, crunchy flakes. They can be found in most large supermarkets in the Asian foods section of the international aisle.

Pepperoncini (Peperoncini) Also called Tuscan peppers, these thin, 2- to 3-inch-long chilies have a slightly sweet flavor and a heat ranging from medium to medium-hot. They are most often sold pickled, in jars, and can be found in the condiment aisle of most supermarkets.

Polenta Popular in Northern Italy and Latin America, polenta is coarsely ground yellow cornmeal, which is cooked into a porridgelike consistency with broth or water. Regular and instant polenta are both available in many supermarkets, in the international or specialty foods aisle. Coarse-ground yellow cornmeal can be substituted for regular polenta.

Quinoa An ancient whole grain (technically not a true cereal grain) indigenous to South America, originally used by the Incas, quinoa (pronounced KEEN-wah) is unique among grains as it contains essential amino acids that make it a complete protein. It can be found in either the specialty foods aisle or among the rice and other grains in many large supermarkets. For best results, rinse well under cold water before cooking to remove any bitter-tasting resin, or saponin.

Radicchio A popular Italian salad green, radicchio is a red-leaf member of the chicory family, possessing firm yet tender leaves with a slightly bitter flavor. Most commonly eaten raw in salads, it may also be cooked by grilling, sautéing, baking, or braising. Radicchio is available year-round, with a peak season from midwinter to early spring. Choose heads that have crisp, full-colored leaves with no sign of browning. Store in a plastic bag in the refrigerator for up to one week.

Rice *Arborio rice* is rounded, medium-grain rice from Italy that is both firm and creamy when cooked. It is the traditional rice in risotto. *Basmati rice* is fragrant, long-grain rice from Pakistan and India characterized by a nutty flavor and popcornlike aroma. *Jasmine rice* is delicately scented, softly textured, long-grain rice from Thailand, frequently used in Southeast Asian cuisine.

Tahini Tahini, or sesame tahini, is a thick, Middle Eastern paste made of ground raw (sometimes roasted) sesame seeds; it is an essential ingredient in authentic hummus. Tahini can be found in most large supermarkets in the international or specialty foods aisle, as well as the condiment and salad dressing section.

Salt, coarse A larger grained sea salt crystal, which is derived directly from a living ocean or sea. Typically unrefined, it has a bright, pure, clean flavor, and contains traces of other minerals, including iron, magnesium, calcium, potassium, manganese, zinc, and iodine.

Sesame oil, toasted (or dark) An Asian variety of sesame oil with a dark color and an intense, nutty flavor and aroma. Valued as a condiment, it is used sparingly in cooking. Toasted, or dark, sesame oil can be found in the international aisle or condiment and salad dressing section of many large supermarkets. For best results, select those brands consisting only of pure, or 100 percent, sesame oil.

Tamari sauce A Japanese soy sauce that is fermented from one to three years, and has a mellow, intense flavor. Unlike other varieties of soy sauce, which contain wheat, traditional tamari sauce is typically wheat-free; however, those with wheat allergies or gluten intolerance should check the label carefully, as some brands may contain wheat.

Thai curry paste Thai curry paste comes in both red and green forms. Thai red curry paste is a hot-and-spicy concentrated mixture of dried red chilies and seasoned spices, which typically consist of onion, garlic, galangal, lemon grass, kafir lime zest, cilantro root, peppercorn, and salt. Thai green curry paste is made with green chilies and, as a result, is slightly milder; otherwise, it contains the same ingredients as the red variety. Both can be found in the international aisle or condiment section of many large supermarkets.

Tomatoes, sun-dried Sun-dried tomatoes are chewy, intensely flavored, dark red tomatoes that have been dried in the sun or by artificial methods. They are either packed in oil or dry-packed. The dry-packed type should be rehydrated in water or other liquid before use. Both types are available in most large supermarkets: the dry-packed variety can sometimes be found in the produce section, around the dried wild mushrooms, while the oil-packed variety can usually be located in the condiment section, near the marinated artichokes.

Vinegars *Balsamic vinegar* is a mellow Italian vinegar, made from white Trebbiano grape juice. It gets its dark color and pungent sweetness from aging in barrels, made of various woods and in graduating sizes, over a period of years. *Rice vinegar* is made from fermented rice; Japanese rice vinegar is almost colorless and is milder than most Western vinegars. It comes in two types: natural (or plain) and seasoned. Both can be found in either the international aisle or the condiment and salad dressing section of most large supermarkets.

Wheat germ Derived from the heart of the wheat berry, wheat germ is a good source of protein, B vitamins, vitamin E, and iron. It has a nutty flavor and crunchy texture, and is often added to baked goods, or sprinkled on cereal, casseroles, and gratins. It can be found in the cereal aisle of most supermarkets.

ABOUT THE NUTRITIONAL NUMBERS

All of the nutritional analyses in this book were compiled using MasterCook Deluxe 4.06 Software, from SierraHome. However, as certain ingredients (gnocchi, instant miso soup) were unknown to the software at the time of compilation, substitutes of equivalent caloric and nutritional value were used in their place. All of the recipes using broth have been analyzed using low-sodium canned vegetable broth. All of the recipes using rinsed and drained canned beans have been analyzed using freshly cooked dried beans. Unless salt is listed as a measured ingredient (versus to taste, with no preceding suggested measurement) in the recipe, or unless otherwise indicated, no salt has been included in the analysis; this applies to other seasonings (black pepper, cayenne, etc.) as well. None of the recipes' optional ingredients, unless otherwise indicated, has been included in the nutritional analyses. If there is a choice of two or more ingredients in a recipe (for example, pine nuts or slivered almonds), the first ingredient has been used in the analysis. Likewise, if there is a choice in the amounts of a particular ingredient in a recipe (for example, 2 to 4 tablespoons low-sodium vegetable broth, plus additional, as necessary), the first amount has been used in the analysis. If there is a range in the number of servings a recipe yields (for example, 4 to 6 servings), the analysis has been based on the first amount.

Appetizers and Snacks

First impressions count, and the appetizers and hors d'oeuvres in this chapter aim to please. With a minimal amount of time and effort, most can be thrown together while your stew simmers on the stove or your dessert bakes in the oven. Several can be made the night before. All are a wonderful way to begin a meal, whether it's the Golden Tomato Bruschetta to complement your pasta party, the Curried Spinach Fondue with pita to presage your Indian feast, or the Chipotle Guacamole with tortilla chips to kick-off your Super Bowl fiesta. But if it's a snack you're looking for, why wait for a party?

Artichoke, Chickpea, and Spinach Dip

 Makes 6 to 8 servings

This dip or spread is also delicious served with crispy store-bought flatbread and bagel chips.

1 (15-ounce) can chickpeas, rinsed and drained

1 cup baby spinach leaves

1 (6-ounce) jar quartered marinated artichoke hearts, drained

¼ cup extra-virgin olive oil

2 large cloves garlic, finely chopped

1 to 2 tablespoons fresh lemon juice

½ teaspoon salt, or to taste

Freshly ground black pepper, to taste

Pita bread, pita chips, toasted baguette rounds, bread sticks, or raw vegetables, to serve

In a food processor fitted with the knife blade, or in a blender, process all the ingredients, except the bread, until smooth and pureed. Transfer to a serving bowl and serve at room temperature, accompanied with the pita bread. Alternatively, cover and refrigerate a minimum of 1 hour or up to 2 days and serve chilled, or return to room temperature.

Per serving (without pita bread): Calories 166 | Protein 5g | Total Fat 10g | Sat. Fat 1g | Cholesterol 0mg | Carbohydrate 15g | Dietary Fiber 2g | Sodium 215mg

Avocado-Tahini Dip with Lemon

 Makes 8 servings

Here is a great party dip you can make the night before; the lemon juice prevents the avocado from becoming brown.

Juice of 2 medium lemons (about 6 tablespoons)

¼ cup sesame tahini

4 large cloves garlic, finely chopped

½ teaspoon salt, or to taste

Freshly ground black pepper, to taste

Cayenne pepper, to taste (optional)

2 large ripe avocados, peeled, pitted, and mashed

1 to 2 tablespoons finely chopped fresh flat-leaf parsley (optional)

Sweet paprika (optional)

Raw vegetables, pita chips, pita bread, crispy flatbread, bagel chips, or crackers, to serve

In a medium bowl, stir together the lemon juice, tahini, garlic, salt, black pepper, and cayenne (if using). Add the avocado and parsley (if using), stirring well to thoroughly combine. Sprinkle lightly with the paprika (if using). Cover and refrigerate a minimum of 1 hour or up to 1 day and serve chilled, accompanied with the raw vegetables.

Per serving (without raw vegetables): Calories 131 | Protein 3g | Total Fat 12g | Sat. Fat 2g | Cholesterol 0mg | Carbohydrate 7g | Dietary Fiber 2g | Sodium 140mg

Spicy Red Bean Dip

Makes 4 to 6 servings

This also makes a delicious topping for tostadas and baked potatoes, or a filling for burritos, wraps, and tacos.

1 tablespoon extra-virgin olive oil

1 cup chopped onion

1 to 2 jalapeño chilies, seeded and finely chopped

2 large cloves garlic, finely chopped

½ teaspoon ground cumin

½ teaspoon salt, or to taste

¼ teaspoon sweet paprika

Freshly ground black pepper, to taste

1 (15-ounce) can red kidney beans, rinsed and
    drained

¼ cup low-sodium vegetable broth, or more, as
    necessary

Plantain chips or tortilla chips, to serve

In a small saucepan, heat the oil over medium heat. Add the onion and cook, stirring, until softened, about 3 minutes. Add the chili, garlic, cumin, salt, paprika, and pepper; cook, stirring constantly, 1 minute. Stir in the beans and broth and bring to a brisk simmer over medium-high heat, stirring often. Remove from heat and set aside to cool slightly.

In a food processor fitted with the knife blade, or in a blender, process the bean mixture until smooth, adding broth as necessary to achieve desired consistency. Serve warm, accompanied with the plantain chips. The dip can be stored, covered, in the refrigerator up to 3 days before reheating over low heat.

Per serving (without chips): Calories 140 | Protein 7g | Total Fat 4g | Sat. Fat 1g | Cholesterol 0mg | Carbohydrate 20g | Dietary Fiber 5g | Sodium 170mg

Tuscan-Style Crostini with White Beans and Sage

Makes 4 servings

This rustic crostini topping is also wonderful served with crispy flatbread and breadsticks or spread over plain focaccia and prebaked pizza shells. Rosemary can replace the sage, if desired.

1½ tablespoons extra-virgin olive oil

1 to 2 large cloves garlic, finely chopped

1 (15-ounce) can cannellini or other white
    beans, rinsed and drained

2 to 4 tablespoons low-sodium vegetable
    broth, or more, as necessary

1 tablespoon finely chopped fresh sage,
    or about ½ teaspoon dry rubbed sage

½ teaspoon coarse salt, or to taste

Freshly ground black pepper, to taste

Toasted baguette rounds or toasted halved
    Italian bread, to serve (see Cook's Tip,
    below)

In a small heavy-bottomed saucepan, heat the oil over medium-low heat. Add the garlic and cook, stirring, until fragrant and softened but not browned, about 2 minutes. Add the beans, 2 tablespoons broth, sage, salt, and pepper; cook, stirring, until heated through, about 5 minutes, mashing the beans with the back of a wooden spoon (some should remain whole) and adding additional broth, as necessary, to achieve a spreadable consistency. Serve warm, spread over the baguette rounds.

Per serving (without bread): Calories 142 | Protein 7g | Total Fat 5g | Sat. Fat 1g | Cholesterol 0mg | Carbohydrate 17g | Dietary Fiber 6g | Sodium 255mg

Cook's Tip: *To toast the bread slices, preheat oven to 400F (205C). Arrange ½-inch-thick rounds of bread in a single layer on an ungreased, light-colored baking sheet. Bake on the middle oven rack 5 minutes, until lightly toasted.*

Curried Toasted Cashews

Makes 8 to 12 servings

Toss these curry-spiced cashews with golden and dark raisins to create a healthy and delicious party mix. They also lend pizzazz to hot cooked rice or couscous.

- 2 cups whole raw cashews
- 2 teaspoons canola oil
- 2 teaspoons mild curry powder
- ½ teaspoon salt, or to taste
- Pinch cayenne pepper, or to taste (optional)

Preheat oven to 300F (150C).

Place cashews in a shallow baking dish large enough to accommodate them in a single layer. Add the oil, curry powder, salt, and cayenne (if using) and toss well to thoroughly coat. Bake on the center rack about 25 minutes, until lightly toasted, turning halfway through cooking. Transfer baking dish to a wire rack and let cashews cool to room temperature before serving. Completely cooled nuts can be stored in an airtight container at room temperature up to 2 weeks.

Per ¼ cup: Calories 225 | Protein 8g | Total Fat 20g | Sat. Fat 2g | Cholesterol 0mg | Carbohydrate 7g | Dietary Fiber 3g | Sodium 138mg

Variations: *To make Cumin Toasted Cashews, use ground cumin in lieu of the curry powder. Blanched whole almonds can replace the cashews.*

Edamame Dip with Raw Vegetables

Makes 8 servings

This exotic jade-green dip also makes a terrific spread for rice crackers. Frozen edamame, or green soybeans, are increasingly available in major supermarkets. Frozen baby lima beans can be substituted, if necessary.

- 1 pound frozen shelled edamame (green soybeans), cooked according to package directions, drained
- ½ to ¾ cup low-sodium vegetable broth, or more, as necessary
- 2½ tablespoons extra-virgin olive oil
- ½ tablespoon toasted (dark) sesame oil
- 3 to 4 large cloves garlic, finely chopped
- 1 tablespoon fresh lime juice, or to taste
- 1 teaspoon sugar
- ½ teaspoon salt, or to taste
- Freshly ground black pepper, to taste
- ¼ cup chopped fresh cilantro or basil (optional)
- Assorted raw vegetables, to serve

Rinse the edamame under cold running water until cold. Drain again. Transfer to a food processor fitted with the knife blade, or to a blender. Add ½ cup broth, olive oil, sesame oil, garlic, lime juice, sugar, salt, and pepper; process or blend until smooth, adding additional broth, if desired, for a creamier consistency. Transfer to a medium bowl and add the cilantro (if using), stirring well to combine. Serve at room temperature, accompanied with the raw vegetables. Alternatively, cover and refrigerate a minimum of 2 hours or up to 1 day and serve chilled, or return to room temperature.

Per serving (without raw vegetables): Calories 150 | Protein 10g | Total Fat 10g | Sat. Fat 1g | Cholesterol 0mg | Carbohydrate 7g | Dietary Fiber 4g | Sodium 167mg

Eggplant and Black Olive Dip

 Makes 6 servings

This delicious dip or spread also makes a great stuffing for pita bread, or filling for wraps.

1 large eggplant (about 1 pound), halved
   lengthwise, flesh scored a few times in
   a crisscross pattern (salting is not
   necessary)
¼ to ⅓ cup pitted kalamata or other
   good-quality black olives (see Cook's Tip,
   page 16)
2 tablespoons extra-virgin olive oil
1 to 2 tablespoons drained capers
1 tablespoon fresh lemon juice, or to taste
½ teaspoon salt, or to taste
Freshly ground black pepper, to taste
Cayenne pepper, to taste (optional)
Assorted raw vegetables, pita bread, pita
   chips, or crispy flatbread, to serve

Preheat oven to 475F (245C). Lightly grease a baking sheet.

Place the eggplant halves, cut sides down, on prepared baking sheet. Prick the skin in several places with the tines of a fork. Bake 15 to 20 minutes, until the skin begins to shrivel. Place, cut sides down, on several layers of paper towel to drain.

When the eggplant is cool enough to handle, scoop flesh from each half and transfer to a food processor fitted with the knife blade; discard skin. Add the olives, oil, capers, lemon juice, salt, black pepper, and cayenne (if using). Process until smooth. Transfer to a covered container and refrigerate a minimum of 2 hours, or up to 2 days, and serve chilled, accompanied with the raw vegetables.

Per serving (without raw vegetables): Calories 83 | Protein 1g | Total Fat 7g | Sat. Fat 1g | Cholesterol 0mg | Carbohydrate 5g | Dietary Fiber 2g | Sodium 349mg

Green Olive and Almond Crostini

 Makes 4 servings

This classic Provençal combination of briny green olives and crunchy toasted almonds is also fabulous tossed with pasta or steamed vegetables.

½ cup pitted green olives, with or without
   pimento (see Cook's Tip, page 16)
¼ cup toasted slivered almonds (see Cook's
   Tip, below)
1 teaspoon chopped fresh tarragon or about
   ¼ teaspoon dried tarragon
Freshly ground black pepper, to taste
1½ tablespoons extra-virgin olive oil
Toasted baguette rounds or toasted halved
   Italian bread, to serve (see Cook's Tip,
   page 11)

In a food processor fitted with the knife blade, combine the olives, almonds, tarragon, and pepper; pulse until coarsely chopped. Add oil in a steady stream and process until smooth. Transfer to a small bowl or crock and let stand at room temperature about 15 minutes to allow the flavors to blend. Serve at room temperature, accompanied by the bread, providing a relish knife for spreading.

Per serving (without bread): Calories 108 | Protein 2g | Total Fat 11g | Sat. Fat 1g | Cholesterol 0mg | Carbohydrate 3g | Dietary Fiber 1g | Sodium 149mg

Cook's Tip: *To toast slivered almonds, pine nuts, or other small nut shapes or pieces in the oven: Preheat the oven to 350F (175C). Spread the nuts in a single layer on an ungreased light-colored baking sheet. Bake about 5 minutes, until lightly golden, stirring halfway through the cooking time. Immediately remove from the baking sheet and set aside briefly to cool.*

To toast on the stovetop: Heat a small skillet over medium heat. Add the nuts and cook, stirring constantly, until lightly golden, 3 to 5 minutes. Immediately remove from the skillet and set aside briefly to cool.

For larger whole nuts and nut pieces, increase the cooking time by a few minutes.

Chipotle Guacamole

 Makes 8 servings

This spicy guacamole is also tasty with plantain chips.

> 2 ripe avocados, peeled, pitted, and mashed
> ½ cup finely chopped plum tomatoes
> ¼ cup finely chopped onion
> 1 tablespoon fresh lime juice, or to taste
> 1 tablespoon fresh orange juice (optional)
> 1 to 2 canned chipotle chilies in adobo sauce, finely chopped
> 1 to 2 cloves garlic, finely chopped
> ¼ teaspoon salt, or to taste
> Freshly ground black pepper, to taste
> Tortilla chips, to serve

In a small bowl, mix together all the ingredients, except the chips, until thoroughly combined. Serve at room temperature, or cover and refrigerate 2 to 12 hours and serve chilled, accompanied with the chips.

Per serving (without chips): Calories 88 | Protein 1g | Total Fat 8g | Sat. Fat 1g | Cholesterol 0mg | Carbohydrate 6g | Dietary Fiber 2g | Sodium 73mg

Quick Guacamole

 Makes 8 servings

To ensure the proper consistency of this popular dip, use ripe avocados and good-quality, chunky-style salsa.

> 2 ripe avocados, peeled and pitted, 1 mashed, 1 chopped
> ⅓ cup chunky-style mild or medium tomato salsa
> 2 large cloves garlic, finely chopped
> 1 tablespoon fresh lime juice, or to taste
> Salt and freshly ground black pepper, to taste
> Tortilla chips, to serve

In a small bowl, stir together all the ingredients, except the chips, until thoroughly combined. Mash lightly with a fork and then stir again. Serve at room temperature, or cover and refrigerate 2 to 12 hours and serve chilled, accompanied with the chips.

Per serving (without chips): Calories 85 | Protein 1g | Total Fat 8g | Sat. Fat 1g | Cholesterol 0mg | Carbohydrate 5g | Dietary Fiber 2g | Sodium 33mg

Variation: *To make Quick Tomatillo Guacamole, substitute green tomatillo salsa, or salsa verde, for the standard tomato variety.*

Guacamole-Stuffed Cherry Tomatoes

 Makes 4 to 6 servings

Because of their smaller size, grape tomatoes are not recommended substitutes for the cherry variety in this particular recipe. However, about one dozen small plum tomatoes (about 1 ounce each), halved lengthwise, pulp and seeds discarded, will work beautifully.

> 24 cherry tomatoes
> Salt
> ½ cup prepared guacamole
> Chopped fresh cilantro, for garnish

Cut a thin slice from the stem end of each tomato and discard. Using a melon baller or small spoon, remove and discard all pulp and seeds. Season the insides lightly with salt and turn upside down on paper towels to drain about 15 minutes. (At this point, the drained tomatoes can be stored, covered, in an upright position in the refrigerator up to 12 hours before continuing with the recipe.)

Fill each tomato with 1 teaspoon guacamole. Transfer to a serving platter and garnish each top with cilantro. Serve at once.

Per 6 tomatoes: Calories 66 | Protein 1g | Total Fat 5g | Sat. Fat 1g | Cholesterol 0mg | Carbohydrate 7g | Dietary Fiber 2g | Sodium 47mg

Variation: *To make Cherry Tomatoes Stuffed with Hummus, substitute prepared hummus for the guacamole and garnish lightly with paprika in lieu of the cilantro.*

Mushrooms Stuffed with Breadcrumbs, Lemon, and Thyme

Makes 4 to 6 servings

The timeless elegance of these thyme-scented mushrooms makes them a superb choice for a special occasion. Best of all, they can be assembled up to 12 hours before baking. Cremini or wild mushrooms are not recommended substitutes for the cultivated white variety in this particular recipe.

12 to 16 large white cultivated mushrooms (12 to 14 ounces), washed and stemmed, stems reserved

2 tablespoons extra-virgin olive oil

2 tablespoons fresh lemon juice

1 tablespoon finely chopped fresh thyme, or about ¾ teaspoon dried thyme

2 cloves garlic, finely chopped

½ teaspoon coarse salt

¼ teaspoon lemon-pepper seasoning

¾ cup finely ground soft breadcrumbs, preferably from whole wheat baguette

Preheat the oven to 375F (190C). Lightly oil a baking sheet. Cut off and discard the tough tips of the reserved mushroom stems. Finely chop the trimmed stems and reserve.

Heat 1 tablespoon of the oil in a medium nonstick skillet over medium-high heat. Add the mushroom stems and cook, stirring occasionally, until most of the liquid released from the stems has evaporated, 2 to 3 minutes. Carefully add the lemon juice. Cook, stirring often, until most of the liquid has evaporated, about 2 minutes, adding the thyme, garlic, salt, and lemon-pepper seasoning the last 30 seconds or so. Remove from the heat and add the breadcrumbs, stirring well to thoroughly combine.

Rub the rounded sides of the mushroom caps with half of the remaining oil. Arrange the mushroom caps, gill sides up, in a single layer on the prepared baking sheet. Spoon the filling evenly into the caps, and dab the tops with the remaining oil. (At this point, the mushrooms can be held at room temperature up to 1 hour before continuing with the recipe, or covered and refrigerated up to 12 hours before returning to room temperature and baking.) Bake on the center oven rack about 30 minutes, until nicely browned. Allow the mushrooms to cool about 5 minutes before serving warm.

Per 3 to 4 stuffed mushrooms: Calories 108 | Protein 3g | Total Fat 8g | Sat. Fat 1g | Cholesterol 0mg | Carbohydrate 9g | Dietary Fiber 1g | Sodium 303mg

Warm Cilantro Dipping Sauce with Plantain Chips

Makes 6 servings

The cilantro sauce is also an excellent dip for warm boiled or steamed new potatoes, raw zuc-

chini sticks, or raw bell pepper strips. Leftovers are wonderful brushed over toasted baguette or tossed with pasta.

- ½ cup fresh cilantro leaves, finely chopped
- 1 tablespoon cider vinegar
- ½ tablespoon fresh lime juice
- 2 large cloves garlic, finely chopped
- ¼ teaspoon hot sauce, or to taste
- ¼ teaspoon salt, or to taste
- Freshly ground black pepper, to taste
- 6 tablespoons extra-virgin olive oil
- Plantain chips, to serve

In a small heatproof bowl, combine the cilantro, vinegar, lime juice, garlic, hot sauce, salt, and black pepper. Set aside.

In a small saucepan, heat the oil over medium heat until just hot; slowly whisk into the cilantro mixture. Serve warm or at room temperature, accompanied with the chips. Completely cooled sauce can be stored, covered, in the refrigerator up to 2 days before returning to room temperature, or heating over low heat, and serving.

Per serving (without chips): Calories 128 | Protein 1g | Total Fat 14g | Sat. Fat 2g | Cholesterol 0mg | Carbohydrate 2g | Dietary Fiber 0g | Sodium 99mg

Red Onion and Black Olive Tapenade

Makes 6 to 8 servings

This tasty tapenade is also delicious tossed with rice, pasta, or cooked vegetables such as asparagus, green beans, eggplant, and zucchini.

- ¾ cup pitted kalamata or other good-quality black olives (see Cook's Tip, opposite)
- ½ cup chopped red onion
- 1 tablespoon drained capers

- 1 to 1½ tablespoons fresh lemon juice
- 1 tablespoon extra-virgin olive oil
- ½ teaspoon Dijon mustard
- 1 large clove garlic, finely chopped
- ¼ teaspoon dried oregano
- ¼ teaspoon dried thyme
- Freshly ground black pepper, to taste

Toasted baguette rounds or toasted halved Italian bread, to serve (see Cook's Tip, page 11)

In a food processor fitted with the knife blade, combine all the ingredients, except the bread. Pulse until almost smooth. Serve at room temperature, accompanied with the bread. Mixture can be stored, covered, in the refrigerator up to 3 days before returning to room temperature and serving.

Per serving (without bread): Calories 106 | Protein 0g | Total Fat 10g | Sat. Fat 0g | Cholesterol 0mg | Carbohydrate 4g | Dietary Fiber 0g | Sodium 490mg

Cook's Tip: *For easy olive pitting, place each olive on its side and place the flat side of a large knife over top; using your palm, strike the knife swiftly. The olive usually splits in half and the pit pops out.*

Roasted Red Pepper and Eggplant Confit

 Makes 6 servings

Use this popular Provençal appetizer as a topping for toasted baguette rounds, focaccia, or polenta; a stuffing for pita bread; or a filling for sandwich wraps. It is also excellent tossed with penne or other short pasta.

- 2 large red bell peppers (about 8 ounces each), cored, seeded, cut into 1-inch pieces
- 1 medium eggplant (about 12 ounces), peeled, cut into 1-inch pieces (salting is not necessary)

2 large cloves garlic, peeled and thinly sliced

1 (14-ounce) can whole peeled tomatoes in
   juice, drained and coarsely chopped

6 tablespoons extra-virgin olive oil

¾ teaspoon coarse salt, or to taste

Freshly ground black pepper, to taste

Preheat oven to 425F (220C).

On an ungreased baking sheet with sides, toss together all the ingredients until thoroughly combined. Spread in a single layer. Bake on the center oven rack 45 to 60 minutes, until the vegetables are very tender and lightly charred, stirring and turning every 15 minutes. Let cool to room temperature before serving. Completely cooled confit can be stored, covered, in the refrigerator up to 3 days before returning to room temperature and serving.

Per serving: Calories 165 | Protein 2g | Total Fat 14g | Sat. Fat 2g | Cholesterol 0mg | Carbohydrate 11g | Dietary Fiber 4g | Sodium 379mg

Mediterranean-Style Salsa with Pita Chips

Makes 6 servings

This is a tasty alternative to standard tomato salsa and tortilla chips. The salsa also makes a terrific relish for veggie burgers, topping for grilled portobello mushrooms, or spread for crispy flatbread. For best results, serve at room temperature.

2 tablespoons extra-virgin olive oil

2 large cloves garlic, finely chopped

1 (8-ounce) Italian eggplant, peeled and
   chopped (salting is not necessary)

1 large red bell pepper (about 8 ounces), cored,
   seeded, and chopped

1 small zucchini (about 4 ounces), chopped

1 large tomato (about 8 ounces), seeded and
   chopped

½ cup low-sodium vegetable broth, or more, if
   necessary

2 tablespoons cider vinegar

1 teaspoon sugar

½ teaspoon dried thyme leaves

½ teaspoon salt, or to taste

¼ teaspoon crushed red pepper flakes, or to
   taste (optional)

Freshly ground black pepper, to taste

¼ cup finely chopped fresh basil or flat-leaf
   parsley

½ tablespoon fresh lemon juice, or to taste

Pita chips, to serve

In a large nonstick skillet, heat the oil over medium heat. Add the garlic and cook, stirring constantly, 1 minute. Add the eggplant, bell pepper, and zucchini; cook, stirring, until softened, 5 to 7 minutes. Add the tomato, broth, vinegar, sugar, thyme, salt, red pepper flakes (if using), and black pepper; cook, stirring, until all the vegetables are just tender, about 5 minutes. Remove from heat and let cool a few minutes.

Transfer eggplant mixture to a food processor fitted with the knife blade; process in on/off pulses until fairly smooth but still chunky. Transfer to a serving bowl and toss with the basil and lemon juice, adding more broth by the tablespoon to achieve a saucier consistency, if necessary. Let cool to room temperature. (At this point, the mixture can be refrigerated, covered, up to 2 days before returning to room temperature and serving.) Serve with the pita chips.

Per serving (without pita chips): Calories 77 | Protein 2g | Total Fat 5g | Sat. Fat 1g | Cholesterol 0mg | Carbohydrate 8g | Dietary Fiber 3g | Sodium 226mg

Greek-Style Spinach Puffs

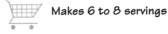 **Makes 9 appetizers**

Frozen puff pastry (the leading brand is vegan) makes quick work of this scrumptious appetizer. For even easier entertaining, the spinach filling can be prepared a day in advance, but allow it to come to room temperature before assembling the pastries.

½ tablespoon extra-virgin olive oil

1 cup chopped onion

2 large cloves garlic, finely chopped

8 ounces frozen chopped spinach, cooked according to package directions, drained and squeezed dry between paper towels

½ tablespoon finely chopped fresh dill or about ½ teaspoon dried dill

½ teaspoon salt

⅛ teaspoon crushed fennel seed or pinch of crushed anise seed

Freshly ground black pepper, to taste

Pinch, or more, ground nutmeg (optional)

½ (about 17-ounce) package (1 sheet) frozen puff pastry, thawed according to package directions

Preheat oven to 400F (205C).

In a medium nonstick skillet, heat the oil over medium heat. Add the onion and cook, stirring, until just beginning to brown, about 5 minutes. Add the garlic and cook, stirring constantly, 30 seconds. Add the spinach, dill, salt, fennel, and black pepper and cook, stirring, 2 minutes. Remove from the heat and add the nutmeg (if using), stirring well to combine. Set aside to cool about 15 minutes.

Cut the pastry sheet into 9 equal squares. Place about 2 heaping tablespoons of the spinach filling in the middle of a square. Pinch 2 opposite corners together to seal. Repeat with remaining filling and pastry. Transfer to an ungreased baking sheet and

prick each parcel on both sides once with a fork. Bake on the center oven rack 18 to 20 minutes, until golden brown. Serve warm.

Per puff: Calories 154 | Protein 3g | Total Fat 8g | Sat. Fat 2g | Cholesterol 0mg | Carbohydrate 18g | Dietary Fiber 3g | Sodium 228mg

Curried Spinach Fondue with Pita

Makes 6 to 8 servings

This creamy fondue is wonderful served with crusty French or Italian bread, as well. It also makes a fabulous sauce for boiled new potatoes, or topping for grilled portobello mushrooms and eggplant.

⅔ cup light coconut milk

1 cup low-sodium vegetable broth or water, plus additional, as necessary

1 tablespoon cornstarch

½ teaspoon mild curry powder, or to taste

¼ teaspoon sugar (optional)

2 (9-ounce) bags ready-washed baby spinach

Salt and freshly ground black pepper, to taste

Pita bread, to serve

In a small container, stir together the coconut milk, ½ cup of the broth, cornstarch, curry powder, and sugar (if using) until thoroughly blended. Set aside.

In a large deep-sided nonstick skillet with a lid, add the remaining ½ cup broth and top with half the spinach. Cover and turn the heat to medium-high; cook, without stirring, for 2 minutes, until spinach is beginning to wilt. Toss and add the remaining spinach; cover and cook 2 more minutes without stirring. Uncover and cook, tossing and cutting through the spinach with the edge of a large spatula, until most of the liquid has evaporated and the spinach is greatly reduced in volume, 2 to 3 minutes. Reduce the heat to medium and add the coconut milk mixture, salt, and pepper. Cook until thickened and bubbly, stirring often, 2 to 3 minutes. Transfer to a fondue pot, chafing dish, or top of a double boiler and serve at once, accompanied with the pita bread. For a thinner fondue, or if mixture becomes too dry, add additional broth or water, as necessary.

Per serving (without bread): Calories 57 | Protein 5g | Total Fat 2g | Sat. Fat 2g | Cholesterol 0mg | Carbohydrate 6g | Dietary Fiber 3g | Sodium 165mg

Golden Tomato Bruschetta

Makes 4 servings

Many major supermarkets carry tiny, golden-hued pear tomatoes during the summer months. If yours doesn't, substitute with the cherry or grape variety for an equally tasty appetizer.

1 pint (2 cups) golden pear or ½ to ¾ pound golden baby Roma tomatoes, chopped
2 to 3 tablespoons finely chopped fresh basil
1 tablespoon extra-virgin olive oil
1 teaspoon balsamic or red wine vinegar
1 large clove garlic, finely chopped
½ teaspoon coarse salt
Freshly ground black pepper, to taste
Slices Italian bread, toasted (see Cook's Tip, page 11), rubbed on one side with a halved clove garlic, to serve

In a medium bowl, toss all the ingredients, except the bread, until thoroughly combined. Let stand about 15 minutes at room temperature to allow the flavors to blend. Toss again and serve at room temperature, accompanied with the bread. Alternatively, the topping can be covered and refrigerated up to 24 hours before returning to room temperature and serving.

Per serving (without bread): Calories 54 | Protein 1g | Total Fat 4g | Sat. Fat 1g | Cholesterol 0mg | Carbohydrate 5g | Dietary Fiber 1g | Sodium 245mg

Sun-Dried Tomato–Pesto Toast

Makes 6 pieces

This scrumptious pesto topping is also delicious tossed with hot pasta or steamed vegetables, namely green beans, or spread over grilled egg-plant and zucchini.

¼ cup chopped fresh basil
3 tablespoons julienned, drained, oil-packed sun-dried tomatoes
2 tablespoons pine nuts
1 tablespoon extra-virgin olive oil
1 tablespoon tomato paste
1 large clove garlic, finely chopped
½ teaspoon coarse salt
Freshly ground black pepper, to taste
6 slices Italian bread (about 1.25 ounces each), preferably Tuscan pane

Preheat oven to 375F (190C).

In a food processor fitted with the knife blade, process all the ingredients, except the bread, until fairly smooth. (At this point, mixture can be refrigerated, covered, up to 3 days before continuing with the recipe.) Spread evenly over the bread slices and transfer to an ungreased baking sheet. Bake on the center oven rack about 7 minutes, until heated through but not browned. Serve warm or at room temperature.

Per piece: Calories 144 | Protein 4g | Total Fat 6g | Sat. Fat 1g | Cholesterol 0mg | Carbohydrate 20g | Dietary Fiber 1g | Sodium 395mg

Walnut–Red Pepper Dip

 Makes 6 servings

Serve this versatile and delicious dip as a spread for crispy flatbread or toasted baguette rounds. It also makes a fabulous sauce for hot cooked pasta.

1 (12-ounce) jar roasted red bell peppers, well drained

1 cup fresh breadcrumbs (preferably from a whole wheat baguette)

¼ cup walnut pieces

2 tablespoons extra-virgin olive oil

2 large cloves garlic, finely chopped

½ teaspoon coarse salt, or to taste

½ teaspoon ground cumin

Freshly ground black pepper, to taste

Pinch, or to taste, cayenne pepper (optional)

Assorted raw vegetables, pita chips, or bread sticks, to serve

In a food processor fitted with the knife blade, process all the ingredients, except the raw vegetables, until smooth. Serve at room temperature, accompanied with the raw vegetables. Dip can be covered and refrigerated up to 2 days before returning to room temperature and serving.

Per serving (without raw vegetables): Calories 109 | Protein 3g | Total Fat 8g | Sat. Fat 1g | Cholesterol 0mg | Carbohydrate 8g | Dietary Fiber 2g | Sodium 197mg

White Bean Hummus

Makes 4 to 6 servings

While delicious hummus spin-offs abound, this particular variation of the classic Middle Eastern chickpea-and-tahini dip is one of my favorites.

1 (15-ounce) can cannellini or other white beans, rinsed and drained

2 tablespoons fresh lemon juice, or to taste

1 tablespoon sesame tahini

1 tablespoon extra-virgin olive oil

1 tablespoon water, or more, as necessary

1 to 2 large cloves garlic, finely chopped

½ teaspoon coarse salt

Freshly ground black pepper, to taste

Cayenne pepper to taste (optional)

2 tablespoons chopped fresh flat-leaf parsley (optional)

Sweet paprika, for dusting (optional)

Pita bread or pita chips, to serve

In a food processor fitted with knife blade, process the beans, lemon juice, tahini, oil, water, garlic, salt, black pepper, and cayenne (if using) until smooth, adding more water, if necessary, and lemon juice to achieve the desired consistency and tartness. Transfer to a serving bowl and add the parsley (if using), stirring well to combine. Lightly dust with the paprika (if using). Serve at room temperature, or cover and refrigerate a minimum of 1 hour or up to 3 days and serve chilled, or return to room temperature, accompanied with the pita bread.

Per serving (without the bread): Calories 148 | Protein 7g | Total Fat 6g | Sat. Fat 1g | Cholesterol 0mg | Carbohydrate 19g | Dietary Fiber 4g | Sodium 240mg

Variation: *To make Spicy Black Bean Hummus, substitute 1 (15-ounce) can rinsed and drained black beans for the white beans and omit the optional parsley and paprika. Process 1 to 2 jalapeño chilies, seeded and chopped, and 1 teaspoon ground cumin along with the other ingredients. Serve with pita bread, pita chips, or tortilla chips.*

Soups, Stews, and Chilis

Quick, hot, and satisfying aptly describes the soups in this chapter—with a few notable exceptions, that is, such as chilled Watermelon Gazpacho, a summertime luncheon staple in my household. A dependable cold-weather dinner is Tuscan Chickpea Soup with Sun-Dried Tomatoes and Rosemary; ready in just about twenty minutes, its comforting aroma will linger in your kitchen for hours, and banish any winter blahs. For a reliable first course in the springtime, nothing beats the elegance of Easy Cream of Asparagus Soup; your guests will never guess the asparagus came from a can unless you tell them. If you need a crowd-pleaser for the fall football season, pull out your tallest stockpot and cook up a double batch of Kansas City–Style Two-Bean Chili. Even confirmed meat-eaters usually dig in for seconds.

Easy Cream of Asparagus Soup

Makes 6 servings

Present this simply elegant soup to commence a special meal.

    2 (15-ounce) cans asparagus, liquids included
    2 (14-ounce) cans (3½ cups) low-sodium
        vegetable broth
    6 to 8 fresh pencil-thin asparagus, tough
        ends trimmed, tips separated from stalks,
        stalks cut into 1-inch pieces (optional)
    Salt and freshly ground black pepper, to taste
    1 cup light coconut milk
    Pinch ground nutmeg (optional)

In a food processor fitted with the knife blade, or in a blender, place the canned asparagus and their liquids; process or blend until smooth and pureed. Transfer to a medium stockpot and add the broth, fresh asparagus (if using), salt, and pepper. Bring to a boil over high heat, stirring occasionally. Reduce the heat to low and add the coconut milk and nutmeg (if using); cook, stirring, until heated through, about 2 minutes. Serve hot.

Per serving: Calories 92 | Protein 10g | Total Fat 4g | Sat. Fat 3g | Cholesterol 0mg | Carbohydrate 6g | Dietary Fiber 4g | Sodium 790mg

Creamy Curried Broccoli Soup

Makes 4 to 6 servings

Using frozen broccoli makes this scrumptious soup quick and easy to prepare.

    2 tablespoons extra-virgin olive oil
    1 cup chopped onion
    2 (14-ounce) cans (3½ cups) low-sodium
        vegetable broth
    1 (16-ounce) bag frozen broccoli florets
    1 teaspoon mild curry powder, or to taste
    ¼ teaspoon salt, or to taste
    Freshly ground black pepper, to taste
    ½ to 1 cup light coconut milk (optional)

In a medium stockpot, heat the oil over medium heat. Add the onion and cook, stirring, until softened, about 3 minutes. Add the broth, broccoli, curry powder, salt, and pepper and bring to a boil over high heat. Reduce the heat, partially cover, and simmer gently until the broccoli is tender, stirring occasionally, about 15 minutes. Working in batches, if necessary, transfer to a food processor fitted with the knife blade, or to a blender; process until smooth and pureed. Return to the stockpot and add the coconut milk (if using); cook, stirring, over low heat, until heated through, about 5 minutes. Serve hot.

Per serving: Calories 153 | Protein 14g | Total Fat 7g | Sat. Fat 1g | Cholesterol 0mg | Carbohydrate 12g | Dietary Fiber 7g | Sodium 607mg

Variation: *Frozen chopped cauliflower can replace all or part of the broccoli, if desired.*

Buddhist Hot-and-Sour Soup with Tofu

Makes 4 to 6 servings

This fragrant vegetable soup is an ideal first course to begin an Asian-themed meal. For an even lighter soup, omit the tofu.

    4 cups water
    2 cups low-sodium vegetable broth
    2 tablespoons chopped fresh ginger
    2 tablespoons hoisin sauce

1½ tablespoons low-sodium soy or tamari sauce, or to taste

1 tablespoon black bean sauce

1 tablespoon toasted (dark) sesame oil

Freshly ground black pepper, to taste

8 ounces fresh broccoli florets (about 2½ cups), cut into bite-size pieces, or 8 ounces frozen chopped broccoli (about 2 cups), thawed

2 small zucchini (about 4 ounces each), cut lengthwise in half, thinly sliced crosswise

8 ounces shredded coleslaw mix

8 ounces extra-firm tofu, cut into ½-inch cubes

2 tablespoons finely chopped fresh cilantro (optional)

½ teaspoon Chinese chili paste, or to taste (optional)

In a medium stockpot, bring the water, broth, ginger, hoisin sauce, soy sauce, black bean sauce, sesame oil, and pepper to a boil over high heat. Add the broccoli and return to a boil; boil 1 minute. Add the zucchini and coleslaw mix and return to a boil; boil 1 minute. Add the tofu and return to a boil. Reduce the heat, add the cilantro (if using) and chili paste (if using), and simmer gently, uncovered, until all the vegetables are tender, about 5 minutes, stirring occasionally. Serve hot.

Per serving: Calories 164 | Protein 14g | Total Fat 7g | Sat. Fat 1g | Cholesterol 0mg | Carbohydrate 15g | Dietary Fiber 6g | Sodium 686mg

Butternut Squash and Roasted Red Pepper Soup

Makes 6 servings

This is a warming opener for a Thanksgiving or other winter holiday celebration.

2 tablespoons extra-virgin olive oil

1 cup chopped onion

3 large cloves garlic, finely chopped

2½ cups low-sodium vegetable broth

½ cup water, plus additional, as necessary

2 (12-ounce) packages frozen butternut squash, thawed

1 (12-ounce) jar roasted red bell peppers, preferably fire-roasted, drained

1 teaspoon sugar

½ teaspoon poultry seasoning

½ teaspoon dried thyme leaves

¼ teaspoon dried rosemary

½ teaspoon salt, or to taste

Freshly ground black pepper, to taste

Chopped fresh chives or the green parts of scallions (optional)

In a medium stockpot, heat the oil over medium heat. Add the onion and cook, stirring, until softened, about 3 minutes. Add the garlic and cook, stirring constantly, 1 minute. Add the broth, water, squash, bell peppers, sugar, poultry seasoning, thyme, rosemary, salt, and black pepper; bring to a boil over high heat, breaking up the bell peppers with a large wooden spoon. Reduce the heat, cover, and simmer 20 minutes, stirring occasionally. Working in batches, as necessary, transfer to a food processor fitted with the knife blade, or to a blender; process until smooth and pureed. Return to the pot and reheat over low heat as necessary, adding additional water if a thinner soup is desired. Serve warm, garnished with the chives (if using).

Per serving: Calories 156 | Protein 8g | Total Fat 5g | Sat. Fat 1g | Cholesterol 0mg | Carbohydrate 24g | Dietary Fiber 5g | Sodium 398mg

Moroccan-Style Gingered Carrot Soup with Orange

🛒 **Makes 4 servings**

If serving this fragrant and refreshing soup chilled, freshly squeezed orange juice is highly recommended.

2 tablespoons extra-virgin olive oil

1 cup chopped onion

1 tablespoon chopped fresh ginger

1½ pounds chopped carrots

3 cups low-sodium vegetable broth

¼ teaspoon salt, or to taste

Freshly ground black pepper, to taste

1½ cups orange juice, preferably freshly squeezed

Pinch ground nutmeg

Chopped chives or the green parts of scallions, for garnish (optional)

In a medium stockpot, heat the oil over medium heat. Add the onion and ginger and cook, stirring, until softened, about 3 minutes. Add the carrots and cook, stirring, 2 more minutes. Add the broth, salt, and pepper and bring to a simmer over high heat. Reduce the heat, partially cover, and simmer gently, stirring occasionally, until carrots are tender, about 40 minutes. Stir in the orange juice and remove from heat.

Working in batches, as necessary, transfer the soup mixture to a food processor fitted with the knife blade, or to a blender; process until smooth and pureed. Return to the pot and add the nutmeg and additional salt and pepper, if necessary, stirring well to combine. If serving warm, reheat as necessary over low heat, stirring occasionally. If serving chilled, let cool to room temperature before refrigerating. Refrigerate, covered, a minimum of 3 hours or up to 2 days. Garnish with the chives (if using) just before serving.

Per serving: Calories 220 | Protein 11g | Total Fat 7g | Sat. Fat 1g | Cholesterol 0mg | Carbohydrate 30g | Dietary Fiber 8g | Sodium 577mg

Cauliflower and Potato Soup

🛒 **Makes 5 to 6 servings**

Fresh broccoli can replace all or part of the cauliflower, if desired.

1½ tablespoons extra-virgin olive oil

1 cup chopped onion

½ cup chopped carrot

2 large cloves garlic, finely chopped

1 large head cauliflower (about 2 pounds), cored and separated into florets, cut into bite-size pieces

1 large russet potato (about 8 ounces), peeled and cut into bite-size chunks

4 cups low-sodium vegetable broth

1 large bay leaf, broken in half

½ teaspoon salt, or to taste

Freshly ground black pepper, to taste

Pinch ground nutmeg (optional)

In a medium stockpot, heat the oil over medium heat. Add the onion and carrot and cook, stirring, until softened, about 3 minutes. Add the garlic and cook, stirring constantly, 1 minute. Add the cauliflower and potato and cook, stirring, 2 minutes. Add the broth, bay leaf, salt, and pepper and bring to a boil over high heat. Reduce the heat to between low and medium-low, cover, and simmer, stirring occasionally, until cauliflower and potatoes are tender, 20 to 25 minutes. Remove and discard the bay leaf halves.

Working in batches, if necessary, transfer the soup mixture to a food processor fitted with the knife blade, or to a blender; process until smooth and pureed. Return to the pot and reheat over low heat as necessary. Add the nutmeg (if using), stirring well to combine. Serve warm.

Per serving: Calories 167 | Protein 14g | Total Fat 5g | Sat. Fat 1g | Cholesterol 0mg | Carbohydrate 21g | Dietary Fiber 9g | Sodium 689mg

Quick Southwestern-Style Kidney Bean and Corn Soup

Makes 6 servings

Straight from the pantry, this soup is as delicious to eat as it is easy to prepare.

2 (15-ounce) cans red kidney beans, rinsed and drained

1 (15-ounce) can no-salt added tomato sauce

1 (14-ounce) can (1¾ cups) low-sodium vegetable broth

1 (14.5-ounce) can diced tomatoes with chilies, juices included

1 (11-ounce) can yellow corn, drained

1 cup mild or medium salsa, preferably fire-roasted

1 tablespoon extra-virgin olive oil

1 teaspoon ground cumin, or to taste

Salt and freshly ground black pepper, to taste

Crushed tortilla chips, for garnish (optional)

In a medium stockpot, combine all ingredients, except the tortilla chips, and bring to a boil over high heat, stirring occasionally. Reduce the heat and simmer gently, uncovered, 20 minutes, stirring occasionally. Serve warm, garnished with the tortilla chips (if using).

Per serving: Calories 233 | Protein 14g | Total Fat 3g | Sat. Fat 1g | Cholesterol 0mg | Carbohydrate 40g | Dietary Fiber 9g | Sodium 542mg

Potato and Leek Soup

Makes 4 servings

This thick and comforting soup is in order on a cold winter's day.

2 tablespoons canola oil

1 pound leeks (about 2 large), trimmed, cleaned, and coarsely chopped

1 cup sliced cultivated white mushrooms

2 (14-ounce) cans (3½ cups) low-sodium vegetable broth

½ cup water

1 pound russet potatoes (about 2 large), peeled and coarsely chopped

¼ teaspoon salt, or to taste

Freshly ground black pepper, to taste

In a medium stockpot, heat the oil over medium heat. Add the leeks and mushrooms and cook, stirring, until leeks are softened and mushrooms begin to release their liquids, about 5 minutes. Add the broth, water, potatoes, salt, and black pepper; bring to a boil over high heat. Reduce the heat to medium and simmer briskly, uncovered, until potatoes are tender, about 15 minutes, stirring occasionally. Working in batches, if necessary, transfer to a food processor fitted with the knife blade, or to a blender; process until smooth and pureed. Return to the pot and reheat over low heat as necessary. Serve hot.

Per serving: Calories 206 | Protein 13g | Total Fat 7g | Sat. Fat 1g | Cholesterol 0mg | Carbohydrate 25g | Dietary Fiber 5g | Sodium 602mg

Vegetable-Miso Soup

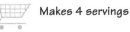 **Makes 4 servings**

Packets of instant Japanese miso soup can be located in the international foods aisle of most well-stocked conventional supermarkets. While most brands are vegan, check the label carefully, as some contain fish products. To reduce the sodium, replace the vegetable broth with water.

1 tablespoon plus 1 teaspoon toasted (dark)
    sesame oil
1 stalk celery, chopped
3 scallions, thinly sliced, white and green
    parts separated
1 medium zucchini (about 6 ounces), cut
    lengthwise in half, thinly sliced crosswise
1 small carrot (about 2 ounces), thinly sliced
1 (15-ounce) can straw mushroom pieces,
    drained well
1 cup low-sodium vegetable broth
3 cups water
2 (.53-ounce) packets instant red or white
    miso soup
1 tablespoon low-sodium soy sauce, plus
    additional, to serve
Freshly ground black pepper, to taste
2 ounces fresh spinach leaves, coarsely torn

In a medium stockpot, heat the 1 tablespoon oil over medium heat. Add the celery and white parts of the scallions; cook, stirring, until just softened, about 2 minutes. Add the zucchini and carrot; cook, stirring, until just softened, about 2 minutes. Add the mushrooms and cook, stirring, 2 minutes. Add the broth and water and bring to a boil over high heat. Add the miso soup packets, soy sauce, and pepper. Reduce the heat to medium-low and cook, stirring occasionally, 7 to 10 minutes, until zucchini and carrot are tender. Add the spinach, scallion greens, and remaining 1 teaspoon sesame oil; cook, stirring, until the spinach is wilted but still bright green, about 2 minutes. Serve hot, with additional soy sauce passed separately.

Per serving: Calories 103 | Protein 6g | Total Fat 5g | Sat. Fat 1g | Cholesterol 0mg | Carbohydrate 10g | Dietary Fiber 3g | Sodium 993mg

Tomato Soup with Thyme

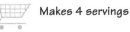 **Makes 4 servings**

This virtually effortless soup is an excellent accompaniment to sandwiches, pizza, and focaccia.

1 tablespoon extra-virgin olive oil
½ cup chopped onion
1 large clove garlic, finely chopped
1 (14.5 ounce) can whole peeled tomatoes,
    juices included
1½ cups low-sodium vegetable broth
1 (8-ounce) can no-salt added tomato sauce
2 teaspoons fresh thyme leaves, or about ½
    teaspoon dried thyme
1 teaspoon sugar
¼ teaspoon salt, or to taste
Freshly ground black pepper, to taste

In a large saucepan or medium stockpot, heat the oil over medium heat. Add the onion and cook, stirring, until softened, 2 to 3 minutes. Add the garlic and cook, stirring constantly, 30 seconds. Add the remaining ingredients and bring to a boil over high heat. Reduce the heat to between low and medium-low, cover, and simmer 30 minutes, stirring occasionally. Working in batches, if necessary, puree the soup in a food processor fitted with the knife blade, or in a blender. Return to the pan and reheat as necessary. Serve warm.

Per serving: Calories 102 | Protein 6g | Total Fat 4g | Sat. Fat 1g | Cholesterol 0mg | Carbohydrate 12g | Dietary Fiber 3g | Sodium 491mg

Roasted Red Pepper and Potato Soup with Cumin

Makes 4 servings

For a Mediterranean flair, use dried rosemary leaves in lieu of the cumin seed.

    1 tablespoon extra-virgin olive oil
    1 cup chopped onion
    ½ cup chopped carrot
    ¼ cup chopped celery
    1 teaspoon whole cumin seed
    2 large cloves garlic, finely chopped
    2 cups low-sodium vegetable broth
    2 cups water
    1 (15-ounce) can sliced potatoes, rinsed and
        drained
    1 (12-ounce) jar roasted red bell peppers,
        drained
    Salt and freshly ground black pepper, to taste
    Cayenne pepper, to taste (optional)

In a medium stockpot, heat the oil over medium heat. Add the onion, carrot, celery, and cumin; cook, stirring, until softened and fragrant, about 3 minutes. Add the garlic and cook, stirring constantly, 1 minute. Add the remaining ingredients and bring to a boil over high heat, breaking up the bell peppers with a large wooden spoon. Reduce the heat to low, cover, and simmer 20 minutes, stirring occasionally.

Working in batches, if necessary, transfer the soup mixture to a food processor fitted with the knife blade, or to a blender; process until smooth and pureed. Return to the pot and reheat as necessary. Serve hot.

Per serving: Calories 134 | Protein 8g | Total Fat 4g | Sat. Fat 1g | Cholesterol 0mg | Carbohydrate 19g | Dietary Fiber 6g | Sodium 611mg

Watermelon Gazpacho

Makes 4 servings

Slightly sweet and slightly salty, this very delicious variation of gazpacho uses watermelon in lieu of tomato as its primary ingredient. Like the tomato, the watermelon is a good source of lycopene, which may help protect against certain cancers.

    3 cups chopped seedless watermelon (about
        1 pound cubed)
    1 medium cucumber (about 10 ounces), peeled,
        unseeded, and chopped
    1 medium red or yellow bell pepper (about
        6 ounces) cored, seeded, and chopped
    4 scallions, white and green parts, thinly
        sliced
    1 jalapeño chili, seeded and chopped (optional)
    1½ to 2 tablespoons fresh lemon juice
    1 tablespoon extra-virgin olive oil
    ½ teaspoon salt, or to taste
    Freshly ground black pepper, to taste
    2 tablespoons chopped fresh parsley

In a food processor fitted with the knife blade, or in a blender, place about two-thirds of the watermelon, half of the cucumber, half of the bell pepper, half of the scallions, and the chili (if using). Add the lemon juice, oil, salt, and black pepper; process until smooth and pureed. Transfer to a large bowl and add the remaining ingredients, stirring well to combine. Cover and refrigerate a minimum of 1 hour, or overnight. Stir well and adjust the seasonings, if necessary, and serve chilled.

Per serving: Calories 102 | Protein 2g | Total Fat 4g | Sat. Fat 1g | Cholesterol 0mg | Carbohydrate 16g | Dietary Fiber 3g | Sodium 276mg

Three-Bean Barley Chili

Makes 8 servings

This protein-packed, fiber-rich chili is always a crowd-pleaser. Pinto beans or black-eyed peas can replace one of the suggested bean varieties. For a milder dish, use plain canned tomatoes.

4 cups water

2 cups mild or medium salsa

1 (14.5-ounce) can diced tomatoes with jalapeño chilies, juices included

1 (14-ounce) can (1¾ cups) low-sodium vegetable broth

1 cup pearl barley

2 tablespoons extra-virgin olive oil

1½ tablespoons chili powder, or to taste

½ tablespoon ground cumin

½ teaspoon salt, or to taste

Freshly ground black pepper, to taste

Cayenne pepper, to taste (optional)

1 (19-ounce) can red kidney beans, rinsed and drained

1 (15-ounce) can black beans, rinsed and drained

1 (15-ounce) can Great Northern, navy, or other white beans, rinsed and drained

1 cup frozen yellow corn, partially thawed (optional)

Chopped onion (optional)

In a medium stockpot, combine the water, salsa, tomatoes and their liquids, broth, barley, oil, chili powder, cumin, salt, black pepper, and cayenne (if using); bring to a boil over high heat, stirring occasionally. Reduce the heat to between low and medium-low, cover, and simmer until the barley is just tender, stirring occasionally, about 40 minutes.

Add the beans and corn (if using) and return to a boil over high heat. Reduce the heat to between low and medium-low and simmer, uncovered, until the barley is tender and mixture is slightly thickened, stirring occasionally, about 5 minutes. Serve warm, garnished with the onion (if using).

Per serving: Calories 297 | Protein 16g | Total Fat 5g | Sat. Fat 1g | Cholesterol 0mg | Carbohydrate 51g | Dietary Fiber 13g | Sodium 539mg

Caribbean-Style Black Bean and Hominy Soup with Plantain Chips

Makes 6 servings

Crushed tortilla or taco chips can replace the plantain chips, if desired. For a lighter but equally delicious soup, omit the chips altogether.

1 tablespoon extra-virgin olive oil

1 cup chopped red onion

4 cloves garlic, finely chopped

1 (14-ounce) can (1¾ cups) low-sodium vegetable broth

1¾ cups water

1 (15-ounce) can vegetarian refried black beans

1 (15-ounce) can black beans, rinsed and drained

1 (15-ounce) can white hominy, drained

1 (14.5-ounce) can diced tomatoes with jalapeño chilies, juices included

2 teaspoons ground cumin

Salt and freshly ground black pepper, to taste

2 ounces plantain chips, crushed, for garnish

In a medium stockpot, heat the oil over medium heat. Add the onion and cook, stirring, until softened, about 3 minutes. Add the garlic and cook, stirring constantly, 1 minute. Add the remaining ingredients, except the plantain chips, and bring to a boil over high heat, stirring well to thoroughly incorporate the refried beans. Reduce the heat to medium-low and simmer gently, uncovered, 15 minutes, stirring occasionally. Serve hot, garnished with the plantain chips.

Per serving: Calories 264 | Protein 13g | Total Fat 7g | Sat. Fat 4g | Cholesterol 0mg | Carbohydrate 40g | Dietary Fiber 8g | Sodium 647mg

Kansas City–Style Two-Bean Chili

 Makes 8 servings

Ready in just about thirty minutes, this smoky-sweet two-bean chili is superb with Southwestern-Style Cornbread (page 68) and an ice-cold beer. Liquid smoke can be located near the barbecue sauces in most major supermarkets; if yours doesn't carry it, use hickory-smoke barbecue sauce in lieu of the regular variety.

1 tablespoon canola oil

1 cup chopped onion

2 (15-ounce) cans kidney beans, rinsed and drained

1 (15-ounce) can butter beans, rinsed and drained

1 (15-ounce) can white hominy, drained

½ cup tomato ketchup

½ cup barbecue sauce

½ cup molasses

½ cup prepared yellow mustard

½ cup water, plus additional, as necessary

¼ cup cider vinegar

1 teaspoon liquid smoke, or more, to taste

1 to 1½ tablespoons chili powder, or to taste

¼ teaspoon cayenne pepper, or to taste (optional)

Salt and freshly ground black pepper, to taste

In a medium stockpot, heat the oil over medium heat. Add the onion and cook, stirring, until the onion is just beginning to brown, about 4 minutes. Add the remaining ingredients and bring to a simmer over medium-high heat. Reduce the heat and simmer gently, uncovered, about 25 minutes, stirring every few minutes from the bottom to prevent sticking. If a thinner consistency is desired, add additional water as necessary. Serve warm.

Per serving: Calories 342 | Protein 16g | Total Fat 4g | Sat. Fat 0g | Cholesterol 0mg | Carbohydrate 64g | Dietary Fiber 14g | Sodium 601mg

Roasted Tomato–Garlic Soup with Orzo and Basil

Makes 4 servings

No one will ever guess this delicious soup comes virtually out of a jar unless you tell them. Uncooked long-grain white rice can replace the orzo, if desired; however, you will need to boil it a few minutes longer.

1 (24-ounce) jar roasted garlic pasta sauce

2 cups water

1 cup low-sodium vegetable broth

2 tablespoons extra-virgin olive oil

¼ teaspoon dried rosemary leaves

¼ teaspoon dried thyme leaves

½ cup orzo pasta

¼ cup finely chopped fresh basil leaves

In a medium stockpot, bring the pasta sauce, water, broth, oil, rosemary, and thyme to a boil over medium-high heat. Add the orzo and half the basil and boil, stirring occasionally, until the orzo is tender yet firm to the bite, about 9 minutes. Serve hot, garnished with the remaining basil.

Per serving: Calories 298 | Protein 7g | Total Fat 15g | Sat. Fat 2g | Cholesterol 0mg | Carbohydrate 36g | Dietary Fiber 7g | Sodium 974mg

African Cabbage, Carrot, Potato, and Chickpea Stew

Makes 4 servings

To feed a crowd, serve this delicious winter vegetable medley over rice or couscous. For a soupier stew, add more broth or water, as desired.

2 tablespoons peanut oil and/or extra-virgin
    olive oil
1 (16-ounce) bag baby carrots
1 cup chopped onion
2 to 3 large cloves garlic, finely chopped
1 pound boiling potatoes, peeled, cut into
    1-inch cubes
1 (15-ounce) can chickpeas, rinsed and drained
8 ounces shredded cabbage
1 cup low-sodium vegetable broth
½ cup water
2 to 3 tablespoons tomato paste
1 teaspoon sugar, or to taste (optional)
1 teaspoon ground cumin
½ teaspoon ground turmeric
½ teaspoon salt, or to taste
¼ teaspoon crushed red pepper flakes, or to
    taste (optional)
Freshly ground black pepper, to taste

In a large deep-sided nonstick skillet with a lid, heat the oil over medium heat. Add the carrots and onion and cook, stirring, until softened, about 5 minutes, adding the garlic the last minute or so of cooking. Add the potatoes, chickpeas, cabbage, broth, water, tomato paste, sugar (if using), cumin, turmeric, salt, red pepper flakes (if using), and black pepper; bring to a boil over high heat. Reduce the heat to medium-low, cover, and cook until potatoes and carrots are tender, about 20 to 30 minutes, stirring occasionally. Serve warm.

Per serving: Calories 325 | Protein 13g | Total Fat 9g | Sat. Fat 1g | Cholesterol 0mg | Carbohydrate 52g | Dietary Fiber 8g | Sodium 518mg

French-Canadian Cabbage and Navy Bean Soup with Escarole

Makes 4 servings

Serve this hearty soup with a tossed green salad and lots of crusty, whole grain baguette for a cozy, winter-warming meal. Mature fresh spinach can replace the escarole, if desired.

2 tablespoons extra-virgin olive oil
½ cup chopped onion
¼ cup chopped carrot
¼ cup chopped celery
2 garlic cloves, finely chopped
2 (14-ounce) cans (3½ cups) low-sodium
    vegetable broth
1 cup water
1 (16-ounce) package shredded cabbage
1 (19-ounce) can navy, Great Northern, or
    other white beans, rinsed and drained
¼ teaspoon salt, or to taste
Freshly ground black pepper, to taste
½ head escarole (about 8 ounces), coarsely
    chopped
½ teaspoon sweet paprika

In a medium stockpot, heat the oil over medium heat. Add the onion, carrot, and celery and cook, stirring, until softened, about 3 minutes. Add the garlic and cook, stirring constantly, 1 minute. Add the broth, water, cabbage, beans, salt, and pepper; bring to a boil over high heat. Reduce the heat and simmer gently, uncovered, stirring occasionally, until the cabbage is just tender, about 15 minutes. Add the escarole and paprika and cook, stirring, until the cabbage and escarole are tender, about 10 minutes. Serve warm.

Per serving: Calories 284 | Protein 21g | Total Fat 8g | Sat. Fat 1g | Cholesterol 0mg | Carbohydrate 37g | Dietary Fiber 12g | Sodium 627mg

Curried Roasted Carrot Soup with Coconut

Makes 4 to 6 servings

A preliminary roasting of carrots and garlic lends this soup a delicious depth of flavor.

1 (16-ounce) bag baby carrots

3 large cloves garlic, peeled, left whole

2 tablespoons canola or other mild vegetable oil

Salt, to taste, plus ¼ teaspoon

Freshly ground black pepper, to taste

1 (14-ounce) can light coconut milk

2 (14-ounce) cans (3½ cups) low-sodium vegetable broth

1 tablespoon mango chutney

½ to 1 teaspoon curry powder

¼ cup chopped scallion greens

Preheat oven to 450F (230C). On an ungreased baking sheet with a rim, toss the carrots and garlic with the oil. Sprinkle lightly with salt and black pepper and toss well to combine. Bake about 20 minutes, until browned and tender, turning twice.

Transfer the carrot mixture to a food processor fitted with the knife blade. Add the coconut milk and process until smooth. Transfer to a medium stockpot and add the broth, chutney, curry powder, ¼ teaspoon salt, and pepper; bring to a simmer over medium-high heat, stirring occasionally. Reduce the heat and add the scallion greens; simmer gently, 2 minutes, stirring occasionally. Serve warm.

Per serving: Calories 259 | Protein 14g | Total Fat 14g | Sat. Fat 7g | Cholesterol 0mg | Carbohydrate 21g | Dietary Fiber 6g | Sodium 668mg

Hummus Soup

Makes 4 servings

Ready in just about fifteen minutes, this marvelous Middle Eastern–style soup makes a filling supper, accompanied with lots of pita bread and a tossed green salad.

2 (14-ounce) cans (3½ cups) low-sodium vegetable broth

1½ cups prepared plain (classic) hummus

1 (15-ounce) can chickpeas, rinsed and drained

Salt and freshly ground black pepper, to taste

Cayenne pepper, to taste (optional)

¼ cup chopped fresh flat-leaf parsley (see Cook's Tip, below)

1 to 2 tablespoons fresh lemon juice, or to taste

2 teaspoons extra-virgin olive oil

1 teaspoon toasted (dark) sesame oil

In a medium stockpot, bring the broth and hummus to a boil over medium-high heat, stirring often to incorporate the hummus. Add the chickpeas, salt, pepper, and cayenne (if using); reduce the heat and simmer, covered, 10 minutes, stirring a few times. Stir in the parsley, lemon juice, olive and sesame oils. Serve hot.

Per serving: Calories 335 | Protein 20g | Total Fat 13g | Sat. Fat 2g | Cholesterol 0mg | Carbohydrate 38g | Dietary Fiber 8g | Sodium 684mg

Cook's Tip: *When shopping for flat-leaf parsley, be careful not to confuse it with fresh cilantro, which it closely resembles.*

Tuscan Chickpea Soup with Sun-Dried Tomatoes and Rosemary

Makes 6 servings

This hearty soup is a meal in itself accompanied with lots of crusty Italian bread and a tossed green salad. For a delicious first course, omit the pasta. Alternatively, for a more substantial main dish, double the amount of pasta.

2 tablespoons extra-virgin olive oil

2 cups chopped onions

½ cup chopped carrot

6 large cloves garlic, finely chopped

2 (14-ounce) cans (3½ cups) low-sodium
   vegetable broth

1 to 2 cups water

2 (15-ounce) cans chickpeas, rinsed and drained

½ cup drained oil-packed sun-dried tomatoes,
   chopped, ½ tablespoon marinade reserved

2 teaspoons dried rosemary

1 large bay leaf

½ teaspoon salt, or to taste

¼ teaspoon crushed red pepper flakes, or to
   taste (optional)

Freshly ground black pepper, to taste

1 cup small elbow macaroni or similar pasta
   (4 ounces), preferably whole wheat, cooked
   according to package directions until just
   al dente, drained

¼ cup chopped fresh basil or flat-leaf parsley
   (optional)

In a medium stockpot, heat the oil over medium heat. Add the onions and carrot and cook, stirring, until softened, about 3 minutes. Add the garlic and cook, stirring constantly, 1 minute. Add the broth, 1 cup water, chickpeas, tomatoes and reserved marinade, rosemary, bay leaf, salt, red pepper flakes (if using), and black pepper; bring to a boil over high heat, stirring occasionally. Reduce the heat and simmer, covered, 10 minutes, stirring occasionally. Remove and discard the bay leaf.

Working in batches, as necessary, transfer the soup mixture to a food processor fitted with the knife blade, or to a blender; process until smooth and pureed. Return to the pot and add the cooked macaroni and basil (if using); cook over low heat, stirring occasionally, until heated through, about 3 minutes, adding additional water if a thinner consistency is desired. Serve hot.

Per serving: Calories 327 | Protein 18g | Total Fat 8g | Sat. Fat 1g | Cholesterol 0mg | Carbohydrate 48g | Dietary Fiber 4g | Sodium 519mg

Sweet Potato and Red Pepper Soup with Toasted Corn

Makes 4 servings

Toasting the corn lends this homey soup a restaurant-quality flavor.

2 tablespoons extra-virgin olive oil

1½ cups frozen yellow corn, thawed

1 cup chopped onion

2 large cloves garlic, finely chopped

2 cups low-sodium vegetable broth

1 cup water, plus additional, as necessary

2 tablespoons tomato paste

1 large sweet potato (about 8 ounces), peeled
   and cut into bite-sized chunks

1 (12-ounce) jar roasted red bell peppers,
   preferably fire-roasted, drained

½ tablespoon chili powder, or to taste

1 teaspoon ground cumin

½ teaspoon salt, or to taste

Freshly ground black pepper, to taste

¼ cup finely chopped fresh cilantro, basil, or
   parsley (optional)

Hot sauce, to taste (optional)

In a medium stockpot, heat 1 tablespoon of the oil over medium-high heat. Add the corn and cook, stirring and tossing constantly, until browned and fragrant, about 3 minutes. Transfer the corn to a holding plate and set aside. Reduce the heat to medium and add the remaining 1 tablespoon oil and onion to the pot; cook, stirring, until softened, about 3 minutes. Add the garlic and cook, stirring constantly, 1 minute. Add the broth, water, tomato paste, sweet potato, red bell peppers, chili powder, cumin, salt, and black pepper; bring to a boil over high heat, breaking up the bell peppers with a large wooden spoon. Reduce the heat to medium and simmer briskly, partially covered, until potato is tender, about 15 minutes, stirring occasionally.

Working in batches, as necessary, transfer the soup mixture to a food processor fitted with the knife blade, or to a blender; process until smooth and pureed. Return to the pot and add the reserved corn and cilantro (if using); cook over medium-low heat, stirring, until heated through, about 3 minutes, adding additional water, if desired, to achieve a thinner consistency. Serve hot, with the hot sauce passed separately (if using).

Per serving: Calories 250 | Protein 10g | Total Fat 8g | Sat. Fat 1g | Cholesterol 0mg | Carbohydrate 39g | Dietary Fiber 8g | Sodium 613mg

Curried Eggplant and Black-Eyed Pea Stew

 Makes 4 servings

To stretch this delicious stew, serve over basmati rice. Chickpeas can replace the black-eyed peas, if desired.

1 large eggplant (about 1 pound), peeled, cut into 1-inch cubes, sprinkled with salt, and set in a colander to drain for 30 minutes (salting is optional) (see Cook's Tip, below)

2 tablespoons extra-virgin olive oil

2 cups chopped onions

4 large cloves garlic, finely chopped

1 (15-ounce) can black-eyed peas, rinsed and drained

1 cup low-sodium vegetable broth

¼ cup mild (American-style) chili sauce or ketchup

¼ cup raisins (optional)

2 to 3 teaspoons mild curry powder

½ teaspoon salt, or to taste

Freshly ground black pepper, to taste

½ cup chopped fresh cilantro

¼ cup mango chutney

Rinse the eggplant cubes under cold running water and drain.

In a large nonstick skillet with a lid, heat the oil over medium heat. Add the eggplant and onions; cook, stirring, until vegetables are just softened, about 3 minutes. Cover and cook, stirring a few times, until the eggplant is just tender, about 5 minutes. Add the garlic and cook, stirring constantly, 2 minutes. Add the black-eyed peas, broth, chili sauce, raisins (if using), curry powder, salt, and pepper; bring to a brisk simmer over medium-high heat, stirring occasionally. Reduce the heat to low and simmer, covered, until eggplant is very tender, about 5 minutes, stirring a few times. Stir in the cilantro and chutney and cook, stirring, until heated through, about 2 minutes. Serve warm.

Per serving: Calories 279 | Protein 11g | Total Fat 9g | Sat. Fat 1g | Cholesterol 0mg | Carbohydrate 42g | Dietary Fiber 6g | Sodium 415mg

Cook's Tip: *Salting helps draw out the eggplant's bitter juices. However, if you are short on time, the step can be omitted here and in other recipes where the eggplant is to be simmered or baked with several ingredients, as any bitterness is typically masked by the other flavors.*

Quick Tomato-Rice Soup with Zucchini and Basil

 Makes 4 to 6 servings

If you happen to have a leftover pint container of Chinese take-out rice, consider using it in this easy version of the Mediterranean classic.

- 1 tablespoon extra-virgin olive oil
- 2 tablespoons all-purpose flour
- 4 cups no-salt-added canned tomato sauce
- 2 cups low-sodium vegetable broth or water, plus additional, as necessary
- ½ tablespoon sugar
- 1 teaspoon onion powder
- ½ teaspoon salt, or to taste
- Freshly ground black pepper, to taste
- 1 medium zucchini (about 6 ounces), coarsely chopped
- 2 cups cooked white or brown rice (see Cook's Tip, page 100)
- 2 tablespoons chopped fresh basil

In a large saucepan or medium stockpot, heat the oil over medium-low heat. Add the flour and cook, stirring constantly, until lightly browned, 3 to 5 minutes. Gradually whisk in the tomato sauce, broth, sugar, onion powder, salt, and pepper. Add the zucchini and bring to a simmer over medium-high heat, stirring constantly. Reduce the heat to low and cook, uncovered, stirring occasionally, 15 minutes. Add the rice and cook, stirring, until heated through, about 3 minutes, adding additional broth or water if a thinner consistency is desired. Stir in the basil and serve hot.

Per serving: Calories 294 | Protein 13g | Total Fat 4g | Sat. Fat 1g | Cholesterol 0mg | Carbohydrate 51g | Dietary Fiber 6g | Sodium 594mg

Asian-Style Lentil Stew

 Makes 4 servings

For added crunch and texture, add about 1 cup of fresh snow peas, cut diagonally in half, the last fifteen minutes of simmering, if desired.

- ½ tablespoon peanut oil
- 1½ cups chopped onion
- 2 to 3 large cloves garlic, finely chopped
- 2¼ cups water
- 1 (14-ounce) can (1¾ cups) low-sodium vegetable broth
- 1 cup dried lentils, rinsed and picked over
- ⅓ cup brown rice
- ¼ teaspoon salt, or to taste
- Freshly ground black pepper, to taste
- 2 tablespoons plain rice vinegar
- 2 tablespoons low-sodium soy or tamari sauce, or to taste
- 1 tablespoon light brown sugar
- 1 tablespoon toasted (dark) sesame oil
- 1 to 2 teaspoons Chinese chili paste, or to taste (optional)

In a medium stockpot, heat the peanut oil over medium heat. Add the onion and cook, stirring, until softened, about 3 minutes. Add the garlic and cook, stirring constantly, 1 minute. Add the water, broth, lentils, rice, salt, and pepper; bring to a boil over high heat. Reduce the heat to between low and medium-low and simmer, covered, 30 minutes, stirring occasionally. Add the remaining ingredients and simmer, covered, stirring occasionally, until the lentils and rice are tender, about 15 minutes. Serve hot.

Per serving: Calories 331 | Protein 21g | Total Fat 6g | Sat. Fat 1g | Cholesterol 0mg | Carbohydrate 51g | Dietary Fiber 18g | Sodium 669mg

White-Bean Minestrone with Zucchini and Rosemary

Makes 4 to 6 servings

This smoky variation of minestrone is one of my favorites.

2 tablespoons extra-virgin olive oil

½ cup chopped onion

½ cup chopped carrot

1 large zucchini (about 8 ounces), cut into small dice

2 large cloves garlic, finely chopped

4 cups low-sodium vegetable broth

2 cups water

1 (19-ounce) can cannellini or other white beans, rinsed and drained

1 cup grape tomatoes, halved, or cherry tomatoes, quartered

½ teaspoon dried rosemary

¼ teaspoon salt, or to taste

¼ teaspoon liquid smoke

Freshly ground black pepper, to taste

In a medium stockpot, heat the oil over medium heat. Add the onion, carrot, and zucchini and cook, stirring, until softened, about 5 minutes. Add the garlic and cook, stirring, 1 minute. Add the remaining ingredients and bring to a boil over high heat. Reduce the heat to medium-low and simmer, uncovered, until vegetables are tender, about 10 minutes, stirring occasionally. Serve warm.

Per serving: Calories 270 | Protein 21g | Total Fat 7g | Sat. Fat 1g | Cholesterol 0mg | Carbohydrate 32g | Dietary Fiber 13g | Sodium 669mg

Easy Lentil Soup

Makes 4 servings

Lentils are one of the healthiest and cheapest sources of vegetable protein and iron on the planet. This simple, warming soup is another of my favorites.

1 tablespoon extra-virgin olive oil

1 cup chopped onion

¼ cup chopped carrot

4 cups low-sodium vegetable broth

1 cup water

1 cup dried lentils, rinsed and picked over

½ teaspoon dried thyme leaves

¼ teaspoon salt, or to taste

Freshly ground black pepper, to taste

1 large bay leaf, broken in half, or 2 small bay leaves

In a medium stockpot, heat the oil over medium heat. Add the onion and carrot and cook, stirring, until softened, about 3 minutes. Add the broth, water, lentils, thyme, salt, pepper, and bay leaf; bring to a boil over high heat. Reduce the heat to between low and medium-low, cover, and simmer until the lentils are tender, about 45 minutes, stirring occasionally. Remove and discard the bay leaf halves. Serve warm.

Per serving: Calories 262 | Protein 25g | Total Fat 4g | Sat. Fat 1g | Cholesterol 0mg | Carbohydrate 34g | Dietary Fiber 19g | Sodium 659mg

Salads

Not very long ago, salads in America consisted of some torn iceberg lettuce leaves, a few tomato wedges, and a couple of onion slices (if you were lucky), all drowning in a sea of Green Goddess or Thousand Island dressing. These days, the expansion of the global food market has dramatically increased the selection—nearly every ethnic cuisine, from the Asian-Style Spinach and Mushroom Salad with Hoisin Vinaigrette to the Spanish-Style Zucchini Salad with Poppy Seed Vinaigrette, are represented in this chapter. Several, such as Cinco de Mayo Mexican Salad, Spicy Thai Tofu Salad with Cherry Tomatoes and Basil, and Grilled Tuscan Bread Salad with Summer Vegetables, are the focal points of memorable meals.

Italian-Style Artichoke and White Bean Salad

Makes 4 servings

Red kidney beans can be substituted for the white beans, if desired.

1 (15-ounce) can cannellini or other white
    beans, rinsed and drained
1 (6-ounce) jar marinated quartered artichoke
    hearts, drained
½ cup chopped red onion
2 tablespoons finely chopped fresh basil
2 tablespoons finely chopped fresh flat-leaf
    parsley
1 tablespoon extra-virgin olive oil
½ tablespoon white wine vinegar or cider
    vinegar
Salt and freshly ground black pepper, to taste

In a medium bowl, gently toss all the ingredients until well combined. Let stand 15 minutes at room temperature to allow the flavors to blend. Toss again and serve at room temperature. Alternatively, cover and refrigerate a minimum of 2 hours or up to 2 days and serve chilled, or return to room temperature.

Per serving: Calories 153 | Protein 8g | Total Fat 4g | Sat. Fat 1g | Cholesterol 0mg | Carbohydrate 24g | Dietary Fiber 9g | Sodium 46mg

Variation: *To make Italian-Style Artichoke and White Bean Bruschetta, chop the artichokes and prepare the recipe as otherwise directed. Serve at room temperature, accompanied with slices of Italian bread, toasted (see Cook's Tip, page 11), rubbed on one side with a halved garlic clove.*

Avocado, Corn, Tomato, and Zucchini Salad

Makes 6 servings

This is a fine accompaniment to any of the book's Mexican-style entrees, namely the Sweet Potato and Black Bean Burritos (page 70). It also makes an excellent main course salad for four, tossed with 1 (15-ounce) can rinsed and drained black beans.

⅓ cup mild or medium salsa, preferably the
    chunky variety
2 tablespoons chopped fresh cilantro or flat-
    leaf parsley
2 tablespoons extra-virgin olive oil
1 tablespoon fresh lime juice
½ teaspoon salt
¼ teaspoon ground cumin
Freshly ground black pepper, to taste
2 medium vine-ripened tomatoes (about
    6 ounces each), seeded and chopped
1 medium zucchini (about 6 ounces), chopped
1 cup cooked fresh or frozen yellow corn, at
    room temperature
1 ripe avocado, peeled, pitted, and coarsely
    chopped
4 scallions, white and green parts, thinly
    sliced

In a large bowl, stir together the salsa, cilantro, oil, lime juice, salt, cumin, and pepper until thoroughly combined. Add the remaining ingredients and toss gently yet thoroughly to combine. Let stand about 10 minutes to allow the flavors to blend. Toss gently again and serve at room temperature. Alternatively, cover and refrigerate a minimum of 2 hours or overnight and serve chilled.

Per serving: Calories 144 | Protein 3g | Total Fat 10g | Sat. Fat 2g | Cholesterol 0mg | Carbohydrate 14g | Dietary Fiber 3g | Sodium 227mg

Southwestern-Style Marinated Four-Bean Salad

 Makes 8 servings

Here is a super-quick and ever-popular side salad that holds up well at picnics and barbecues. Pinto beans can replace either the black beans or kidney beans, if desired.

1 (15-ounce) can black beans, rinsed and
    drained
1 (15-ounce) can red kidney beans, rinsed and
    drained
1 (8-ounce) can green beans, rinsed and
    drained
1 (8-ounce) can yellow wax beans, rinsed and
    drained
1 cup chopped red onion
¼ cup chopped fresh cilantro
1 jalapeño chili, seeded and finely chopped
    (optional)
5 tablespoons cider vinegar
2½ tablespoons extra-virgin olive oil
1 tablespoon light brown sugar
½ tablespoon ground cumin, or to taste
½ teaspoon salt, or to taste
Freshly ground black pepper, to taste

In a large bowl, toss together all the ingredients until well combined. Let stand 30 minutes at room temperature to allow the flavors to blend, tossing a few times. Toss again and serve at room temperature. Alternatively, cover and refrigerate a minimum of 1 hour or up to 3 days and serve chilled, or return to room temperature.

Per serving: Calories 152 | Protein 7g | Total Fat 5g | Sat. Fat 1g | Cholesterol 0mg | Carbohydrate 22g | Dietary Fiber 4g | Sodium 322mg

Spanish-Style Zucchini Salad with Poppy Seed Vinaigrette

 Makes 4 to 6 servings

Use the versatile poppy seed vinaigrette to dress countless salads and slaws.

¼ cup extra-virgin olive oil
4 teaspoons red wine vinegar
1 tablespoon orange juice
½ tablespoon poppy seeds
½ teaspoon sugar
¼ teaspoon dry mustard
¼ teaspoon salt, or to taste
Freshly ground black pepper, to taste
2 to 4 scallions, white and green parts, thinly
    sliced
4 medium zucchini (about 5 ounces each),
    halved lengthwise, thinly sliced crosswise

In a large bowl, whisk together the oil, vinegar, orange juice, poppy seeds, sugar, mustard, salt, and pepper until thoroughly blended. Stir in the scallions and let stand about 5 minutes to allow the flavors to blend. Add the zucchini and toss well to thoroughly coat; let stand about 5 minutes to allow the flavors to blend. Toss again and serve at room temperature. Alternatively, cover and refrigerate a minimum of 2 hours or up to 1 day and serve chilled, or return to room temperature.

Per serving: Calories 153 | Protein 2g | Total Fat 14g | Sat. Fat 2g | Cholesterol 0mg | Carbohydrate 6g | Dietary Fiber 2g | Sodium 139mg

Variation: *To make Spanish-Style Cucumber Salad with Poppy Seed Vinaigrette, substitute 2 medium seedless cucumbers, about 10 ounces each, for the zucchini; prepare as otherwise directed in the recipe.*

Moroccan-Style Carrot, Currant, and Orange Salad with Sunflower Seeds

Makes 4 servings

Tahini, an oily, nutlike paste made from ground sesame seeds, can be found in most well-stocked supermarkets among the sauces and condiments. Natural peanut butter can be substituted, if necessary.

½ cup unsweetened apple juice

2 tablespoons sesame tahini

1 tablespoon pure maple syrup

1 tablespoon cider vinegar

½ teaspoon salt

Freshly ground black pepper, to taste

Pinch ground cinnamon

¼ cup Zante currants or raisins

1 (10-ounce) bag shredded carrots

1 (11-ounce) can mandarin orange segments, drained

¼ cup sunflower seeds

2 tablespoons finely chopped fresh flat-leaf parsley

In a large bowl, whisk together the juice, tahini, maple syrup, vinegar, salt, pepper, and cinnamon until smooth. Add the currants and let stand about 10 minutes to soften. Add the remaining ingredients and toss gently yet thoroughly to combine. Serve at room temperature. Alternatively, cover and refrigerate a minimum of 2 hours or overnight and serve chilled.

Per serving: Calories 199 | Protein 5g | Total Fat 9g | Sat. Fat 1g | Cholesterol 0mg | Carbohydrate 29g | Dietary Fiber 5g | Sodium 293mg

Tuscan-Style Chickpea and Spinach Salad with Artichokes and Sun-Dried Tomatoes

Makes 4 to 6 servings

This festive chickpea and spinach salad is an ideal first course for easy entertaining, as the chickpea mixture can be made up to a day ahead of serving.

2 tablespoons extra-virgin olive oil

¼ cup drained and julienned marinated sun-dried tomatoes, 1 tablespoon marinade reserved

1 tablespoon fresh lemon juice

1 teaspoon Dijon mustard

1 large clove garlic, finely chopped

½ teaspoon salt, preferably the coarse variety, or to taste

Freshly ground black pepper, to taste

1 (15-ounce) can chickpeas, rinsed and drained

1 (6-ounce) jar marinated quartered artichoke hearts, drained

4 scallions, white and green parts, thinly sliced

2 to 4 tablespoons chopped fresh basil

1 (9-ounce) bag baby spinach

In a medium bowl, whisk together the oil, reserved sun-dried tomato marinade, lemon juice, mustard, garlic, salt, and pepper until thoroughly blended. Add the remaining ingredients, except the spinach, and toss well to combine. Let stand about 10 minutes at room temperature to allow the flavors to blend; toss again. (At this point, mixture can be covered and refrigerated up to 1 day before returning to room temperature and continuing with the recipe.) Serve at room temperature, over the spinach leaves.

Per serving: Calories 234 | Protein 10g | Total Fat 11g | Sat. Fat 2g | Cholesterol 0mg | Carbohydrate 27g | Dietary Fiber 5g | Sodium 360mg

Cucumber and Tomato Salad with Tahini

 Makes 6 servings

To turn this tasty salad into a main dish for four, toss with 1 (15-ounce) can rinsed and drained chickpeas.

½ cup sesame tahini

¼ to ½ cup water

Juice of ½ to 1 whole lemon

2 large cloves garlic, finely chopped

½ teaspoon salt, or to taste

Freshly ground black pepper, to taste

2 large tomatoes (about 8 ounces each), seeded and chopped

2 medium cucumbers (about 8 ounces each), seeded and chopped

¼ cup chopped fresh flat-leaf parsley (optional)

2 to 4 scallions, white and green parts, thinly sliced (optional)

Romaine lettuce leaves (optional)

In a medium bowl, whisk together the tahini, ¼ cup water, juice of ½ lemon, garlic, salt, and pepper until thoroughly blended. Add additional water and lemon juice to achieve desired consistency and tartness. Add the remaining ingredients, except the lettuce (if using), and toss gently yet thoroughly to combine. Season with additional salt and pepper, if necessary. Let stand about 15 minutes at room temperature to allow the flavors to blend. Toss again and serve at room temperature, over the lettuce (if using). Alternatively, cover and refrigerate a minimum of 1 hour or up to 1 day and serve chilled, or return to room temperature.

Per serving: Calories 145 | Protein 5g | Total Fat 11g | Sat. Fat 2g | Cholesterol 0mg | Carbohydrate 11g | Dietary Fiber 3g | Sodium 188mg

Fennel and Pink Grapefruit Salad with Balsamic-Orange Vinaigrette

 Makes 4 servings

Regularly stocked in most major supermarkets throughout the fall and winter months, fennel is often mislabeled anise, which is an annual herb grown primarily for its similar licorice-flavored seeds.

3 tablespoons prepared nonfat balsamic vinaigrette

2 tablespoons orange juice

1 tablespoon extra-virgin olive oil

½ tablespoon sugar, or to taste

Salt and freshly ground black pepper, to taste

1 large fennel bulb (about 1 pound), trimmed, cored, cut in half lengthwise, and thinly sliced crosswise

1 (15-ounce) can pink grapefruit in light syrup, well drained

2 tablespoons chopped fennel fronds

In a medium bowl, whisk together the vinaigrette, orange juice, oil, sugar, salt, and pepper. Let stand a few minutes to allow the flavors to blend; whisk again. Add the remaining ingredients and toss gently yet thoroughly to combine. Let stand about 10 minutes at room temperature to allow the flavors to blend. Toss gently again and serve. Alternatively, cover and refrigerate a minimum of 1 hour or overnight and serve chilled.

Per serving: Calories 98 | Protein 2g | Total Fat 4g | Sat. Fat 1g | Cholesterol 0mg | Carbohydrate 17g | Dietary Fiber 1g | Sodium 202mg

Quick Greek Salad

 Makes 4 to 5 servings

This versatile Mediterranean salad can serve as a light first course or filling main dish with the addition of the optional ingredients.

  5 tablespoons extra-virgin olive oil
  1 to 2 tablespoons fresh lemon juice
  1 tablespoon red wine vinegar
  1 to 2 cloves garlic, finely chopped
  ½ teaspoon dried oregano
  ½ teaspoon lemon-pepper seasoning
  ½ teaspoon salt, or more, to taste
  Freshly ground black pepper, to taste
  1 (10-ounce) bag romaine lettuce leaves
  Sliced plum tomatoes or halved cherry or
     grape tomatoes, sliced cucumbers, sliced
     red onion, pitted kalamata olives, chickpeas
     (optional)

In a large bowl, whisk together the oil, lemon juice, vinegar, garlic, oregano, lemon-pepper seasoning, salt, and pepper until thoroughly blended. Let stand about 10 minutes to allow the flavors to blend. Whisk again and add the lettuce and optional ingredients (if using), tossing well to thoroughly coat. Serve at once.

Per serving: Calories 164 | Protein 1g | Total Fat 17g | Sat. Fat 2g | Cholesterol 0mg | Carbohydrate 3g | Dietary Fiber 1g | Sodium 315mg

Mixed Greens with Fresh Herb Vinaigrette

 Makes 4 servings

This classic herbed vinaigrette is also wonderful brushed over broiled or grilled vegetables, such as bell peppers, eggplant, mushrooms, and zucchini.

  3 tablespoons extra-virgin olive oil
  1 tablespoon red wine vinegar
  ½ teaspoon Dijon mustard
  1 clove garlic, finely chopped
  ¼ teaspoon salt
  Freshly ground black pepper, to taste
  1 teaspoon finely chopped fresh chives or the
     green parts of scallions
  1 teaspoon finely chopped fresh parsley
  1 teaspoon finely chopped fresh basil
  1 teaspoon finely chopped fresh mint
  1 (10-ounce) bag mixed greens or other lettuce

In a large bowl, whisk together the oil, vinegar, mustard, garlic, salt, and pepper until thoroughly blended. Stir in the chives, parsley, basil, and mint. Let stand a few minutes to allow the flavors to blend, and then whisk again. Add the greens, tossing well to thoroughly coat. Serve at once.

Per serving: Calories 111 | Protein 2g | Total Fat 10g | Sat. Fat 1g | Cholesterol 0mg | Carbohydrate 4g | Dietary Fiber 2g | Sodium 144mg

Variation: *To make Mixed Greens with Fresh Chive Vinaigrette, omit the basil and mint and double the amounts of chives and parsley.*

Mesclun Salad with Strawberry-Balsamic Vinaigrette

 Makes 4 servings

Here is a lovely first-course salad special enough for company. Raspberry jam and whole raspberries can replace the strawberry jam and sliced strawberries, if desired.

  4½ tablespoons extra-virgin olive oil
  1½ tablespoons balsamic vinegar
  1 tablespoon strawberry jam

¼ teaspoon salt

Freshly ground black pepper, to taste

1 (10-ounce) bag mesclun or other mixed
    greens

1 cup sliced fresh strawberries

In a large bowl, whisk together the oil, vinegar, jam, salt, and pepper until thoroughly blended. Add the mesclun to the bowl and toss to evenly coat. Divide evenly among each of 4 salad bowls or plates and garnish with equal amounts of strawberries. Serve at once.

Per serving: Calories 177 | Protein 2g | Total Fat 16g | Sat. Fat 2g | Cholesterol 0mg | Carbohydrate 10g | Dietary Fiber 2g | Sodium 153mg

Jicama, Bell Pepper, and Red Onion Salad

 Makes 4 to 6 servings

Jicama, sometimes called the Mexican potato, is a large bulbous root vegetable available in most major supermarkets.

2 tablespoons cider vinegar

2 tablespoons extra-virgin olive oil

1 tablespoon fresh lime juice

1 tablespoon sugar

½ teaspoon salt

Freshly ground black pepper, to taste

1 medium jicama (about 12 ounces), peeled
    and coarsely chopped

1 medium red bell pepper (about 6 ounces),
    cored, seeded, and chopped

½ medium cucumber (about 4 ounces), peeled,
    seeded, and chopped

½ cup chopped red onion

¼ cup chopped fresh cilantro

In a large bowl, whisk together the vinegar, oil, lime juice, sugar, salt, and black pepper. Let stand a few

minutes to allow the sugar and salt to dissolve; whisk again. Add the remaining ingredients, tossing well to combine. Let stand 15 minutes at room temperature to allow the flavors to blend. Toss again and serve. Alternatively, cover and refrigerate a minimum of 2 hours or up to 2 days and serve chilled, or return to room temperature.

Per serving: Calories 135 | Protein 2g | Total Fat 7g | Sat. Fat 1g | Cholesterol 0mg | Carbohydrate 18g | Dietary Fiber 6g | Sodium 273mg

Greek-Style Black-Eyed Pea Salad with Scallions and Dill

Makes 4 servings

For a special first course or appetizer, serve these tasty black-eyed peas in radicchio or Belgian endive leaves.

1 (15-ounce) can black-eyed peas, rinsed and
    drained

2 scallions, white and green parts, thinly
    sliced

Juice of ½ lemon (about 1½ tablespoons)

1 tablespoon extra-virgin olive oil

2 teaspoons chopped fresh dill or about
    ½ teaspoon dried

¼ teaspoon salt, or to taste

Freshly ground black pepper, to taste

In a medium bowl, toss together all the ingredients until well combined. Let stand about 15 minutes at room temperature to allow the flavors to blend. Toss again and serve at room temperature. Alternatively, cover and refrigerate 1 hour or up to 2 days and serve chilled, or return to room temperature.

Per serving: Calories 109 | Protein 5g | Total Fat 4g | Sat. Fat 1g | Cholesterol 0mg | Carbohydrate 15g | Dietary Fiber 5g | Sodium 138mg

Marinated Mushroom Salad

Makes 6 servings

For an earthier dish, sliced cremini mushrooms can replace all or part of the cultivated variety, if desired.

  ¼ cup extra-virgin olive oil

  2 tablespoons white wine vinegar

  1 tablespoon Dijon mustard

  ½ teaspoon dried oregano

  ½ teaspoon dried tarragon

  ½ teaspoon salt

  Freshly ground black pepper, to taste

  4 cups sliced fresh cultivated white mushrooms

  1½ cups cherry or grape tomatoes, halved

  8 to 12 pitted kalamata olives, halved
    (see Cook's Tip, page 16) (optional)

  ¼ cup chopped fresh flat-leaf parsley

In a medium bowl, whisk together the oil, vinegar, mustard, oregano, tarragon, salt, and pepper until thoroughly blended. Add the mushrooms, tomatoes, olives (if using), and parsley; toss to thoroughly coat. Let stand about 5 minutes before tossing again. Cover and refrigerate a minimum of 2 hours, or overnight. Toss thoroughly and serve chilled or return to room temperature.

Per serving: Calories 107 | Protein 2g | Total Fat 10g | Sat. Fat 1g | Cholesterol 0mg | Carbohydrate 5g | Dietary Fiber 1g | Sodium 217mg

Warm Mushroom and Arugula Salad

Makes 4 to 6 servings

This is an ideal first-course salad to serve in the fall, when mushrooms are in season. The mushroom topping is also wonderful tossed with steamed broccoli.

  3½ tablespoons extra-virgin olive oil

  8 ounces sliced fresh cultivated and/or
    cremini mushrooms

  ¼ cup chopped red onion

  2 large cloves garlic, finely chopped

  2½ tablespoons balsamic vinegar

  ½ teaspoon coarse salt, or to taste

  Freshly ground black pepper, to taste

  1 (9-ounce) package arugula

In a large nonstick skillet with a lid, heat 1 tablespoon of the oil over medium heat. Add the mushrooms and onion; cook, stirring, until mushrooms begin to release their liquids, 3 to 4 minutes. Add the garlic and cook, stirring constantly, until mushrooms have released most of their liquids, 3 to 5 minutes. Working quickly, add the remaining 2½ tablespoons oil, vinegar, salt, and pepper, stirring well to combine. Immediately remove skillet from heat, cover, and let stand until just warm, about 15 minutes.

Place half the arugula in a large bowl and add half the warm mushroom mixture and accumulated juices; toss well to combine. Add the remaining ingredients and toss well to combine. Serve at once.

Per serving: Calories 142 | Protein 3g | Total Fat 13g | Sat. Fat 2g | Cholesterol 0mg | Carbohydrate 7g | Dietary Fiber 1g | Sodium 255mg

Variation: *To make Easy Skillet Spinach and Mushroom Salad to serve two to three, divide the recipe ingredients in half and use baby spinach in lieu of the arugula. Cook the mushrooms as directed in the same large nonstick skillet. After the mushroom mixture has cooled, covered, for 15 minutes, add the spinach directly to the skillet and toss well with a spatula to thoroughly combine. Serve at once, directly from the skillet.*

French Potato Salad

 Makes 4 to 6 servings

Superb at room temperature, this classic potato salad is always a hit at picnics or potlucks.

1½ pounds small Yukon gold or red-skin potatoes, scrubbed, left whole

3½ tablespoons low-sodium vegetable broth

1½ tablespoons extra-virgin olive oil

1½ tablespoons tarragon vinegar

½ tablespoon Dijon mustard

¼ teaspoon salt, plus more, to taste

Freshly ground black pepper, to taste

2 tablespoons finely chopped fresh flat-leaf parsley

4 scallions, white and green parts, thinly sliced

In a medium stockpot, bring the potatoes and enough salted water to cover to a boil over high heat. Reduce the heat slightly and boil until potatoes are tender through the center but not mushy, 15 to 20 minutes. Drain and set aside to cool about 15 minutes.

When cool enough to handle but still quite warm, thinly slice the potatoes and transfer to a large bowl. Pour the vegetable broth over the potatoes and toss gently to combine. Let stand until the broth has been absorbed, about 3 minutes. Meanwhile, in a small bowl, whisk together the oil, vinegar, mustard, salt, and pepper. Stir in the parsley. Add to the potatoes, tossing gently to combine. Let stand about 5 minutes, tossing gently once or twice. Add the scallions and toss gently to combine. Let cool to room temperature, about 15 minutes, before tossing gently again and serving. Alternatively, cover and refrigerate up to 24 hours before returning to room temperature and serving.

Per serving: Calories 158 | Protein 4g | Total Fat 5g | Sat. Fat 1g | Cholesterol 0mg | Carbohydrate 25g | Dietary Fiber 3g | Sodium 197mg

Asian-Style Spinach and Mushroom Salad with Hoisin Vinaigrette

 Makes 6 servings

You can use the hoisin vinaigrette to dress countless salads and vegetables. It's particularly delicious tossed with lightly steamed or blanched asparagus, snow peas, or sugar snap peas.

3 tablespoons peanut oil

2 tablespoons hoisin sauce

2 tablespoons plain rice vinegar

1 tablespoon low-sodium soy or tamari sauce

1 tablespoon toasted (dark) sesame oil

1 tablespoon light brown sugar

½ teaspoon salt, or to taste

Freshly ground black pepper, to taste

1 (10-ounce) bag baby spinach

1 cup sliced fresh white mushrooms

½ cup shredded carrot

2 scallions, white and green parts, thinly sliced

In a large bowl, whisk together the peanut oil, hoisin sauce, vinegar, soy sauce, sesame oil, sugar, salt, and pepper until thoroughly blended. Add the spinach, mushrooms, carrot, and scallions and toss well to thoroughly coat. Serve at once.

Per serving: Calories 121 | Protein 2g | Total Fat 10g | Sat. Fat 2g | Cholesterol 0mg | Carbohydrate 9g | Dietary Fiber 2g | Sodium 312mg

Radicchio and Walnut Salad with Cranberry-Balsamic Vinaigrette

Makes 4 servings

Any bitter green (Belgian endive, curly endive, escarole, or frisée) or spinach can replace the radicchio, if desired.

3 tablespoons extra-virgin olive oil

2 tablespoons canned whole cranberry sauce

1 tablespoon balsamic vinegar

1 teaspoon water, or more, as necessary

¼ teaspoon salt

Freshly ground black pepper

6 to 7 cups loosely packed washed and torn radicchio or other bitter greens

¼ cup walnut pieces

In a food processor fitted with the knife blade, or in a blender, process the oil, cranberry sauce, vinegar, water, salt, and pepper until smooth. (For a thinner consistency, add more water, as desired.)

To serve, divide the radicchio evenly among 4 salad bowls or plates and drizzle evenly with the dressing. Sprinkle each with 1 tablespoon of walnut pieces. Serve at once.

Per serving: Calories 165 | Protein 3g | Total Fat 15g | Sat. Fat 2g | Cholesterol 0mg | Carbohydrate 7g | Dietary Fiber 2g | Sodium 157mg

Variation: *To make Endive, Beet, and Walnut Salad with Cranberry-Balsamic Vinaigrette, replace the radicchio with 4 to 6 cups curly endive (or other bitter greens or spinach) and divide equally among 4 salad bowls or plates. Arrange 1 (15-ounce) can sliced beets, drained well, evenly over the endive. Drizzle evenly with the vinaigrette, and then sprinkle evenly with the walnuts. Serve at once.*

Per serving: Calories 186 | Protein 3g | Total Fat 15g | Sat. Fat 2g | Cholesterol 0mg | Carbohydrate 13g | Dietary Fiber 3g | Sodium 389mg

Southwestern-Style Sweet Potato and Black Bean Salad

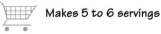 Makes 5 to 6 servings

Chipotle chili powder, made by grinding whole smoked and dried jalapeño chilies, can be located in the spice aisle in many well-stocked supermarkets. Regular chili powder can be substituted; however, you may need to use more, as it is generally less flavorful.

1 pound sweet potatoes (about 2 medium), peeled and cut into 2-inch chunks

2 tablespoons extra-virgin olive oil

1 tablespoon fresh lime juice

1 tablespoon orange juice

1 teaspoon chipotle chili powder

½ teaspoon ground cumin, or to taste

½ teaspoon salt, or to taste

Freshly ground black pepper, to taste

4 scallions, white and green parts, thinly sliced

½ cup chopped fresh cilantro

1 cup rinsed, drained canned black beans

In a large saucepan, bring the sweet potatoes and enough salted water to cover to a boil over high heat. Reduce the heat slightly and cook until potatoes are tender through the center but not mushy, about 15 minutes. Drain and let cool about 15 minutes.

In a large bowl, whisk together the oil, lime juice, orange juice, chili powder, cumin, salt, and pepper. Stir in the scallions and cilantro and set aside to let the flavors blend.

Cut the cooled potatoes into bite-size cubes and add to the dressing mixture, along with the black beans; toss gently yet thoroughly to combine. Let stand about 15 minutes to allow the flavors to blend; toss gently again and serve slightly warm or at room temperature. Alternatively, cover and refrigerate a minimum of 2 hours or up to 1 day and serve chilled, or return to room temperature.

Per serving: Calories 199 | Protein 5g | Total Fat 6g | Sat. Fat 1g | Cholesterol 0mg | Carbohydrate 32g | Dietary Fiber 5g | Sodium 234mg

Grilled Hearts of Romaine with Balsamic-Shallot Vinaigrette

Makes 4 servings

This is a quick and easy no-toss salad sophisticated enough for special occasions. Though it must be eaten shortly after grilling, the dressing can be made up to two days in advance.

½ cup prepared nonfat balsamic vinaigrette

2 tablespoons extra-virgin olive oil

2 small shallots, finely chopped

1 tablespoon light brown sugar

½ teaspoon salt, plus additional, to taste

Freshly ground black pepper, to taste

4 hearts of romaine (about 4 ounces each), rinsed and patted dry with paper towels, left whole

In a small bowl, whisk together the balsamic vinaigrette, 1 tablespoon of the oil, shallots, sugar, salt, and pepper until thoroughly blended. Let stand a few minutes to allow the sugar to dissolve. Whisk again and set aside about 15 minutes to allow the flavors to blend. (At this point, the balsamic-shallot vinaigrette can be stored, covered, in the refrigerator up to 2 days before returning to room temperature and using as directed in the recipe.)

Place a stovetop grilling pan with grids over medium-high heat. Brush romaine hearts with remaining 1 tablespoon oil, and season with salt and pepper. Grill 5 to 10 minutes, turning frequently, until slightly charred but not heated all the way

through. Transfer each romaine heart to a salad plate and drizzle with equal amounts of the balsamic-shallot vinaigrette. (Alternatively, slice the hearts into bite-size chunks and transfer to a large bowl. Add the vinaigrette and toss well to thoroughly combine.) Serve at once.

Per serving: Calories 111 | Protein 2g | Total Fat 7g | Sat. Fat 1g | Cholesterol 0mg | Carbohydrate 11g | Dietary Fiber 2g | Sodium 698mg

Tomato and Parsley Salad

Makes 3 to 4 servings

This simple salad is deceptively delicious. Fresh cilantro or basil can replace the parsley, if desired.

2 cups grape, pearl, or cherry tomatoes, halved

½ teaspoon coarse salt

2 tablespoons extra-virgin olive oil

1 tablespoon fresh lemon juice

1 teaspoon cider vinegar

Freshly ground black pepper, to taste

½ cup chopped fresh flat-leaf parsley

In a large bowl, toss together the tomatoes and salt. Let stand about 5 minutes. Add the oil, lemon juice, vinegar, and pepper; toss well to combine. Let stand about 5 minutes to allow the flavors to blend. Add the parsley and toss well to combine. Serve at room temperature. Alternatively, cover and refrigerate a minimum of 2 hours or up to 1 day and serve chilled, or return to room temperature.

Per serving: Calories 115 | Protein 2g | Total Fat 10g | Sat. Fat 1g | Cholesterol 0mg | Carbohydrate 8g | Dietary Fiber 2g | Sodium 332mg

Edamame, Chickpea, and Kidney Bean Salad

 Makes 8 servings

This is a perfect picnic or potluck salad to feed a crowd. Black beans can replace the kidney beans, if desired.

2 cups frozen shelled edamame (green soybeans), cooked according to package directions, drained

¼ cup extra-virgin olive oil

Juice of 2 limes (about ¼ cup)

1 teaspoon ground cumin

½ teaspoon salt, or to taste

Freshly ground black pepper, to taste

½ cup thinly sliced red onion, soaked in cold water to cover 10 minutes, drained (see Cook's Tip, below)

½ cup chopped fresh cilantro

1 (15-ounce) can red kidney beans, rinsed and drained

1 (15-ounce) can chickpeas, rinsed and drained

Rinse the edamame under cold running water until cooled. Drain again.

In a large bowl, whisk together the oil, lime juice, cumin, salt, and pepper. Stir in the onion and cilantro and let stand at room temperature about 10 minutes. Add the edamame, kidney beans, and chickpeas and toss well to combine. Let stand another 10 minutes at room temperature before tossing again and serving. Alternatively, cover and refrigerate a minimum of 2 hours or up to 2 days and serve chilled or return to room temperature.

Per serving: Calories 234 | Protein 13g | Total Fat 12g | Sat. Fat 2g | Cholesterol 0mg | Carbohydrate 22g | Dietary Fiber 4g | Sodium 138mg

Cook's Tip: *Soaking raw onion rings in cold water for 10 minutes helps minimize their pungency.*

MAIN-COURSE SALADS

Arborio Rice Salad with Black Beans and Toasted Corn

 Makes 4 main-dish or 6 to 8 side-dish servings

The use of the starchier arborio variety of rice ensures the grains will not harden in the refrigerator.

⅔ cup arborio rice

½ tablespoon canola oil

1½ cups frozen yellow corn, thawed

Garlic salt, to taste

Freshly ground black pepper, to taste

1 (15-ounce) can black beans, rinsed and drained

1½ cups prepared mild or medium salsa or picante sauce

4 scallions, white and green parts, thinly sliced

Bring a medium stockpot of salted water to a boil over high heat. Add the rice and boil until tender yet firm to the bite, stirring a few times, 12 to 15 minutes. Drain in a colander. Rinse under cold running water to cool; drain well.

Meanwhile, in a medium nonstick skillet, heat the oil over medium-high heat. Add the corn and cook, tossing and stirring often, until browned and fragrant, 3 to 5 minutes. Remove skillet from heat and toss the corn with the garlic salt and pepper; set aside to cool about 15 minutes.

In a large bowl, toss together the rice and corn with the remaining ingredients until thoroughly combined. Season with additional garlic salt and pepper, to taste. Serve at room temperature, or cover and refrigerate a minimum of 2 hours or up to 1 day and served chilled, or return to room temperature.

Per serving: Calories 293 | Protein 11g | Total Fat 3g | Sat. Fat 0g | Cholesterol 0mg | Carbohydrate 59g | Dietary Fiber 7g | Sodium 263mg

Grilled Tuscan Bread Salad with Summer Vegetables

Makes 4 to 6 main-dish servings

This grilled version of panzanella, Tuscany's famous bread salad, may well be my favorite.

4½ tablespoons extra-virgin olive oil

2 tablespoons fresh lemon juice

1 tablespoon red wine vinegar

2 large cloves garlic, 1 finely chopped, 1 peeled and cut in half

½ teaspoon salt, plus additional, to taste

Freshly ground black pepper, to taste

2 medium bell peppers (about 6 ounces each), preferably 1 green and 1 red, cored, seeded, and cut into 1½-inch-wide strips

2 medium zucchini (about 6 ounces each), preferably 1 green and 1 yellow, cut lengthwise into ⅓-inch-thick slices

1 medium red onion (about 6 ounces), cut into ¼-inch-thick rounds

6 ounces Italian bread, cut crosswise into 1-inch-thick slices

2 medium vine-ripened tomatoes (about 6 ounces each), coarsely chopped

½ cup chopped fresh basil

Italian seasoning, dried oregano, and/or crushed red pepper flakes, to serve (optional)

Prepare a medium-hot charcoal or gas grill, or preheat a broiler. Position the grill rack or oven rack 4 to 6 inches from the heat source. If broiling, lightly oil a large baking sheet and set aside. Alternatively, place a stovetop grilling pan with grids over medium-high heat.

Meanwhile, in a small bowl, whisk together 3 tablespoons of the oil, lemon juice, vinegar, the chopped garlic, salt, and black pepper until thoroughly blended. Set aside.

Brush both sides of the bell peppers, zucchini, onion, and bread slices evenly with the remaining 1½ tablespoons oil; sprinkle the vegetables lightly with salt and black pepper. Set aside the bread.

Grill or broil the vegetables until browned and tender, working in batches as necessary. As a general rule, cook the bell peppers 3 to 4 minutes per side, and the zucchini and onion 2 to 3 minutes per side. Place the vegetables on a baking sheet (another baking sheet, if broiling) as they finish cooking.

When all the vegetables have been cooked, grill the bread until lightly browned, 1 to 2 minutes per side. Cool slightly, and then rub on one or both sides with the cut sides of the halved garlic. Tear bread into bite-size pieces and transfer to a large bowl. Cut the grilled vegetables into 1-inch pieces and add to the bread bowl, along with the tomatoes and basil. Add the reserved dressing, salt, and black pepper and toss well to thoroughly combine. Let stand 20 minutes. Toss well again and serve at once, with the optional seasonings (if using) passed separately.

Per serving: Calories 321 | Protein 7g | Total Fat 17g | Sat. Fat 3g | Cholesterol 0mg | Carbohydrate 38g | Dietary Fiber 6g | Sodium 528mg

Variations: *To make Grilled Tuscan Bread Salad with Summer Vegetables and White Beans, add 1 (15-ounce) can cannellini or other white beans, rinsed and drained, along with the tomatoes and basil.*

To make Tuscan-Style Grilled Summer Vegetable Wraps, omit the Italian bread and the halved garlic clove from the recipe. Proceed as otherwise directed, adding white beans, if desired, as suggested in the variation, above. Divide the vegetable mixture equally among 4 to 6 (10-inch) flour tortillas, preferably whole wheat. Roll up each tortilla from the edge nearest you, tucking in the sides as you roll. Serve at once.

Brown Rice Salad with Apples, Celery, Raisins, and Walnuts

 Makes 4 main-dish or 6 to 8 side-dish servings

If desired, 1 cup of quick-cooking couscous (preferably the whole wheat variety) can replace the brown rice; also, slivered almonds or chopped pecans can replace the walnuts.

- 1 medium (about 6 ounces) Macintosh, Fuji, or other crisp red apple, cored, unpeeled, chopped
- ½ tablespoon fresh lemon juice
- 1 cup quick-cooking or regular brown rice, cooked according to package directions (see Cook's Tip, page 100), cooled to room temperature
- 2 stalks celery, thinly sliced
- ⅓ cup walnuts, chopped
- ¼ cup raisins or Zante currants
- ¼ cup chopped fresh parsley
- 2 tablespoons canola or other mild vegetable oil
- 2 tablespoons pure maple syrup
- 2 tablespoons cider vinegar
- Salt and freshly ground black pepper, to taste

In a large bowl, toss together the apple and lemon juice until combined. Add the remaining ingredients and toss well to combine. Let stand about 10 minutes at room temperature to allow the flavors to blend. Toss again and serve at room temperature. Alternatively, cover and refrigerate a minimum of 2 hours or overnight and serve chilled, or return to room temperature.

Per serving: Calories 378 | Protein 7g | Total Fat 14g | Sat. Fat 1g | Cholesterol 0mg | Carbohydrate 59g | Dietary Fiber 3g | Sodium 24mg

Southwestern Cornbread Salad

 Makes 4 main-dish or 6 to 8 side-dish servings

Whenever I bake-up a batch of Southwestern-Style Cornbread (page 68), I cube half the recipe, place in a freezer bag, and store in the freezer for up to two months. Whenever I want to enjoy this sensational bread salad, I thaw the cornbread cubes on the countertop for a few hours and then follow the quick and easy recipe, below.

- ½ recipe Southwestern-Style Cornbread (page 68), cut into 1-inch cubes
- 1 (15-ounce) can black beans, rinsed and drained
- 1 cup mild or medium salsa
- 4 scallions, white and green parts, thinly sliced
- 2 to 4 tablespoons chopped fresh cilantro
- 1 jalapeño chili, seeded and finely chopped (optional)
- 2 tablespoons extra-virgin olive oil
- 1 tablespoon fresh lime juice, or to taste
- 1 teaspoon ground cumin
- 1 teaspoon sugar (optional)
- Salt and freshly ground black pepper, to taste
- Shredded iceberg lettuce (optional)

Preheat the oven to 350F (175C). Place the cubed cornbread on an ungreased baking sheet. Bake for 20 minutes, turning a few times, until lightly toasted. Allow to cool for 15 minutes.

Meanwhile, in a large bowl, combine the black beans, salsa, scallions, cilantro, chili (if using), oil, lime juice, cumin, sugar (if using), salt, and pepper until thoroughly combined. Let stand a few minutes to allow the flavors to blend. Add the cornbread and toss gently yet thoroughly to combine. Let stand about 10 minutes to allow the flavors to blend. Toss gently again and serve at once, over the lettuce, if using.

Per serving: Calories 341 | Protein 11g | Total Fat 10g | Sat. Fat 1g | Cholesterol 0mg | Carbohydrate 56g | Dietary Fiber 9g | Sodium 756mg

Bulgur Salad with Cantaloupe and Walnuts

Makes 4 main-dish or 8 side-dish servings

Honeydew or mango can replace the cantaloupe, if desired. For an even sweeter salad, add up to 2 tablespoons of raisins, currants, or chopped dried apricots.

¾ cup orange juice, preferably freshly
    squeezed
2 tablespoons fresh lemon juice
2 tablespoons water
1 cup fine-grain (fancy) bulgur
2 tablespoons extra-virgin olive oil
1 tablespoon red wine vinegar
½ teaspoon salt, or to taste
Freshly ground black pepper, to taste
4 scallions, white and green parts, thinly
    sliced
½ cup chopped fresh flat-leaf parsley
¼ cup chopped fresh mint
2 cups cubed fresh cantaloupe
¼ cup chopped walnuts, slivered almonds, or
    whole pine nuts

In a medium saucepan over medium heat, bring the juices and water barely to a simmer. Remove from heat and let cool 5 minutes. Add the bulgur, stirring well to combine. Let stand until the bulgur has absorbed all of the liquid and feels dry, about 30 minutes, stirring occasionally.

In a large bowl, whisk together the oil, vinegar, salt, and pepper. Add the scallions, parsley, and mint; stir well to combine. Add the bulgur and stir well to combine. Let stand about 10 minutes to allow the flavors to blend. Add the cantaloupe and walnuts and toss gently yet thoroughly to combine. Season with additional salt and pepper, to taste. Serve at room temperature. Alternatively, cover and refrigerate a minimum of 2 hours or up to 1 day and served chilled, or return to room temperature.

Per serving: Calories 293 | Protein 8g | Total Fat 12g | Sat. Fat 1g | Cholesterol 0mg | Carbohydrate 43g | Dietary Fiber 10g | Sodium 290mg

Pasta Salad with Grilled Balsamic Summer Vegetables

Makes 4 main-dish or 6 to 8 side-dish servings

Best at room temperature, this is an excellent pasta salad to bring to summer picnics and potlucks.

½ recipe Grilled Balsamic Summer Vegetables
    (page 130), cut into bite-size pieces
8 ounces gemelli or rotini pasta, cooked
    according to package directions until al
    dente, drained
1 (6-ounce) jar marinated artichoke hearts,
    drained and chopped
1 tablespoon extra-virgin olive oil

In a large bowl, toss together all the ingredients until well combined. Serve warm or at room temperature. Completely cooled pasta salad can be refrigerated, covered, up to 2 days before returning to room temperature and serving.

Per serving: Calories 384 | Protein 11g | Total Fat 12g | Sat. Fat 2g | Cholesterol 0mg | Carbohydrate 61g | Dietary Fiber 7g | Sodium 300mg

Cinco de Mayo Mexican Salad

 Makes 4 main-dish servings or 6 side-dish servings

You don't have to wait for the fifth of May to enjoy this festive, fabulous Mexican salad.

2½ tablespoons extra-virgin olive oil

2½ tablespoons fresh lime juice

1 tablespoon country-style whole-grain mustard

1 teaspoon ground cumin

½ teaspoon salt, or to taste

Freshly ground black pepper, to taste

1 (15-ounce) can black beans, rinsed and drained

1 cup cooked fresh or frozen yellow corn, at room temperature

1 cup chopped red bell pepper

1 cup cherry or grape tomatoes, halved

1 ripe avocado, peeled, pitted, and chopped

4 scallions, white and green parts, thinly sliced

½ cup finely chopped fresh cilantro

Shredded iceberg lettuce (optional)

Crushed taco shell or tortilla chips (optional)

In a large bowl, whisk together the oil, lime juice, mustard, cumin, salt, and black pepper. Add the remaining ingredients, except the optional ingredients, and toss gently yet thoroughly to combine. Serve at room temperature, or cover and refrigerate a minimum of 2 hours or overnight and serve chilled, over the lettuce (if using), garnished with the crushed taco shell (if using).

Per serving: Calories 310 | Protein 10g | Total Fat 18g | Sat. Fat 3g | Cholesterol 0mg | Carbohydrate 35g | Dietary Fiber 7g | Sodium 334mg

Quinoa Tabbouleh Salad

Makes 4 to 6 main-dish servings

Instant couscous (preferably the whole wheat variety), cooked according to package directions, can easily stand in for the quinoa, if desired.

1 cup quinoa, rinsed well under cold running water and drained

3 tablespoons extra-virgin olive oil

Juice of 1 lemon (about 3 tablespoons)

½ teaspoon coarse salt, or to taste

Freshly ground black pepper, to taste

4 medium plum tomatoes (about 3 ounces each), chopped

1 small cucumber (about 8 ounces), seeded and chopped

6 scallions, white and green parts, thinly sliced

1 cup chopped fresh flat-leaf parsley

¼ cup chopped fresh mint

Bring a large saucepan filled with salted water to a boil over high heat. Add the quinoa, reduce heat to medium, and cook until tender yet firm to the bite, about 12 minutes, stirring occasionally. Drain well and let cool about 10 minutes.

Meanwhile, in a large bowl, whisk together the oil, lemon juice, salt, and pepper. Add the tomatoes, cucumber, scallions, parsley, and mint, tossing well to combine. Add the quinoa, tossing well to combine. Let stand about 15 minutes at room temperature to allow the flavors to blend. Toss again and serve at room temperature. Alternatively, cover and refrigerate a minimum of 2 hours or up to 1 day and serve chilled, or return to room temperature.

Per serving: Calories 292 | Protein 8g | Total Fat 13g | Sat. Fat 2g | Cholesterol 0mg | Carbohydrate 39g | Dietary Fiber 6g | Sodium 267mg

Curried Pasta Salad with Grapes and Chutney

 Makes 5 to 6 main-course or 8 to 10 side-dish servings

Any variety of seedless grapes can be used successfully in this refreshing curried pasta salad. Make sure the shells you select are not the large or jumbo size, which are used for stuffings; rather, the pasta should be just large enough to comfortably fit half a grape inside.

12 ounces medium shells or similar pasta

¼ cup raisins

¼ cup mango chutney

2 tablespoons extra-virgin olive oil

1 tablespoon cider vinegar

1 teaspoon mild curry powder, or
    to taste

½ teaspoon salt

Freshly ground black pepper, to taste

1 cup seedless green grapes, halved

1 cup seedless red grapes, halved

¼ cup slivered almonds, toasted
    (see Cook's Tip, page 13)

¼ cup chopped celery

In a large stockpot filled with boiling salted water, cook the pasta according to package directions until al dente. While the pasta is cooking, place the raisins in a colander set in a sink. Drain the pasta slowly over the raisins. Rinse under cold running water until cool. Set aside to drain, tossing a few times (the shells tend to collect water).

In a large bowl, stir together the chutney, oil, vinegar, curry powder, salt, and pepper. Add the pasta and raisins, grapes, almonds, and celery; toss well to combine. Serve at room temperature. Alternatively, cover and refrigerate a minimum of 2 hours or up to 1 day and serve chilled, or return to room temperature.

Per serving: Calories 429 | Protein 11g | Total Fat 10g | Sat. Fat 1g | Cholesterol 0mg | Carbohydrate 76g | Dietary Fiber 4g | Sodium 234mg

Japanese-Style Soba Noodle and Red Cabbage Salad with Pumpkin Seeds

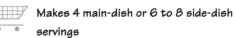 Makes 4 main-dish or 6 to 8 side-dish servings

A significant source of iron and other essential nutrients, pumpkin seeds are good for you. Sunflower seeds or chopped peanuts can be substituted, if desired.

3 tablespoons fresh lime juice

3 tablespoons low-sodium tamari or soy sauce

3 tablespoons toasted (dark) sesame oil

2 tablespoons sugar, or to taste

½ teaspoon ground ginger

Salt and freshly ground black pepper, to taste

9 ounces soba or somen noodles, broken in
    half, cooked according to package
    directions until al dente, rinsed under cold-
    running water, drained well

1 (10-ounce) bag shredded red cabbage

1 cup shredded carrots

4 scallions, mostly green parts, thinly sliced

¼ cup pumpkin seeds, raw or roasted

In a large bowl, whisk together the lime juice, tamari, sesame oil, sugar, ginger, salt, and pepper. Let stand about 5 minutes to allow the sugar to dissolve. Add the noodles and toss well to thoroughly coat. Add the remaining ingredients and toss well to combine. Let stand about 10 minutes before tossing again and serving at room temperature. Alternatively, cover and refrigerate a minimum of 2 hours or up to 1 day and serve chilled.

Per serving: Calories 394 | Protein 12g | Total Fat 12g | Sat. Fat 2g | Cholesterol 0mg | Carbohydrate 67g | Dietary Fiber 6g | Sodium 982mg

Orzo Salad with Lemon, Corn, Olives, and Basil

 Makes 6 main-dish or 8 to 10 side-dish servings

This delightful pasta salad is perfect for a picnic or potluck. Though optional, the pine nuts add additional protein.

¾ pound orzo pasta

1 cup frozen yellow corn, thawed

¼ cup extra-virgin olive oil

2 to 3 tablespoons fresh lemon juice

2 large cloves garlic, finely chopped

½ teaspoon coarse salt, or to taste

½ teaspoon lemon-pepper seasoning

¼ cup pitted kalamata or other good-quality black olives, chopped (see Cook's Tip, page 16)

¼ cup finely chopped fresh basil

2 tablespoons chopped chives or green parts of scallions

2 tablespoons pine nuts or slivered almonds (optional)

Freshly ground black pepper, to taste

1 cup grape tomatoes or cherry tomatoes, halved

In a large stockpot, cook the pasta in boiling salted water according to package directions until al dente. While pasta cooks, place the corn in a colander set in a sink. Slowly drain the cooked pasta over the corn. Drain well.

In the stockpot, whisk together the oil, lemon juice, garlic, salt, and lemon-pepper seasoning until well combined. Add the hot pasta and corn mixture, along with the olives, basil, chives, pine nuts (if using), and black pepper. Toss well to thoroughly combine. Transfer to a serving bowl and let cool about 15 minutes. Add the tomatoes and toss well to combine. Serve slightly warm or at room temperature. Alternatively, cover and refrigerate a minimum of 3 hours or up to 1 day and serve chilled, or return to room temperature.

Per serving: Calories 352 | Protein 9g | Total Fat 13g | Sat. Fat 1g | Cholesterol 0mg | Carbohydrate 51g | Dietary Fiber 3g | Sodium 357mg

Couscous and Chickpea Salad with Olives and Walnuts

 Makes 6 main-dish or 8 to 10 side-dish servings

Satisfy a hungry buffet or picnic crowd with this tasty, protein-packed couscous salad.

2 tablespoons extra-virgin olive oil

1 (15-ounce) can chickpeas, rinsed and drained

1 bunch scallions (about 6), thinly sliced, white and green parts separated

½ cup pitted kalamata or other good-quality black olives, chopped (see Cook's Tip, page 16)

½ tablespoon dried oregano

½ teaspoon coarse salt, or to taste

2 cups low-sodium vegetable broth

1½ cups instant couscous, preferably whole wheat

¼ cup finely chopped walnuts, almonds, or pine nuts

¼ cup red wine vinegar

2 tablespoons chopped fresh flat-leaf parsley (optional)

Freshly ground black pepper, to taste

In a large deep-sided nonstick skillet with a lid, heat 1 tablespoon oil over medium heat. Add the chickpeas, white parts of the scallions, olives, oregano, and salt; cook, stirring, until scallions are softened, about 3 minutes. Add the broth and bring to a boil over high heat. Stir in the couscous, cover, and remove from heat. Let stand until all the liquid has been absorbed, about 7 minutes. Uncover and fluff with a fork.

Transfer couscous mixture to a large bowl. While still warm, add the remaining 1 tablespoon of oil and all other ingredients, tossing well to combine. Let stand 15 minutes to allow the flavors to blend. Toss again and serve slightly warm or at room temperature. Alternatively, cover and refrigerate a minimum of 3 hours, or up to 1 day, and serve chilled, or return to room temperature.

Per serving: Calories 379 | Protein 15g | Total Fat 14g | Sat. Fat 1g | Cholesterol 0mg | Carbohydrate 50g | Dietary Fiber 4g | Sodium 654mg

Spicy Thai Tofu Salad with Cherry Tomatoes and Basil

Makes 4 main-dish servings

For a milder dish, use a pinch or two of crushed red pepper flakes in lieu of the Thai red curry paste, or substitute with Chinese chili paste, which is less hot.

1 pound extra-firm tofu, drained
Salt and freshly ground black pepper,
    to taste
2 tablespoons peanut oil
1 large clove garlic, finely chopped
Juice of 2 limes (about ¼ cup)
1 tablespoon light brown sugar
1 teaspoon Thai red curry paste, or to taste
4 to 6 scallions, white and green parts,
    thinly sliced

1½ cups cherry or grape tomatoes, halved
¼ to ½ cup chopped fresh basil
2 tablespoons chopped fresh cilantro
Bean sprouts (optional)

Place the tofu on a deep-sided plate or shallow bowl. Top with a second plate and weight with a heavy can. Let stand a minimum of 15 minutes (preferably 1 hour). Drain excess water. Cut the tofu into ¾-inch cubes and season with salt and pepper.

In a wok or large nonstick skillet, heat 1 tablespoon of the oil over medium-high heat. Add the tofu and cook, stirring often, until crispy and golden, 5 to 7 minutes, adding the garlic the last minute or so of cooking. Remove from heat and let cool slightly.

In a medium bowl, stir together the lime juice, remaining 1 tablespoon oil, brown sugar, curry paste, salt, and pepper. Let stand a few minutes to allow the sugar to dissolve. Stir in the scallions and let stand another few minutes to allow the flavors to blend. Add the warm tofu mixture and toss well to combine. Let cool to room temperature. Add the remaining ingredients, except the bean sprouts, and toss well to combine. Serve at room temperature over the bean sprouts (if using), or cover and refrigerate a minimum of 2 hours or up to 1 day and serve chilled, or return to room temperature.

Per serving: Calories 195 | Protein 11g | Total Fat 13g | Sat. Fat 2g | Cholesterol 0mg | Carbohydrate 13g | Dietary Fiber 3g | Sodium 57mg

Bow Tie Pasta Salad with Peas and Sun-Dried Tomatoes

 Makes 5 to 6 main-dish or 8 to 10 side-dish servings

Immature legumes, green peas are a good source of protein in a vegan diet. They also provide a nice contrast of color to the sun-dried tomatoes in this pretty pasta salad, which is festive enough for the holidays.

12 ounces bow tie pasta (farfalle) or similar short pasta

1½ cups frozen peas

5 tablespoons prepared nonfat balsamic vinaigrette

2 tablespoons extra-virgin olive oil

1½ tablespoons Dijon mustard

½ cup oil-packed sun-dried tomato halves, drained and chopped, ½ tablespoon marinade reserved

½ teaspoon salt, or to taste

Freshly ground black pepper, to taste

½ cup chopped red onion

½ cup chopped fresh basil

In a large stockpot filled with boiling salted water, cook the pasta until al dente, adding the peas during the last few minutes of cooking. Drain in a colander and rinse under cold running water; drain well again.

In a large bowl, whisk together the balsamic vinaigrette, oil, mustard, reserved marinade, salt, and pepper. Stir in the onion and let stand a few minutes to allow the flavors to blend. Add the pasta and pea mixture, sun-dried tomatoes, and basil, tossing well to combine. Let stand a few minutes before tossing again and serving at room temperature. The salad can be stored, covered, in the refrigerator up to 2 days before returning to room temperature and serving.

Per serving: Calories 385 | Protein 12g | Total Fat 10g | Sat. Fat 1g | Cholesterol 0mg | Carbohydrate 63g | Dietary Fiber 4g | Sodium 563mg

Pot-Sticker Salad with Sugar Snap Peas and Carrots

 Makes 4 main-dish servings

Cabbage is typically the main ingredient in vegetable pot stickers, the Asian equivalent of ravioli, which are increasingly available in well-stocked conventional supermarkets. Check the labels carefully, however, as some products may contain egg.

¼ cup low-sodium soy sauce, plus additional, to serve

1 tablespoon toasted (dark) sesame oil

2 scallions, white and green parts, thinly sliced

16 ounces frozen vegetable pot stickers

8 ounces baby carrots, halved lengthwise

1 (12-ounce) bag (about 3 cups) fresh sugar snap peas

8 ounces mung bean sprouts

In a large heat-proof bowl with a lid, combine the soy sauce and sesame oil. Add the scallions and stir to combine. Set aside to marinate about 15 minutes at room temperature.

Meanwhile, lightly oil a steamer basket. Fill a large saucepan or medium stockpot with about 1 inch of water and fit with the prepared steamer basket. Bring the water to a boil over high heat. Place the pot stickers in the basket, cover, and reduce the heat to medium-high; cook for 4 minutes. Add the carrots, cover, and cook for 2 more minutes. Add the snap peas, cover, and cook until the pot stickers are cooked through but still firm and the vegetables are crisp-tender, 2 to 4 more minutes.

Transfer hot pot stickers and vegetables to the bowl with the soy sauce–scallion mixture; toss gently to combine. Cover and let stand about 5 minutes; toss gently again. To serve, divide the sprouts evenly among 4 deep-rimmed plates or bowls. Top with equal amounts of pot stickers, vegetables, and sauce. Serve warm or at room temperature, with additional soy sauce passed separately.

Per serving: Calories 288 | Protein 11g | Total Fat 5g | Sat. Fat 1g | Cholesterol 0mg | Carbohydrate 53g | Dietary Fiber 7g | Sodium 962mg

Sandwiches, Wraps, Pizza, Breads, and Other Lighter Fare

There is nothing more convenient than food on bread—whether it's a traditional sandwich, wrap, burrito, fajita, taco, tostada, enchilada, quesadilla, pita, pizza, or focaccia. This chapter doesn't disappoint, whether it's Pinto Bean Sloppy Joe Sandwiches, Sweet Potato and Black Bean Burritos, Grilled Portobello Mushroom and Vegetable Fajitas, Lentil Tacos, Hummus Pizza with Sun-Dried Tomatoes and Kalamata Olives, or Provençal-Style Focaccia with Red Pepper Coulis and Rosemary. There are also a fabulous Artichoke Garlic Bread and Southwestern-Style Cornbread to accompany your favorite soups, stews, and chilis or, better yet, to snack on—yum!

Artichoke Garlic Bread

 Makes 16 pieces

This is one of my favorite ways to serve garlic bread, particularly with Mediterranean-style soups.

2 tablespoons extra-virgin olive oil

3 to 4 large cloves garlic, finely chopped

1 (6-ounce) jar marinated artichoke hearts, drained well and chopped

½ teaspoon dried oregano

½ teaspoon coarse salt

1 (10-ounce) baguette, preferably whole wheat, sliced lengthwise in half

Preheat oven to 375F (190C).

In a small skillet, heat the oil over medium heat. Add the garlic and cook, stirring constantly, 1 minute, until fragrant and just beginning to brown. Remove the skillet from the heat and add the artichokes, oregano, and salt, tossing well to combine. Return the skillet to the heat and cook, stirring, 30 seconds. Set aside.

Pull most of the bread from both halves of the baguette, leaving ½-inch-thick shells. Set the shells aside and crumble the bread into a medium bowl. Add the artichoke mixture to the crumbs and toss well to combine. Spoon the artichoke-bread crumb mixture into the bottom bread shell and replace the top. Cut in half crosswise and wrap with foil. Place on a baking sheet and bake 20 minutes, until heated through. Remove the foil and slice each half crosswise into 8 equal pieces for a total of 16 pieces. Serve warm.

Per piece: Calories 70 | Protein 2g | Total Fat 2g | Sat. Fat 0g | Cholesterol 0mg | Carbohydrate 11g | Dietary Fiber 1g | Sodium 177mg

Variations: *To make Artichoke and Sun-Dried Tomato Garlic Bread, add 2 tablespoons drained, chopped oil-packed sun-dried tomatoes to the skillet along with the artichokes. Proceed as otherwise directed.*

To make Artichoke and Sun-Dried Tomato Garlic Bread Sandwiches with White Beans, substitute dried rosemary for the oregano and add 1 cup rinsed, drained canned cannellini or other white beans along with the artichokes and sun-dried tomatoes. Season with freshly ground black pepper. After replacing the top of the bread shell, cut into quarters crosswise and wrap with foil. Proceed as otherwise directed, but do not slice. Makes 4 sandwiches.

Per sandwich: Calories 347 | Protein 12g | Total Fat 10g | Sat. Fat 2g | Cholesterol 0mg | Carbohydrate 54g | Dietary Fiber 7g | Sodium 719mg

Avocado Tostadas

 Makes 4 servings

While you will need 2 tablespoons of oil to fry the tortillas, about half of it is absorbed by the paper towels.

2 tablespoons canola oil

4 (6-inch) corn tortillas

¼ teaspoon salt, plus additional, to taste

2 ripe avocados, peeled, pitted, and mashed

1 cup cherry tomatoes, quartered, or grape tomatoes, halved

¼ cup chopped fresh cilantro

¼ cup chopped red onion

1 to 2 jalapeño chilies, seeded and finely chopped

1 tablespoon fresh lime juice, or more, to taste

2 large cloves garlic, finely chopped

Freshly ground black pepper, to taste

Salsa or taco sauce, for garnish (optional)

Line a baking sheet with several layers of paper towels and set aside. In a small 7- or 8-inch skillet, heat the oil over medium-high heat. Working with 1 tortilla at a time, fry each tortilla 20 to 30 seconds on each side or until light golden. Transfer the tortillas to prepared baking sheet and blot between paper towels. Remove paper towels and sprinkle lightly with salt, if desired.

In a medium bowl, mix the avocados, tomatoes, cilantro, onion, chilies, lime juice, garlic, ¼ teaspoon salt, and pepper. (At this point, mixture can be stored, covered, in the refrigerator up to 12 hours before returning to room temperature and continuing with the recipe.) Mound equal amounts (about ½ cup) of the avocado mixture over each tortilla. Garnish with the salsa (if using) and serve at once.

Per tostado: Calories 270 | Protein 4g | Total Fat 20g | Sat. Fat 3g | Cholesterol 0mg | Carbohydrate 24g | Dietary Fiber 5g | Sodium 190mg

Variation: *To make Avocado Tacos to serve four, omit the canola oil and tortillas from the recipe. Heat 8 taco shells in a preheated 350F (175C) oven 3 to 5 minutes, until crisp. Fill with equal amounts (about ¼ cup) of the avocado mixture and garnish with shredded lettuce, if desired, as well as the optional salsa or taco sauce.*

Wild Mushroom and Pinto Bean Burritos with Tomatillo Salsa

Makes 6 servings

If you like mushrooms as much as I do, you will love these juicy burritos. Green tomatillo salsa, or salsa verde, is available in many well-stocked supermarkets; in a pinch, a chunky-style, tomato-based variety can be substituted. Black beans can replace the pinto beans, if desired.

6 (10-inch) flour tortillas

1 tablespoon extra-virgin olive oil

1 medium red or yellow onion (about 6 ounces each), sliced into thin half-moons

1 medium red bell pepper (about 6 ounces), cored, seeded, and cut into thin strips

8 ounces sliced cremini mushrooms

2 cloves garlic, finely chopped

¼ teaspoon salt, or to taste

½ tablespoon chili powder, or to taste

1 cup rinsed, drained canned pinto beans

6 tablespoons prepared tomatillo salsa (salsa verde)

Freshly ground black pepper, to taste

Cayenne pepper, to taste (optional)

¼ cup chopped fresh cilantro

Preheat oven to 350F (175C).

Wrap tortillas in foil and place in oven 15 minutes.

Meanwhile, in a large nonstick skillet, heat ½ tablespoon oil over medium-high heat. Add the onion and bell pepper and cook, stirring, until lightly browned, about 7 minutes. Reduce the heat to medium and add the remaining ½ tablespoon oil, the mushrooms, garlic, and salt; cook, stirring, until mushrooms begin to release their liquids, about 4 minutes. Add the chili powder and cook, stirring, until the liquids from the mushrooms have evaporated, about 4 minutes. Add the beans, salsa, black pepper, and cayenne (if using); cook, stirring, until heated through, about 3 minutes. Remove from the heat and add the cilantro, stirring well to combine. Season with additional salt and black pepper, if necessary.

To assemble, place 1 heated tortilla on each of 6 dinner plates. Spoon equal portions (about ½ cup) of the mushroom mixture down the center of each tortilla. Roll up each tortilla from the edge nearest you, tucking in the sides as you roll. Serve at once.

Per serving: Calories 207 | Protein 7g | Total Fat 5g | Sat. Fat 1g | Cholesterol 0mg | Carbohydrate 34g | Dietary Fiber 6g | Sodium 308mg

Black Bean and Avocado Wraps with Shredded Cabbage

Makes 4 servings

In South America, raw cabbage, an important cruciferous vegetable, is frequently used as a filling or topping in various tortilla dishes. For a delicious lower-carb alternative, omit the tortillas and shredded cabbage and spoon the bean mixture into cabbage cups.

1 (15-ounce) can black beans, rinsed and drained

1 ripe avocado, peeled, pitted, and chopped

½ cup mild or medium prepared salsa

3 to 4 scallions, white and green parts, thinly sliced

Juice of ½ lime (about 1 tablespoon), or to taste

1 teaspoon ground cumin

½ teaspoon sugar, or to taste (optional)

Salt and freshly ground black pepper, to taste

Cayenne pepper, to taste (optional)

4 (10-inch) flour tortillas, preferably whole wheat

1⅓ cups shredded green cabbage

In a small bowl, toss together the beans, avocado, salsa, scallions, lime juice, cumin, sugar (if using), salt, black pepper, and cayenne (if using) until thoroughly combined. Spoon equal amounts (about ½ cup) over each tortilla, leaving about a 1-inch border all around the edge. Scatter ⅓ cup cabbage over the bean mixture. Tightly roll up each tortilla from the edge nearest you, tucking in the sides as you roll. Cover tightly with plastic wrap and refrigerate a minimum of 30 minutes, or up to 1 day. Serve chilled.

Per serving: Calories 301 | Protein 11g | Total Fat 11g | Sat. Fat 2g | Cholesterol 0mg | Carbohydrate 43g | Dietary Fiber 7g | Sodium 264mg

Cajun-Style Black-Eyed Pea and Corn Patties

Makes 6 servings

I like to tuck these tasty patties inside hamburger buns and top with lettuce, tomato, red onion, and ketchup.

2 tablespoons extra-virgin olive oil or canola oil

1½ cups fresh or thawed frozen yellow corn

1 cup chopped onion

1 teaspoon Cajun seasoning

1 (15-ounce) can black-eyed peas, rinsed and drained

¼ cup fresh breadcrumbs, preferably whole wheat

¼ cup instant oats

2 tablespoons plus 4 teaspoons cornmeal

1 tablespoon barbecue sauce, preferably hickory smoked, or ketchup

½ teaspoon salt

Freshly ground black pepper, to taste

In a large nonstick skillet, heat ½ tablespoon of the oil over medium heat. Add the corn, onion, and Cajun seasoning; cook, stirring, until corn and onion are lightly browned, about 5 minutes. Remove from heat and set aside to cool a few minutes.

In a food processor fitted with the knife blade, pulse the corn mixture, black-eyed peas, breadcrumbs, oats, the 2 tablespoons cornmeal, barbecue sauce, salt, and pepper until well combined but still chunky. Divide mixture into 6 portions and shape into ½-inch-thick patties. Dredge patties in remaining cornmeal and set aside.

Wipe out the skillet and add the remaining 1½ tablespoons of oil; heat over medium heat. Add the patties and cook until golden, 4 to 5 minutes on each side. Serve at once.

Per serving: Calories 187 | Protein 6g | Total Fat 7g | Sat. Fat 1g | Cholesterol 0mg | Carbohydrate 28g | Dietary Fiber 2g | Sodium 232mg

Indian-Style Chickpea Patties

Makes 4 servings

Delicious on their own, or with a smear of chutney, these chickpea patties are also fabulous stuffed into pita bread or tucked inside hamburger buns, garnished with lettuce, sliced tomatoes, sliced cucumber, or sliced onion.

1 (15-ounce) can chickpeas, rinsed and drained

⅓ cup crispy rice cereal

⅓ cup old-fashioned or quick-cooking rolled oats

2 to 4 tablespoons water, or more, if necessary

2 tablespoons wheat germ

2 tablespoons chopped fresh cilantro or parsley

2 large cloves garlic, finely chopped

1 teaspoon ground cumin

½ teaspoon ground turmeric

½ teaspoon salt, or taste

Freshly ground black pepper, to taste

Cayenne pepper, to taste (optional)

1 tablespoon canola or other mild vegetable oil

Mango chutney, to serve (optional)

In a food processor fitted with the knife blade, process the chickpeas, rice cereal, rolled oats, 2 tablespoons of the water, wheat germ, cilantro, garlic, cumin, turmeric, salt, black pepper, and cayenne (if using) until smooth and moistened, adding more water, as necessary, to achieve a workable consistency. Divide mixture into 4 portions and shape into about ½ inch-thick patties.

In a large nonstick skillet, heat the oil over medium heat. Add the patties and cook until golden, 4 to 5 minutes on each side. Serve at once, topped with the chutney (if using).

Per serving (without chutney): Calories 189 | Protein 8g | Total Fat 6g | Sat. Fat 1g | Cholesterol 0mg | Carbohydrate 27g | Dietary Fiber 1g | Sodium 315mg

Chutney-Peanut Pita Pizzas with Broccoli

Makes 4 servings

These exotic personal pizzas are also tasty with an additional topping of thinly sliced onion.

¼ cup creamy peanut butter

3 tablespoons mango chutney

1 tablespoon low-sodium soy or tamari sauce

½ tablespoon water

1 teaspoon fresh lime juice

2 teaspoons toasted (dark) sesame oil

2 large cloves garlic, finely chopped

Salt and freshly ground black pepper, to taste

4 (6-inch) whole wheat pita breads

1 cup chopped fresh broccoli

Preheat oven to 375F (190C).

In a small bowl, stir together the peanut butter, chutney, soy sauce, water, lime juice, 1 teaspoon sesame oil, garlic, salt, and pepper. Set aside.

Arrange the pita on a large ungreased baking sheet and spread evenly with the chutney mixture. Top with equal amounts of the broccoli. Season with salt and pepper, and drizzle each with ¼ teaspoon of the remaining oil. Bake on the center oven rack about 10 to 12 minutes, until broccoli is tender and just beginning to brown. Serve at once.

Per serving: Calories 284 | Protein 10g | Total Fat 12g | Sat. Fat 2g | Cholesterol 0mg | Carbohydrate 40g | Dietary Fiber 6g | Sodium 492mg

Grilled Portobello Mushroom Burgers with Black Bean–Guacamole Sauce

Makes 4 sandwiches

These juicy, succulent burgers require a large, crusty roll, such as the Kaiser variety, to contain the scrumptious sauce.

- 4 tablespoons refried black beans
- 3 tablespoons prepared guacamole, plus additional, if desired
- 1½ tablespoons salsa, plus additional, if desired
- ¼ teaspoon ground cumin (optional)
- 4 large (about 2 ounces each) portobello mushroom caps
- 2 teaspoons extra-virgin olive oil
- Salt and freshly ground black pepper, to taste
- 4 large Kaiser rolls, preferably whole wheat, split
- Iceberg or other lettuce leaves, sliced tomato, and sliced red onion, for topping (optional)

Prepare a medium-hot charcoal or gas grill, or heat a nonstick grill pan over medium-high heat.

In a small bowl, mix together the refried beans, guacamole, salsa, and cumin (if using) until thoroughly blended. Set aside.

Brush each mushroom on the gills and rim with ½ teaspoon of the oil; season with salt and pepper. Place the mushrooms, gill sides down, on the grill and grill 3 minutes. Turn over and grill 3 to 4 minutes longer, rotating each mushroom a half turn after 2 minutes, until bottoms are nicely browned. As they are grilling, fill the mushroom cavity with equal amounts (about 2 tablespoons) of the bean mixture.

Place a filled mushroom, gill side up, on the bottom half of each roll. Top with lettuce, tomato, and onion (if using). Close each roll and serve at once, with additional guacamole and/or salsa passed separately, if desired.

Per serving (includes roll): Calories 210 | Protein 8g | Total Fat 8g | Sat. Fat 1g | Cholesterol 0mg | Carbohydrate 31g | Dietary Fiber 4g | Sodium 345mg

Grilled Portobello Mushroom and Vegetable Fajitas

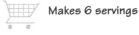

Makes 6 servings

Thick and juicy portobello mushrooms are natural meat substitutes that typically satisfy all but the most confirmed carnivore.

- 3 tablespoons balsamic vinegar
- 3 tablespoons extra-virgin olive oil
- 2 to 3 large cloves garlic, finely chopped
- ½ teaspoon salt, plus additional, to taste
- Freshly ground black pepper, to taste
- 4 large portobello mushroom caps (about 2 ounces each)
- 2 medium red onions (about 6 ounces each), sliced into ½-inch-thick rounds
- 2 medium red bell peppers (about 6 ounces each) cored, seeded, and quartered lengthwise
- 2 medium green bell peppers (about 6 ounces each) cored, seeded, and quartered lengthwise
- ¼ to ½ cup chopped fresh cilantro
- 12 (6-inch) snack-size flour tortillas, warmed
- Salsa, to serve (optional)

In a small bowl, whisk together the vinegar, oil, garlic, salt, and black pepper. Place the mushrooms, onions, and bell peppers on a large baking sheet with sides and drizzle with the vinegar and oil mixture; toss well to coat. Let marinate at room temperature 15 to 30 minutes, tossing a few times.

Meanwhile, prepare a medium-hot charcoal or gas grill, or preheat a broiler. Position the grill rack or oven rack 4 to 6 inches from the heat source. If broiling, lightly oil another large baking sheet and set aside. Alternatively, place a stovetop grilling pan with grids over medium-high heat.

Working in batches, if necessary, transfer vegetables from marinade to the grill rack or prepared baking sheet, leaving behind and reserving any remaining marinade. Grill or broil the vegetables until browned and tender, 3 to 5 minutes per side (the onions are typically done first, followed by the bell peppers, then the mushrooms). As they finish cooking, return the vegetables to the first baking sheet containing the reserved marinade.

When all the vegetables are done, cut into thin strips. Transfer the vegetables and any reserved marinade and accumulated juices to a warmed serving platter with a deep rim, or a warmed large shallow serving bowl. Sprinkle with the cilantro and season with additional salt and pepper, as necessary; toss gently with a large spatula to combine. Serve at once, allowing diners to build their own fajitas by filling tortillas with the grilled vegetables and topping them with a little salsa (if using).

Per serving (per 2 fajitas): Calories 282 | Protein 7g | Total Fat 11g | Sat. Fat 2g | Cholesterol 0mg | Carbohydrate 42g | Dietary Fiber 5g | Sodium 420mg

Hummus Pizza with Sun-Dried Tomatoes and Kalamata Olives

Makes 4 to 6 main-dish or 8 to 12 appetizer servings

The versatility of hummus is showcased in this delicious pizza, perfect for a casual weeknight supper or special party appetizer. Classic hummus is a dairy-free Middle Eastern puree of chickpeas, sesame tahini, and lemon juice; it can be located in the refrigerated section among the dips and spreads.

1¼ cups prepared plain (classic) hummus
1 to 2 cloves garlic, finely chopped
1 (10- or 13-ounce) can refrigerated pizza dough (see Cook's Tip, below)
⅓ cup julienned, drained oil-packed sun-dried tomatoes, 1 tablespoon marinade reserved
6 pitted kalamata or other good-quality black olives, halved (see Cook's Tip, page 16)

Preheat oven to 350F (175C). Lightly oil a standard-size baking sheet and set aside. In a small bowl, mix together the hummus and garlic until thoroughly blended; set aside.

Unroll the pizza dough onto the prepared baking sheet and press to fit. Brush the reserved sun-dried tomato marinade evenly over the dough, and then prick with a fork in several places. Bake in the center of the oven 12 to 15 minutes, until very lightly browned. Remove from the oven and spread evenly with the hummus-garlic mixture. Top evenly with the sun-dried tomatoes and olives. Place on the bottom rack and bake 5 minutes, until the edges are nicely browned. Cut into wedges and serve warm or at room temperature.

Per serving: Calories 383 | Protein 10g | Total Fat 13g | Sat. Fat 2g | Cholesterol 0mg | Carbohydrate 57g | Dietary Fiber 4g | Sodium 304mg

Cook's Tip: *Refrigerated 10- or 13-ounce cans of pizza dough can be found alongside the canned biscuits in the refrigerated section of most supermarkets. Fresh or frozen 16-ounce bags of pizza dough, also available in most stores, can be used as well, but you will need to thaw the dough first, if necessary, and work a bit harder to stretch and fit it into the baking sheet. Also, the pizza will have a thicker crust and may take an extra five minutes or so to brown.*

Stuffed Pitas with Curried Chickpea Spread

 Makes 4 sandwiches

Use this delicious spread as a dip for raw vegetables and pita chips, as well.

 1 (15-ounce) can chickpeas, rinsed and drained
 2 to 4 tablespoons low-sodium vegetable broth, plus additional, as necessary
 2 tablespoons extra-virgin olive oil
 1 tablespoon fresh lemon juice, or more, to taste
 1 to 2 large cloves garlic, finely chopped
 ¼ teaspoon mild curry powder, or to taste
 ¼ teaspoon ground cumin
 ¼ teaspoon salt
 Freshly ground black pepper, to taste
 ¼ cup freshly chopped fresh flat-leaf parsley or cilantro
 4 (6-inch) pita breads, preferably whole wheat, split crosswise in half
 Lettuce, sliced cucumbers, sliced tomatoes, and sprouts

In a food processor fitted with the knife blade, process the chickpeas, 2 tablespoons broth, oil, lemon juice, garlic, curry powder, cumin, salt, and pepper until smooth, adding more broth, if necessary, to achieve desired consistency. Transfer to a small bowl and add the parsley, stirring well to combine. Spread each pita half with equal amounts of the chickpea mixture (about 2 tablespoons). Stuff with the lettuce and other garnishes and serve.

Per sandwich: Calories 337 | Protein 12g | Total Fat 10g | Sat. Fat 1g | Cholesterol 0mg | Carbohydrate 53g | Dietary Fiber 5g | Sodium 497mg

Mexican Torta Sandwiches

 Makes 4 sandwiches

A torta is a Mexican-style sandwich similar to a burrito; however, it uses a hollowed-out roll instead of a flour tortilla. These make great grab-and-go sandwiches to take to work, the beach, or picnics.

 1 cup vegetarian refried beans
 2 tablespoons prepared salsa
 1 to 2 scallions, white and green parts, thinly sliced
 1 jalapeño chili, seeded and finely chopped (optional)
 1 (10-ounce, 24-inch-long) baguette, preferably whole wheat, cut crosswise into 4 (6-inch) pieces
 6 tablespoons prepared guacamole
 1⅓ cups shredded green cabbage

In a small bowl, mix together the beans, salsa, scallions, and chili (if using) until thoroughly blended. Set aside.

Cut each piece of baguette horizontally in half. Pull out most of the soft bread from the center (reserve for other use, such as fresh breadcrumbs). Fill the bottom halves with equal portions of the bean mixture, followed with equal portions (1½ tablespoons) of the guacamole. Top with equal portions (⅓ cup) of the cabbage. Replace the tops, cut in half, if desired, and serve. (At this point, sandwiches can be wrapped in plastic and refrigerated up to 1 day before serving chilled or returning to room temperature.)

Per sandwich: Calories 309 | Protein 11g | Total Fat 6g | Sat. Fat 1g | Cholesterol 0mg | Carbohydrate 53g | Dietary Fiber 7g | Sodium 755mg

Pinto Bean Sloppy Joe Sandwiches

 Makes 6 sandwiches

These sandwiches are delicious topped with Maple Coleslaw (page 123). The pinto bean mixture also makes a great topping for baked potatoes.

1 tablespoon extra-virgin olive oil

1 cup chopped onion

½ cup chopped green bell pepper

2 cloves garlic, finely chopped

1 (15-ounce) can pinto beans, rinsed and drained

1 (6-ounce) can tomato paste

¾ cup water

⅓ cup wheat germ

¼ cup molasses

1 tablespoon chili powder, or more, to taste

½ to 1 teaspoon liquid smoke (optional)

½ teaspoon salt, or to taste

Freshly ground black pepper, to taste

Hot sauce, to taste (optional)

6 hamburger buns or large rolls, preferably whole wheat, split

In a medium nonstick skillet, heat the oil over medium heat. Add the onion and bell pepper and cook, stirring, until softened, about 3 minutes. Add the garlic and cook, stirring, 1 minute. Add the remaining ingredients, except the hamburger buns. Bring to a gentle simmer over medium-high heat, stirring occasionally. Reduce the heat to between low and medium-low and simmer gently, uncovered, until thickened, 8 to 10 minutes, stirring occasionally and mashing the beans with the back of a large spoon. To serve, spoon equal amounts of the bean mixture on the bottom of each hamburger bun. Close the tops and serve at once.

Per sandwich: Calories 292 | Protein 11g | Total Fat 6g | Sat. Fat 1g | Cholesterol 0mg | Carbohydrate 52g | Dietary Fiber 9g | Sodium 619mg

Quick Moo-Shu Vegetables

Makes 4 servings

Broccoli slaw can replace up to one-fourth of the shredded coleslaw, if desired. For extra protein, add some chopped peanuts during the last two minutes of cooking.

1 tablespoon toasted (dark) sesame oil

2 large cloves garlic, finely chopped

1 (10-ounce) bag shredded coleslaw mix

1 (8-ounce) bag shredded carrots

4 scallions, white and green parts, thinly sliced

¼ cup hoisin sauce, plus additional, to serve

2 tablespoons low-sodium soy or tamari sauce

Salt and freshly ground black pepper, if necessary, to taste

8 (6-inch) snack-size flour tortillas, heated according to package directions

Plum sauce, to serve (optional)

In a wok or large nonstick skillet, heat the oil over medium heat. Add the garlic and cook, stirring constantly, 30 seconds. Add the coleslaw, carrots, and scallions; cook, stirring occasionally, until softened, about 8 minutes. Add the hoisin sauce and soy sauce and cook, stirring, 2 minutes. Transfer to a warmed serving bowl and season with salt and pepper, if necessary. Serve at once, allowing diners to assemble their own wraps by filling tortillas with the vegetable mixture and topping with additional hoisin sauce or plum sauce (if using).

Per serving (2 wraps): Calories 289 | Protein 8g | Total Fat 8g | Sat. Fat 1g | Cholesterol 0mg | Carbohydrate 48g | Dietary Fiber 6g | Sodium 843mg

Three-Bean Barley Enchiladas with Chipotle Cream Sauce

 Makes 6 servings

Here is a delicious and economical way to use up leftovers from Three-Bean Barley Chili (page 28).

12 to 14 (6-inch) corn tortillas
Chipotle Cream Sauce (below)
½ recipe Three-Bean Barley Chili (page 28), slightly warm or at room temperature

Preheat oven to 350F (175C). Lightly oil a 12 x 8-inch baking dish and set aside.

Place the tortillas on a large ungreased baking sheet (some overlap is okay) and place in the oven until just warmed and softened, about 5 minutes.

Spread about ⅓ cup of Chipotle Cream Sauce along the bottom of the prepared baking dish. Spoon equal portions of Three-Bean Barley Chili (about a heaping ⅓ cup) along the center of each tortilla and roll up; snugly arrange tortillas, seam side down, in the baking dish. Pour the remaining sauce evenly over the tortillas. Bake, uncovered, 20 minutes, until the enchiladas are heated through and the sauce is slightly bubbly. Serve at once.

Per serving: Calories 330 | Protein 13g | Total Fat 10g | Sat. Fat 3g | Cholesterol 0mg | Carbohydrate 51g | Dietary Fiber 11g | Sodium 886mg

Chipotle Cream Sauce

Makes about 2⅔ cups

Use this creamy chipotle sauce to blanket all of your favorite enchilada recipes.

2 tablespoons extra-virgin olive oil
¼ cup chopped onion
2 large cloves garlic, finely chopped
2 cups tomato puree
2 canned chipotle chilies in adobo sauce, finely chopped
1 teaspoon sugar
½ teaspoon salt
¾ cup light coconut milk

In a medium saucepan (preferably on a back burner, as the mixture tends to sputter), heat the oil over medium heat; add the onion and cook, stirring, until softened, about 3 minutes. Add the garlic and cook, stirring constantly, 1 minute. Add the tomato puree, chilies, sugar, and salt and let come to a simmer. Reduce the heat to between low and medium-low and simmer, partially covered, until the mixture is reduced to about 1¾ cups, about 15 minutes, stirring occasionally. Stir in the coconut milk and bring to a simmer over medium heat; cook, stirring, 1 minute. Remove from heat and use as directed in chosen recipe.

Per 1/6 of recipe: Calories 117 | Protein 3g | Total Fat 7g | Sat. Fat 3g | Cholesterol 0mg | Carbohydrate 13g | Dietary Fiber 3g | Sodium 524mg

Southwestern-Style Cornbread

 Makes 8 servings

This moist and savory cornbread is excellent with the Kansas City–Style Two-Bean Chili (page 29). Leftovers form the basis of the fabulous South-western Cornbread Salad (page 50).

1½ cups stone-ground yellow cornmeal
½ cup all-purpose flour
1 tablespoon baking powder
1 teaspoon salt
1 cup water
2 (8.5-ounce) cans creamed corn

¼ cup drained chopped mild green chilies

2 tablespoons drained chopped pimento (optional)

1 tablespoon canola oil

Preheat oven to 400F (205C). Lightly oil an 8-inch-square baking dish and set aside.

In a medium bowl, whisk together the cornmeal, flour, baking powder, and salt. In a large bowl, mix together the remaining ingredients until thoroughly blended. Add the cornmeal mixture, stirring well to thoroughly combine. Transfer to the prepared baking dish and bake on the center oven rack 35 to 40 minutes, until golden and a knife inserted in the center comes out almost clean.

Let cool about 15 minutes before cutting into 8 wedges or 16 squares and serving warm or at room temperature.

Per serving: Calories 175 | Protein 4g | Total Fat 3g | Sat. Fat 0g | Cholesterol 0mg | Carbohydrate 36g | Dietary Fiber 5g | Sodium 594mg

Variation: *To enjoy a sweeter variation of this cornbread, add up to ¼ cup sugar to the batter before baking.*

Tuscan-Style White Bean Quesadillas with Artichokes and Sun-Dried Tomatoes

Makes 6 main-dish or 12 appetizer or snack servings

Serve these delicious grilled sandwiches with a tossed green salad for a satisfying meal.

6 tablespoons chopped, drained oil-packed sun-dried tomatoes, ½ tablespoon marinade reserved

1 (6-ounce) jar marinated quartered artichoke hearts, drained and chopped

1 tablespoon extra-virgin olive oil

2 large cloves garlic, finely chopped

1 teaspoon dried rosemary

1 (15-ounce) can cannellini or other white beans, rinsed and drained

½ teaspoon salt, preferably the coarse variety, or to taste

Freshly ground black pepper, to taste

6 (10-inch) flour tortillas

Pizza or pasta sauce, heated, to serve

Preheat oven to 170F (75C).

In a small bowl, combine the tomatoes and artichokes; set aside.

In a small heavy-bottomed saucepan, heat the oil and reserved sun-dried tomato marinade over medium-low heat. Add the garlic and rosemary and cook, stirring, until fragrant and softened, about 2 minutes. Add the beans, salt, and pepper; cook, stirring, until heated through, about 5 minutes, mashing about half the beans with the back of a wooden spoon. Remove from heat and set briefly aside.

Heat a 12-inch nonstick skillet over medium-high heat. Working quickly, place 1 tortilla in the skillet and spread with one-third of the bean mixture. Top with one-third of the sun-dried tomato–artichoke mixture. Top with another tortilla, pressing down lightly. Turn over when bottom is lightly browned, 1 to 2 minutes. Cook until bottom is lightly browned, 1 to 2 minutes more. Transfer to an ungreased baking sheet and place in the warm oven.

Repeat with remaining ingredients, stacking the quesadillas on top of each other on the baking sheet as they are cooked. Cut into wedges and serve at once, accompanied by the warm pizza sauce for topping.

Per serving (½ quesadilla, without sauce): Calories 237 | Protein 9g | Total Fat 7g | Sat. Fat 1g | Cholesterol 0mg | Carbohydrate 36g | Dietary Fiber 7g | Sodium 372mg

Lentil Tacos

 Makes 6 servings

These delicious tacos are especially tasty topped with shredded cabbage and guacamole. The lentil filling can also be used in burritos or tostadas, or spooned over South American—Style Corn Cakes (page 122).

1 tablespoon extra-virgin olive oil

1 cup chopped onion

2½ cups low-sodium vegetable broth

1 cup dried lentils, rinsed and
    picked over

1 tablespoon chili powder, or to taste

2 teaspoons ground cumin

1 teaspoon dried oregano

½ teaspoon salt, or to taste

Freshly ground black pepper, to taste

12 taco shells

1 cup mild or medium salsa

Shredded lettuce, shredded cabbage, chopped
    tomato, chopped onion, taco sauce, or
    guacamole, to serve

In a medium nonstick skillet with a lid, heat the oil over medium heat. Add the onion and cook, stirring, until softened, about 3 minutes. Add the broth, lentils, chili powder, cumin, oregano, salt, and pepper; bring to a boil over high heat. Reduce the heat, cover, and simmer gently until lentils are tender, about 40 minutes, stirring a few times.

Meanwhile, preheat oven to 350F (175C). Place the taco shells on a large ungreased baking sheet. Bake on the middle oven rack 3 to 5 minutes, until crisp. Keep warm in a low-temperature oven until needed.

Uncover and mash the lentils lightly with a potato masher or back of a large spoon. Add the salsa and cook, stirring, 2 minutes. Remove from heat and spoon about ¼ cup of the lentil mixture (you will have about 3 cups) into each taco shell. Fill with desired toppings and serve at once.

Per serving (2 tacos): Calories 279 | Protein 16g | Total Fat 8g | Sat. Fat 1g | Cholesterol 0mg | Carbohydrate 38g | Dietary Fiber 15g | Sodium 604mg

Sweet Potato and Black Bean Burritos

Makes 6 servings

I like to serve these smoky-sweet, yet decidedly spicy burritos with the Avocado, Corn, Tomato, and Zucchini Salad (page 38) as a refreshing counterpoint. Chipotle chilies in adobo sauce, which are essentially smoked jalapeño chilies, can be found in the international aisle of most major supermarkets.

1 tablespoon extra-virgin olive oil

1 cup chopped onion

2 cloves garlic, finely chopped

1 (15-ounce) can cut sweet potatoes or yams
    in light syrup, well drained

1 (15-ounce) can black beans, rinsed and
    drained

2/3 cup water

¼ cup mild chili sauce (American style)

2 to 3 teaspoons chili powder

1 teaspoon ground cumin

½ to 1 teaspoon finely chopped
    or pureed chipotle chilies in
    adobo sauce

½ teaspoon salt

Freshly ground black pepper, to taste

6 (10-inch) flour tortillas, warmed

Salsa, to serve (optional)

In a medium deep-sided skillet, heat the oil over medium heat. Add the onion and cook, stirring, until softened, about 3 minutes. Add the garlic and cook, stirring constantly, 1 minute. Add the potatoes, beans, water, chili sauce, chili powder, cumin, chilies, salt, and pepper; bring to a simmer over medium-high heat. Reduce the heat and simmer gently, uncovered, until reduced and thickened, about 10 minutes, stirring occasionally and mashing the potatoes and beans with the back of a large spoon.

To serve, spoon one-sixth of the sweet potato–bean mixture (⅓ to ½ cup) along the center of each tortilla. Roll up, tucking in the sides as you go. Serve at once, with the salsa (if using).

Per serving: Calories 262 | Protein 8g | Total Fat 6g | Sat. Fat 1g | Cholesterol 0mg | Carbohydrate 46g | Dietary Fiber 6g | Sodium 381mg

Mushroom-Bean Burgers

Makes 4 sandwiches

I like to serve these delicious veggie burgers with Sweet Potato and White Potato Oven Fries (page 127). They are also wonderful without the buns, topped with salsa and/or guacamole. For a more pronounced Mexican flavor, double the amount of cumin and include the optional cilantro in the recipe.

2 tablespoons extra-virgin olive oil

1 cup chopped onion

¾ cup finely chopped fresh cultivated white or cremini mushrooms

3 scallions, white and green parts, thinly sliced

2 large cloves garlic, finely chopped

½ teaspoon ground cumin

Salt and freshly ground black pepper, to taste

2 tablespoons all-purpose flour

1 (15-ounce) can refried vegetarian pinto or black beans

½ cup rolled oats (not instant)

1 tablespoon finely chopped fresh cilantro or parsley (optional)

4 split hamburger buns, preferably whole wheat

Ketchup, mustard, pickles, relish, salsa, or guacamole, for topping

In a medium nonstick skillet, heat ½ tablespoon of the oil over medium heat. Add the onion and cook, stirring, until softened, about 3 minutes. Add the mushrooms, scallions, garlic, cumin, salt, and pepper; cook, stirring, until mushrooms have released most of their liquids, 3 to 4 minutes. Add the flour and cook, stirring constantly, 1 minute. Add the refried beans, oats, and cilantro (if using), stirring well to thoroughly combine; cook, stirring constantly, 2 minutes. Remove from heat and let cool to room temperature. Divide the mixture into 4 portions and shape into about ½-inch-thick patties.

In a large nonstick skillet, heat the remaining oil over medium heat. Add the patties and cook until nicely browned, 3 to 4 minutes per side. Serve at once, in hamburger buns, with desired toppings passed separately.

Per serving (includes bun): Calories 354 | Protein 13g | Total Fat 11g | Sat. Fat 2g | Cholesterol 0mg | Carbohydrate 52g | Dietary Fiber 9g | Sodium 605mg

Provençal-Style Focaccia with Red Pepper Coulis and Rosemary

🛒 Makes 6 main-dish or 12 appetizer servings

This is a true flatbread focaccia made using pizza dough. A loaf of ready-made plain focaccia (about 16 ounces) can be used instead, but reduce the initial baking time by about 5 minutes. The versatile red pepper coulis can also be used as a topping for crostini or bruschetta, filling for grilled portobello mushroom caps, or sauce for pasta.

1 (12-ounce) jar roasted red bell peppers, drained
1½ tablespoons extra-virgin olive oil
½ teaspoon coarse salt
⅛ teaspoon dried rosemary
Freshly ground black pepper, to taste
1 (10- or 13-ounce) can refrigerated pizza dough (see Cook's Tip, page 65)
4 to 6 large cloves garlic, sliced into thin slivers
1 to 2 tablespoons whole fresh rosemary leaves

Preheat oven to 350F (175C). Lightly oil a standard-size baking sheet with a rim and set aside.

In a food processor fitted with the knife blade, or in a blender, process the red peppers, 1 tablespoon of the oil, salt, dried rosemary, and black pepper until smooth and pureed.

Unroll the pizza dough onto the prepared baking sheet and press to fit. Spread evenly with the red pepper mixture. Scatter evenly with the garlic and fresh rosemary leaves. Drizzle evenly with the remaining ½ tablespoon of oil. Bake in the center of the oven 15 minutes. Transfer to the bottom oven rack and bake 5 minutes, until nicely browned. Cut into wedges and serve warm or at room temperature.

Per serving: Calories 186 | Protein 5g | Total Fat 6g | Sat. Fat 1g | Cholesterol 0mg | Carbohydrate 29g | Dietary Fiber 1g | Sodium 502mg

White Bean and Roasted Red Pepper Vegetable Wraps with Spinach

🛒 Makes 6 servings

The white bean and roasted red pepper mixture can be stored in the refrigerator a few days before using. It also makes a great spread for other breads and crackers, and a dip for raw vegetables, as well.

1 (15-ounce) can cannellini or other white beans, rinsed and drained
1 (7.25-ounce) jar roasted red bell peppers, well drained
1 to 2 tablespoons fresh lemon juice
1 tablespoon extra-virgin olive oil
1 to 2 cloves garlic, finely chopped
½ teaspoon salt, or to taste
Freshly ground black pepper, to taste
2 tablespoons finely chopped fresh flat-leaf parsley (optional)
6 (10-inch) flour tortillas, preferably whole wheat
12 large spinach leaves

In a food processor fitted with the knife blade, or in a blender, process the beans, red bell peppers, lemon juice, oil, garlic, salt, and black pepper until smooth and pureed. Transfer to a medium bowl and add the parsley (if using), stirring well to combine.

Place the tortillas on a flat work surface and spread with equal amounts (about ⅓ cup) of the bean mixture, leaving a ¾-inch border all around. Place 2 spinach leaves in the center of each tortilla. Tightly roll up each tortilla from the edge nearest you, tucking in the sides as you roll. Cover tightly with plastic wrap and refrigerate a minimum of 30 minutes, or overnight. Serve chilled.

Per serving: Calories 338 | Protein 18g | Total Fat 6g | Sat. Fat 1g | Cholesterol 0mg | Carbohydrate 57g | Dietary Fiber 13g | Sodium 443mg

Pasta and Noodle Dishes

Delicious, economical, and easy, pasta is the ideal "fast food." Its natural blandness makes it the perfect backdrop for tasty sauces and fillings, such as the Fusilli with Sun-Dried Tomato and Roasted Red Pepper Sauce or Southwestern-Style Lasagna with Refried Beans, Corn, and Hominy. Its versatility lets you dress it up or down, whether presenting the Penne with Broccolini and Capers at your next dinner party or bringing the Baked Beans and Macaroni Casserole with Crunchy Fried Onions to your next potluck. If gluten-free dishes are required, the Cellophane Noodles with Scallions and Chow Sauce, the Chinese-Style Hot-and-Sour Rice Noodles with Snow Peas and Cucumber, or the Japanese-Style Rice Noodles with Spinach, Bean Sprouts, and Pickled Ginger, prepared with wheat-free tamari sauce, are sure to satisfy.

Chilled Chinese-Peanut Noodles

 Makes 4 to 5 main-dish or 6 to 8 side-dish servings

You can make this tasty Asian pasta dish using Japanese soba or somen noodles, as well.

1 tablespoon toasted (dark) sesame oil

1 tablespoon creamy peanut butter

1 tablespoon sesame tahini

1 tablespoon plain rice vinegar

1 tablespoon pure maple syrup

2 teaspoons low-sodium soy or tamari sauce

1 teaspoon water

1 to 2 large cloves garlic, finely chopped

½ teaspoon ground ginger

Salt and freshly ground black pepper, to taste

3 scallions, white and green parts, thinly sliced

10 ounces dry egg-free Chinese noodles or other thin Asian pasta, cooked according to package directions until just al dente, rinsed under cold running water, drained well

In a large bowl, whisk together the sesame oil, peanut butter, tahini, vinegar, maple syrup, soy sauce, water, garlic, ginger, salt, and pepper. Stir in the scallions. Let stand a few minutes to allow the flavors to blend. Add the noodles and toss well to thoroughly coat. Serve at room temperature, or cover and refrigerate a minimum of 2 hours or up to 1 day and serve chilled.

Per serving: Calories 361 | Protein 11g | Total Fat 9g | Sat. Fat 1g | Cholesterol 0mg | Carbohydrate 60g | Dietary Fiber 3g | Sodium 128mg

Cincinnati-Style Chili Mac

 Makes 4 servings

Cincinnati is famous for its cinnamon-spiked chili, which is often ladled atop a bed of spaghetti noodles in a popular dish known as "Chili Mac." If serving without the pasta, begin with the lesser amount of chili powder.

1 tablespoon extra-virgin olive oil

½ cup chopped onion

½ cup chopped green bell pepper

1 (15-ounce) can red kidney beans, rinsed and drained

1 (14.5-ounce) can diced tomatoes with green chilies, juices included

½ to 1 tablespoon chili powder

½ teaspoon sugar, or to taste (optional)

½ teaspoon ground cumin

½ teaspoon dried oregano

¼ teaspoon ground cinnamon

¼ teaspoon salt, or to taste

Freshly ground black pepper, to taste

8 ounces spaghetti or elbow macaroni, cooked according to package directions, drained

In a medium deep-sided nonstick skillet, heat the oil over medium heat. Add the onion and bell pepper and cook, stirring, until lightly browned, about 7 minutes. Add the remaining ingredients, except the spaghetti, and bring to a boil over high heat. Reduce the heat and simmer gently, uncovered, stirring occasionally, until thickened, about 20 minutes. Serve hot, over the spaghetti.

Per serving: Calories 360 | Protein 15g | Total Fat 5g | Sat. Fat 1g | Cholesterol 0mg | Carbohydrate 65g | Dietary Fiber 7g | Sodium 361mg

Baked Ziti with Zucchini, Chickpeas, and Olives

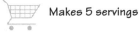

Makes 6 servings

This is a reliable bake-and-take casserole everyone seems to enjoy. Panko bread crumbs, tossed with Italian seasoning, can replace the Italian-seasoned bread crumbs, if desired.

> 8 ounces ziti, rigatoni, or penne pasta
>
> 1 (15-ounce) can chickpeas, rinsed and drained
>
> 1 (14.5-ounce) can diced tomatoes with basil, garlic, and oregano (or similar Italian seasonings), juices included
>
> ½ pound zucchini, coarsely chopped
>
> 1 cup tomato puree
>
> 4 tablespoons chopped kalamata or other good-quality black olives
>
> 1 tablespoon extra-virgin olive oil
>
> 1 tablespoon tomato paste
>
> 2 large cloves garlic, finely chopped
>
> Salt and freshly ground black pepper, to taste
>
> 2 tablespoons Italian-seasoned breadcrumbs

Preheat oven to 350F (175C). Lightly grease an 11 × 7-inch baking dish.

In a large stockpot filled with boiling salted water, cook the ziti according to package directions until just al dente. Drain and return to the pot.

Meanwhile, in a large saucepan or medium stockpot, combine the chickpeas, tomatoes and their juices, zucchini, tomato puree, 2 tablespoons olives, oil, tomato paste, garlic, salt, and pepper; bring to a boil over medium-high heat. Reduce the heat and simmer gently, stirring occasionally, 5 minutes. Add to the ziti, tossing well to combine.

Transfer the ziti mixture to the prepared baking dish. Sprinkle evenly with the breadcrumbs. Top evenly with the remaining 2 tablespoons olives.

Bake about 20 minutes, until heated through and golden. Serve warm.

Per serving: Calories 303 | Protein 11g | Total Fat 7g | Sat. Fat 1g | Cholesterol 0mg | Carbohydrate 51g | Dietary Fiber 5g | Sodium 564mg

Baked Beans and Macaroni Casserole with Crunchy Fried Onions

Makes 5 servings

Here is a kid-friendly casserole that adults will enjoy, as well. Two tablespoons of whole wheat germ or panko bread crumbs (seasoned with garlic salt, to taste, if desired), sprinkled evenly over the top before baking, can replace the fried onions, if desired.

> 1 cup small elbow macaroni or shells, cooked according to package directions until just al dente, drained
>
> 1 (28-ounce) can vegetarian baked beans
>
> 2 to 4 scallions, white and green parts, thinly sliced
>
> ½ cup canned French-fried onions

Preheat oven to 375F (190C). Lightly oil an 8-inch-square baking dish and set aside.

In a large bowl, toss together the macaroni, beans, and scallions until well combined. Transfer to the prepared baking dish and bake, uncovered, 25 minutes. Sprinkle evenly with the onions and bake 2 to 3 minutes more, until onions are golden, taking care not to burn. Serve warm.

Per serving: Calories 271 | Protein 10g | Total Fat 5g | Sat. Fat 2g | Cholesterol 0mg | Carbohydrate 51g | Dietary Fiber 13g | Sodium 755mg

Penne with Broccolini and Capers

 **Makes 4 servings**

Broccolini is baby broccoli, and should not be confused with broccoli rabe, or rapini, a stronger-tasting green, which it closely resembles (see Variation, below). Mature fresh broccoli florets can be substituted, if necessary.

> 1 bunch broccolini (about 1 pound), tough ends trimmed, cut into 1¾-inch lengths
>
> 8 ounces penne or other short tubular pasta
>
> 3 tablespoons extra-virgin olive oil
>
> 6 large cloves garlic, thinly sliced
>
> 2 tablespoons drained capers, 1 tablespoon brine reserved
>
> ¼ teaspoon crushed red pepper flakes, or to taste
>
> ½ teaspoon coarse salt, or to taste
>
> Freshly ground black pepper, to taste

Bring a large pot of salted water to a boil over high heat. Add the broccolini and boil 3 minutes. Transfer with a slotted spoon to a bowl. Add pasta to the pot and cook according to package directions until al dente. Drain, reserving ½ cup of the cooking water.

In a large nonstick skillet, heat the oil over medium-high heat. Add the garlic, capers and brine, and red pepper flakes; cook, stirring constantly, 1 minute. Add broccolini and reserved pasta cooking water; bring to a simmer. Add pasta, salt, and black pepper; cook, stirring constantly, 1 minute. Serve warm or at room temperature.

Per serving: Calories 339 | Protein 11g | Total Fat 11g | Sat. Fat 2g | Cholesterol 0mg | Carbohydrate 50g | Dietary Fiber 5g | Sodium 309mg

Variation: *To make Penne with Broccoli Rabe and Raisins, substitute 1 large bunch broccoli rabe (about 1 pound), trimmed of any discolored leaves and tough bottom stems, for the broccolini, and 2 tablespoons of raisins or currants for the capers (omit the brine). Boil the broccoli rabe as directed for the broccolini and, using tongs or a pasta server, transfer to a colander. While the pasta cooks, rinse the broccoli rabe under cold running water and drain well. Transfer to a cutting board and coarsely chop. Prepare the recipe as otherwise directed, adding the raisins or currants to the skillet along with the cooked broccoli rabe and reserved pasta water. Serve warm or at room temperature, sprinkled with pine nuts, if desired.*

Skillet Lasagna with Cannellini Beans

 **Makes 5 to 6 servings**

You simply can't beat the convenience of this tasty skillet variation of just about everyone's favorite layered casserole.

> 1 tablespoon extra-virgin olive oil
>
> 1 cup chopped onion
>
> 3 large cloves garlic, finely chopped
>
> 1 (15-ounce) can cannellini or other white beans, rinsed and drained
>
> ⅓ cup wheat germ
>
> 1¼ cups water
>
> 1 tablespoon tomato paste
>
> 1 teaspoon dried oregano and/or rosemary
>
> ½ teaspoon salt
>
> ⅛ teaspoon crushed red pepper flakes (optional)
>
> Freshly ground black pepper, to taste
>
> 10 curly-edged lasagna noodles (8 ounces), broken into bite-size pieces
>
> 1 (28-ounce) can no-salt-added diced tomatoes, juices included
>
> 1 cup prepared pizza sauce
>
> ½ cup chopped fresh basil (optional)

In a large nonstick skillet with a lid, heat the oil over medium heat. Add the onion and cook, stirring, until softened, about 3 minutes. Add the garlic and cook, stirring constantly, 1 minute. Add the beans, wheat germ, ¼ cup of the water, tomato paste, oregano, salt, red pepper flakes (if using), and black pepper; cook, stirring, 1 minute. Scatter pasta over bean mixture without stirring. Pour diced tomatoes with juices, pizza sauce, and remaining 1 cup water over pasta without stirring. Cover and bring to a brisk simmer over medium-high heat. Reduce heat to medium-low and simmer, stirring occasionally, until pasta is tender, about 20 minutes, adding the basil (if using) the last few minutes of cooking. Remove skillet from heat and let stand, covered, 5 minutes. Serve at once.

Per serving: Calories 378 | Protein 16g | Total Fat 7g | Sat. Fat 1g | Cholesterol 0mg | Carbohydrate 67g | Dietary Fiber 9g | Sodium 583mg

Variation: *To make Skillet Spinach Lasagna with Cannellini Beans, add 4 ounces of chopped fresh spinach when you add the basil (if using). Proceed as otherwise directed in the recipe.*

Cellophane Noodles with Scallions and Chow Sauce

Makes 2 main-dish or 4 side-dish servings

You can add any variety of vegetables or tofu to this basic Chinese recipe; simply stir-fry them along with the scallions and garlic, increasing the cooking time a minute or two. Frozen vegetables (broccoli is a good choice) can be cooked separately and tossed in at the end. For extra protein, add a garnish of chopped peanuts, almonds, or cashews.

1 (3.75-ounce) package cellophane noodles or mung bean threads

1 tablespoon peanut oil

2 to 4 scallions, white and green parts, thinly sliced

1 to 2 large cloves garlic, finely chopped

Chow Sauce (below)

In a large pot of boiling water, cook the noodles 30 seconds. Drain and rinse briefly under cold running water. Using your fingers, tear the noodles into 4-inch-long clumps and set aside.

In a wok or large nonstick skillet, heat the peanut oil over medium-high heat. Add the scallions and garlic and cook, stirring constantly, until softened and fragrant, 1 to 2 minutes. Reduce the heat to medium and add the noodles and Chow Sauce; cook, tossing and stirring constantly, 2 minutes. Serve at once.

Per serving: Calories 301 | Protein 2g | Total Fat 7g | Sat. Fat 1g | Cholesterol 0mg | Carbohydrate 54g | Dietary Fiber 3g | Sodium 610mg

Chow Sauce

Makes about ¼ cup, or enough for approximately 4 ounces of uncooked noodles

Use this versatile Asian sauce in countless noodle dishes and stir-fries. The ground ginger can be replaced with Chinese five-spice powder, if desired.

2 tablespoons low-sodium tamari or soy sauce

2 tablespoons dry sherry or cooking sherry

1 teaspoon cornstarch

1 teaspoon sugar

⅛ teaspoon ground ginger

In a small bowl, stir together all the ingredients until thoroughly blended. Use as directed in chosen recipe.

Per serving (per tablespoon): Calories 22 | Protein 1g | Total Fat 0g | Sat. Fat 0g | Cholesterol 0mg | Carbohydrate 3g | Dietary Fiber 0g | Sodium 301mg

Japanese-Style Rice Noodles with Spinach, Bean Sprouts, and Pickled Ginger

🛒 Makes 4 servings

Though optional, chopped peanuts add extra protein and crunch to this delicious rice noodle dish. Cellophane noodles can replace the rice vermicelli, if desired; see Cellophane Noodles with Scallions and Chow Sauce (page 79), for the cooking method.

1 (6.75 ounce) package thin rice noodles or
    rice vermicelli
1½ tablespoons toasted (dark) sesame oil
1 tablespoon peanut oil
1 tablespoon sesame seeds
2 large cloves garlic, finely chopped
1 (9-ounce) bag fresh baby spinach
2 cups mung bean sprouts
3 tablespoons low-sodium tamari or soy
    sauce, plus additional, to taste
2 to 3 tablespoons finely chopped pickled
    ginger
1 tablespoon plain rice vinegar
Salt and freshly ground black pepper,
    to taste
¼ cup chopped peanuts (optional)

Bring a large stockpot filled with water to a boil over high heat. Remove from heat and add the rice noodles. Let stand, uncovered, stirring occasionally, until almost al dente, about 5 minutes. Drain well and rinse under cold water for 30 seconds. Drain again.

In a large nonstick skillet, heat ½ tablespoon of the sesame oil and the peanut oil over medium-high heat. Add the sesame seeds and garlic; cook, stirring constantly, until fragrant, 30 to 60 seconds. Add half of the spinach and cook, tossing and stirring constantly, 30 seconds. Add the remaining spinach and cook, tossing and stirring constantly, until just wilted, 1 to 2 minutes. Reduce the heat to medium and add the rice noodles, bean sprouts, tamari sauce, ginger, vinegar, remaining 1 tablespoon sesame oil, salt, and pepper; cook, tossing and cutting through the noodles with the edge of a wide spatula, until heated through, about 3 minutes. Serve warm or at room temperature, garnished with the peanuts (if using).

Per serving: Calories 305 | Protein 5g | Total Fat 10g | Sat. Fat 2g | Cholesterol 0mg | Carbohydrate 51g | Dietary Fiber 3g | Sodium 510mg

Rotelle with Wild Mushroom Ragout

🛒 Makes 5 to 6 servings

Though essentially cultivated brown mushrooms, the cremini variety, also known as baby bellas, nicely mimic the earthy flavor of wild ones. This tasty mushroom ragout is also delicious over polenta. Cultivated white mushrooms can replace half of the creminis, if desired.

2½ tablespoons extra-virgin olive oil
1 cup chopped onion
1 medium red bell pepper (about 6 ounces),
    cored, seeded, and chopped
3 large cloves garlic, finely chopped
16 ounces sliced cremini mushrooms
2 cups canned crushed tomatoes
1 tablespoon red wine (optional)
1½ teaspoons sugar
¾ teaspoon dried oregano
¾ teaspoon salt, or to taste
Freshly ground black pepper, to taste
1 bay leaf
⅛ teaspoon crushed red pepper flakes, or to
    taste (optional)

¼ cup chopped fresh flat-leaf parsley
(optional)

12 ounces rotelle or other short pasta, cooked
according to package directions until al
dente, drained

In a large nonstick skillet, heat the oil over medium heat. Add the onion and bell pepper and cook, stirring, until softened, about 3 minutes. Add the garlic and cook, stirring constantly, 1 minute. Add the mushrooms and cook, stirring, until mushrooms begin to release their liquids, 4 to 5 minutes. Add the tomatoes, wine (if using), sugar, oregano, salt, black pepper, bay leaf, and red pepper flakes (if using), stirring well to combine. Bring to a brisk simmer over medium-high heat. Reduce the heat to medium-low, cover, and simmer, stirring occasionally, until mushrooms are very tender, about 20 minutes.

Uncover the skillet and increase the heat to medium; cook, stirring occasionally, until mixture is slightly thickened, about 5 minutes. Remove the bay leaf and stir in the parsley (if using). Add the pasta, reduce the heat to low, and cook, stirring, until heated through, about 2 minutes. Serve at once.

Per serving: Calories 383 | Protein 12g | Total Fat 9g | Sat. Fat 1g | Cholesterol 0mg | Carbohydrate 66g | Dietary Fiber 5g | Sodium 534mg

Southwestern-Style Lasagna with Refried Beans, Corn, and Hominy

 Makes 8 servings

Refried black beans can replace the standard pinto bean variety, if desired. Serve with a tossed green salad for a well-balanced meal.

1 tablespoon canola oil
1 cup drained canned white hominy

1 cup cooked fresh or frozen yellow corn
4 scallions, white and green parts, thinly
sliced
Garlic salt, to taste
Freshly ground black pepper, to taste
¼ cup finely chopped fresh cilantro
1 (16-ounce) can vegetarian refried beans
2 cups chunky mild or medium salsa
6 oven-ready lasagna noodles
½ cup crushed tortilla chips

Preheat the oven to 375F (190C). Lightly grease an 8-inch-square baking dish and set aside.

In a medium nonstick skillet, heat the oil over medium heat. Add the hominy, corn, scallions, garlic salt, and pepper; cook, stirring, until scallions are softened and mixture is fragrant, 3 to 4 minutes. Remove from heat and toss with the cilantro. Set aside.

In a small bowl, mix together the refried beans and 1 cup of the salsa until well blended. Set aside.

Spread ½ cup of the remaining salsa along the bottom of the prepared baking dish; top with 2 noodles (break, if necessary, to fit). Spread half of the bean mixture on top of the noodles. Top the bean mixture with half of the hominy mixture. Top the hominy mixture with 2 more noodles. Top the noodles with the remaining bean mixture, followed by the remaining hominy mixture. Top with the remaining 2 noodles. Top the noodles with the remaining salsa.

Cover the baking dish with foil (lightly oil the underside if foil will touch the salsa) and bake 35 minutes. Remove the foil and sprinkle evenly with the crushed tortilla chips. Bake another 5 minutes, until topping is lightly browned. Let stand 5 minutes before cutting. Serve warm.

Per serving: Calories 425 | Protein 14g | Total Fat 8g | Sat. Fat 1g | Cholesterol 0mg | Carbohydrate 76g | Dietary Fiber 7g | Sodium 498mg

Chinese-Style Hot-and-Sour Rice Noodles with Snow Peas and Cucumber

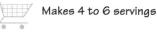 Makes 3 to 4 servings

For added protein, sprinkle each serving with 1 or 2 tablespoons of chopped peanuts or slivered almonds.

- 1 cup fresh snow peas, trimmed
- 8 ounces dried flat (stir-fry or linguine-style) rice noodles, broken in half if bundled
- 2½ tablespoons low-sodium soy or tamari sauce
- 1 tablespoon plain rice vinegar
- 1 teaspoon sugar
- 1½ tablespoons toasted (dark) sesame oil
- 1 teaspoon Chinese hot chili oil
- ½ cup chopped, seeded cucumber
- 2 scallions, white and green parts, thinly sliced

Bring a large stockpot filled with water to a boil. Prepare an ice-water bath. Add the snow peas to the boiling water and cook until crisp-tender, about 2 minutes. Remove with a slotted spoon and transfer to the ice-water bath; refresh 5 minutes. Drain and transfer to a small bowl.

Meanwhile, return the water in the stockpot to a boil. Remove from heat and stir in the rice noodles. Let soak, uncovered, stirring occasionally, until just al dente, or tender yet firm to the bite, about 10 minutes. Drain and rinse under cold running water 30 seconds. Drain well and return to the pot.

Add the soy sauce, vinegar, and sugar to the pot and turn the heat to medium-low; toss a few minutes until the noodles absorb most of the liquid. Add the sesame oil and chili oil and toss well to thoroughly combine. Add the reserved snow peas, cucumber, and scallions and toss until heated through. Remove from heat and serve warm.

Per serving: Calories 376 | Protein 2g | Total Fat 9g | Sat. Fat 1g | Cholesterol 0mg | Carbohydrate 73g | Dietary Fiber 2g | Sodium 512mg

Fusilli with Sun-Dried Tomato and Roasted Red Pepper Sauce

Makes 4 to 6 servings

This sauce is also delicious tossed with gnocchi or spooned over polenta and grilled vegetables.

- 1 tablespoon extra-virgin olive oil
- ½ cup coarsely chopped, well-drained jarred roasted red bell peppers
- ⅓ cup chopped, drained oil-packed sun-dried tomatoes, ½ tablespoon marinade reserved
- 3 large cloves garlic, finely chopped
- ¼ teaspoon crushed red pepper flakes, or to taste
- 1 (28-ounce) can whole peeled tomatoes, juices included
- 1 teaspoon sugar
- ¼ teaspoon salt, or to taste
- Freshly ground black pepper, to taste
- ½ cup chopped fresh basil
- 1 tablespoon balsamic vinegar
- 12 ounces fusilli or similar twist pasta, cooked according to package directions until al dente

In a large nonstick skillet, heat the oil over medium heat. Add the red bell peppers, sun-dried tomatoes, garlic, and red pepper flakes; cook, stirring, until the garlic is fragrant, about 1 minute. Add the canned tomatoes and their juices, reserved marinade, sugar, salt, and black pepper; bring to a boil over high heat, stirring often and breaking up the tomatoes with a large wooden spoon. Reduce the heat to medium-low and simmer, uncovered, until reduced and thickened, 10 to 15 minutes, stirring occasionally and continuing to break up the tomatoes. Stir in the basil and vinegar and add the pasta, tossing well to combine. Serve at once.

Per serving: Calories 432 | Protein 14g | Total Fat 8g | Sat. Fat 1g | Cholesterol 0mg | Carbohydrate 77g | Dietary Fiber 4g | Sodium 587mg

Orzo with Curried Chickpeas and Raisins

 Makes 3 to 4 servings

This eclectic pasta dish is a great choice for a buffet, as it holds up well at room temperature.

2 tablespoons extra-virgin olive oil

1 cup chopped onion

2 cloves garlic, finely chopped

1 teaspoon curry powder, or to taste

1 cup orzo pasta, cooked according to package directions until al dente, drained

1 cup rinsed, drained canned chickpeas

3 tablespoons golden raisins (sultanas), dark raisins, or Zante currants

2 tablespoons pine nuts (optional)

Salt and freshly ground black pepper, to taste

1 cup cherry or grape tomatoes, halved

¼ cup shredded fresh basil leaves

In a large nonstick skillet, heat the oil over medium heat. Add the onion and cook, stirring, until softened, about 3 minutes. Add the garlic and curry powder and cook, stirring constantly, 1 minute. Add the orzo, chickpeas, raisins, pine nuts (if using), salt, and pepper; toss until heated through, about 2 minutes. Remove from the heat and add the tomatoes and basil, tossing well to combine. Serve warm or at room temperature.

Per serving: Calories 366 | Protein 11g | Total Fat 12g | Sat. Fat 2g | Cholesterol 0mg | Carbohydrate 57g | Dietary Fiber 4g | Sodium 16mg

Gnocchi with Roasted Red Pepper Sauce

Makes 4 servings

Gnocchi, chewy Italian potato dumplings, are available frozen or vacuum-packed in most major supermarkets. The red pepper sauce can also be tossed with pasta and is an excellent topping for broiled eggplant, portobello mushrooms, and zucchini.

1 (16-ounce) package frozen or vacuum-packed gnocchi

1 (12-ounce) jar roasted red bell peppers, drained

2 tablespoons extra-virgin olive oil

3 cloves garlic, finely chopped

1 to 2 teaspoons fresh lemon juice

½ teaspoon salt, or to taste

Freshly ground black pepper, to taste

¼ cup finely chopped fresh basil leaves

In a large stockpot filled with boiling salted water, cook the gnocchi according to package directions. Drain in a colander.

Meanwhile, in a food processor fitted with the knife blade, or in a blender, process the bell peppers, oil, garlic, lemon juice, salt, and black pepper until pureed. Set aside.

While the gnocchi is draining, transfer the bell pepper mixture to the stockpot and bring to a simmer over medium heat, stirring frequently. Add the drained gnocchi and basil, stirring well to combine. Remove from heat and serve at once.

Per serving: Calories 412 | Protein 12g | Total Fat 8g | Sat. Fat 1g | Cholesterol 0mg | Carbohydrate 72g | Dietary Fiber 4g | Sodium 275mg

Linguine with Almonds, Breadcrumbs, and Olives

 Makes 6 servings

Serve with a salad of mixed greens and tomatoes for a complete meal.

- 12 ounces linguine or egg-free fettuccine
- ¼ cup extra-virgin olive oil
- ¼ cup panko breadcrumbs or unseasoned (plain) dried regular breadcrumbs
- 1 teaspoon dried oregano
- ½ teaspoon garlic salt
- ¼ teaspoon crushed red pepper flakes, or to taste (optional)
- Freshly ground black pepper, to taste
- ¼ cup coarsely chopped kalamata or other good-quality black olives
- ¼ cup coarsely chopped green olives
- ¼ cup slivered almonds, pine nuts, or walnuts, finely chopped
- 2 tablespoons finely chopped fresh flat-leaf parsley or basil
- Coarse salt, to taste

In a large stockpot filled with boiling salted water, cook the pasta according to package directions until al dente. Drain, reserving ½ cup of the cooking liquid.

Meanwhile, in a large nonstick skillet, heat the oil over medium heat. Add the breadcrumbs, oregano, garlic salt, red pepper flakes (if using), and black pepper; cook, stirring constantly, until breadcrumbs are golden brown, 2 to 3 minutes. Add the pasta and toss well to thoroughly coat. Add the olives, almonds, parsley, coarse salt, and reserved cooking liquid, and toss well to thoroughly combine. Serve at once.

Per serving: *Calories 371 | Protein 9g | Total Fat 16g | Sat. Fat 2g | Cholesterol 0mg | Carbohydrate 48g | Dietary Fiber 2g | Sodium 421mg*

One-Pot Pasta with Spinach, Mushrooms, and Sun-Dried Tomatoes

Makes 3 to 4 servings

This one-pot pasta dish is the perfect rush-hour meal.

- 8 ounces rotelle or other twist pasta
- 4 cups fresh baby spinach leaves, coarsely chopped
- 1 cup sliced fresh cultivated white mushrooms
- 2 tablespoons extra-virgin olive oil
- 3 large cloves garlic, finely chopped
- ½ teaspoon coarse salt, or to taste
- 3 to 4 scallions, white and green parts, thinly sliced
- 2 tablespoons chopped, drained oil-packed sun-dried tomatoes
- 2 tablespoons pine nuts, slivered almonds, or chopped walnuts (optional)
- Freshly ground black pepper, to taste

In a large stockpot filled with boiling salted water, cook the pasta according to package directions until al dente, adding 2 cups spinach and the mushrooms the last 3 minutes or so of cooking. Drain in a colander. Quickly return the stockpot to the same burner (make sure the heat is off) and immediately add the oil, garlic, and salt; stir 10 seconds. Add the scallions and stir constantly until the mixture stops sizzling, 1 to 2 minutes. Add the hot pasta mixture, remaining 2 cups spinach, tomatoes, pine nuts (if using) and pepper; toss over medium-low heat until the fresh spinach begins to wilt. Serve at once.

Per serving: *Calories 403 | Protein 13g | Total Fat 11g | Sat. Fat 2g | Cholesterol 0mg | Carbohydrate 64g | Dietary Fiber 5g | Sodium 394mg*

Quick Pasta Puttanesca

Makes 3 to 4 servings

You'll never miss the anchovies in this speedy vegan variation of the infamous "streetwalker-style" spaghetti alla puttanesca.

8 ounces spaghetti or linguine

1½ tablespoons extra-virgin olive oil

1 cup chopped onion

½ cup chopped green bell pepper

2 to 3 large cloves garlic, finely chopped

1 cup canned crushed tomatoes

2 tablespoons coarsely chopped kalamata or other good-quality black olives

2 tablespoons coarsely chopped green olives

1 to 2 tablespoons coarsely chopped, drained capers

½ teaspoon dried oregano

¼ teaspoon salt, or to taste

¼ teaspoon crushed red pepper flakes, or to taste (optional)

Freshly ground black pepper, to taste

2 tablespoons chopped fresh basil or flat-leaf parsley (optional)

In a large stockpot, cook the spaghetti in boiling salted water according to package directions until al dente; drain.

Meanwhile, in a large nonstick skillet, heat the oil over medium heat. Add the onion and bell pepper and cook, stirring, until softened, about 3 minutes. Add the garlic and cook, stirring constantly, 1 minute. Add the tomatoes, olives, capers, oregano, salt, red pepper flakes (if using), and black pepper; bring to a brisk simmer over medium-high heat. Reduce the heat to medium-low and simmer, stirring occasionally, until slightly reduced and thickened, about 5 minutes. Add the pasta and basil (if using) and toss well to combine. Serve at once.

Per serving: Calories 418 | Protein 11g | Total Fat 12g | Sat. Fat 1g | Cholesterol 0mg | Carbohydrate 67g | Dietary Fiber 4g | Sodium 588mg

Orzo with Mushrooms, Sun-Dried Tomatoes, and Basil

Makes 4 servings

For an earthier pasta dish, use all cremini mushrooms.

2 tablespoons extra-virgin olive oil

1 cup chopped onion

8 ounces sliced fresh cultivated white and/or cremini mushrooms

2 large cloves garlic, finely chopped

1 teaspoon coarse salt

½ teaspoon dried oregano

Freshly ground black pepper, to taste

1 to 2 tablespoons fresh lemon juice

½ pound orzo pasta, cooked according to package directions until al dente, drained

½ cup finely chopped fresh basil

¼ cup julienned, drained oil-packed sun-dried tomatoes, 1 tablespoon marinade reserved

In a medium nonstick skillet, heat the oil over medium heat. Add the onion and cook, stirring, until softened, about 3 minutes. Add the mushrooms, garlic, ½ teaspoon salt, oregano, and pepper; cook, stirring, until mushrooms have released their liquids, 5 to 6 minutes. Stir in the lemon juice. Add the orzo, basil, tomatoes, reserved sun-dried tomato marinade, and remaining ½ teaspoon salt; toss until thoroughly combined and heated through. Remove from heat and serve at once.

Per serving: Calories 349 | Protein 10g | Total Fat 12g | Sat. Fat 2g | Cholesterol 0mg | Carbohydrate 51g | Dietary Fiber 3g | Sodium 496mg

Gingered Somen Noodles with Snow Peas and Teriyaki Sauce

Makes 5 servings

To reduce the sodium in this delicious dish, replace the somen noodles with either rice vermicelli or Italian vermicelli.

2 tablespoons light teriyaki sauce, plus
   additional, to taste
2 tablespoons low-sodium soy or tamari
   sauce
2 tablespoons plain rice vinegar
1 tablespoon toasted (dark) sesame oil
1 teaspoon ground ginger
Freshly ground black pepper, to taste
4 scallions, white and green parts, thinly
   sliced
1 tablespoon peanut oil
2 cups fresh snow peas
1 cup chopped onion
2 large cloves garlic, finely chopped
10 ounces somen or other thin Asian noodle,
   cooked according to package directions
   until al dente, drained and rinsed briefly
   under cold running water

In a small bowl, whisk together the teriyaki sauce, soy sauce, vinegar, sesame oil, ginger, and pepper. Stir in the scallions and set aside.

In a large wok or nonstick skillet, heat the peanut oil over medium-high heat. Add the snow peas and onion and cook, stirring and tossing constantly, 1 minute. Add the garlic and cook, stirring and tossing constantly, until garlic is fragrant and snow peas are crisp-tender, about 2 minutes more. Reduce the heat to medium-low and add the teriyaki sauce–scallion mixture; cook, stirring constantly, 1 minute. Add the noodles and cook, tossing and stirring frequently, until heated through, about 3 minutes.

Serve at once, with additional teriyaki sauce passed separately, if desired.

Per serving: Calories 278 | Protein 10g | Total Fat 6g | Sat. Fat 1g | Cholesterol 0mg | Carbohydrate 50g | Dietary Fiber 2g | Sodium 934mg

Variation: *To make Gingered Somen Noodles with Snap Peas and Teriyaki Sauce, substitute fresh sugar snap peas for the snow peas, and cook them initially with the onion 1 additional minute. Proceed as otherwise directed in the recipe.*

Pasta with Swiss Chard and Red Kidney Beans

Makes 4 servings

Spinach can replace the Swiss chard, and chickpeas or cannellini beans can replace the red kidney beans, if desired.

2 tablespoons extra-virgin olive oil
1 cup chopped onion
2 large cloves garlic, finely chopped
¼ teaspoon crushed red pepper flakes, or to
   taste
1 (15-ounce) can red kidney beans, rinsed and
   drained
4 ounces Swiss chard, stemmed and coarsely
   chopped
¼ cup low-sodium vegetable broth
½ teaspoon salt, or to taste
Freshly ground black pepper, to taste
8 ounces penne or other short tubular pasta,
   cooked according to package directions
   until al dente, drained
½ cup cherry or grape tomatoes, halved

In a large nonstick skillet with a lid, heat the oil over medium heat. Add the onion and cook, stirring, until softened, about 3 minutes. Add the garlic and red pepper flakes and cook, stirring constantly, 1 minute. Add the beans, Swiss chard, broth, salt, and black pepper, tossing well to combine. Cover and simmer, stirring a few times, until the Swiss chard is wilted and tender, 3 to 5 minutes. Add the pasta and tomatoes and cook, uncovered, about 2 minutes, stirring often, until heated through. Serve at once.

Per serving: Calories 386 | Protein 15g | Total Fat 8g | Sat. Fat 1g | Cholesterol 0mg | Carbohydrate 64g | Dietary Fiber 6g | Sodium 364mg

Penne with Roasted Red Pepper and Artichoke Puree

 Makes 5 to 6 servings

The bell pepper and artichoke puree also makes a tasty topping for grilled portobello mushrooms and eggplant.

1 (12-ounce) jar roasted red bell peppers, drained well
2 (6-ounce) jars marinated quartered artichoke hearts, drained well
½ cup loosely packed fresh basil
2 tablespoons extra-virgin olive oil
2 large cloves garlic, finely chopped
½ teaspoon coarse salt, or to taste
Freshly ground black pepper, to taste
12 ounces penne or other short tubular pasta
¼ cup slivered almonds, toasted (see Cook's Tip, page 13)
Shredded fresh basil, for garnish (optional)

In a food processor fitted with the knife blade, process the bell peppers, half the artichokes, basil, oil, garlic, salt, and black pepper until smooth. Set aside.

Meanwhile, in a large stockpot, cook the pasta in boiling salted water according to package directions until al dente; drain and return to the pot. Add the bell pepper mixture, remaining artichokes, and al-

monds. Toss well to thoroughly combine. Serve at once, garnished with the shredded basil (if using).

Per serving: Calories 389 | Protein 13g | Total Fat 10g | Sat. Fat 1g | Cholesterol 0mg | Carbohydrate 64g | Dietary Fiber 8g | Sodium 260mg

Pronto Pasta with Pepperoncini

Makes 4 to 5 servings

Pepperoncini are small, crunchy Italian pickled peppers that are slightly sweet with a moderate degree of heat. They can be located in the condiment section of most major supermarkets.

1 tablespoon extra-virgin olive oil
2 large cloves garlic, finely chopped
2 cups prepared marinara sauce
8 pepperoncini, stemmed and coarsely chopped
⅓ cup sun-dried tomato halves, cut into small pieces with kitchen shears
Freshly ground black pepper, to taste
10 ounces linguine or egg-free fettuccine, cooked according to package directions until al dente, drained

In a large deep-sided nonstick skillet, heat the oil over medium heat. Add the garlic and cook, stirring constantly, until fragrant, about 1 minute. Add the marinara sauce, pepperoncini, sun-dried tomatoes, and pepper; bring to a brisk simmer over medium-high heat. Reduce the heat to medium-low and simmer gently, uncovered, until slightly thickened, about 15 minutes, stirring occasionally. Add the cooked linguine, tossing well to thoroughly coat. Serve at once.

Per serving: Calories 432 | Protein 12g | Total Fat 9g | Sat. Fat 1g | Cholesterol 0mg | Carbohydrate 83g | Dietary Fiber 4g | Sodium 896mg

Sesame-Peanut Fettuccine

Makes 4 servings

You can prepare this Asian-inspired pasta dish with linguine, as well.

- 8 ounces egg-free fettuccine, broken in half
- ⅓ cup creamy peanut butter
- 2 tablespoons low-sodium soy or tamari sauce
- 1 to 2 tablespoons fresh lime juice
- 1 tablespoon toasted (dark) sesame oil
- 2 large cloves garlic, finely chopped
- ¼ teaspoon ground ginger
- ¼ teaspoon cayenne pepper, or to taste (optional)
- Salt and freshly ground black pepper, to taste
- 2 scallions, white and green parts, thinly sliced
- 1 tablespoon sesame seeds

In a large stockpot, cook the pasta in boiling salted water according to package directions until al dente; drain well.

Add the peanut butter, soy sauce, lime juice, sesame oil, garlic, ginger, cayenne (if using), salt, and black pepper to the hot stockpot. Cook over low heat, stirring frequently, until smooth and heated through. Add the drained pasta, scallions, and sesame seeds, tossing until thoroughly combined. Serve warm or at room temperature. Alternatively, cover and refrigerate completely cooled dish up to 2 days and serve chilled, or return to room temperature.

Per serving: Calories 391 | Protein 14g | Total Fat 16g | Sat. Fat 3g | Cholesterol 0mg | Carbohydrate 50g | Dietary Fiber 3g | Sodium 409mg

Spaghetti with Garlic, Onions, and Wheat Germ

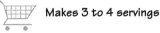 Makes 3 to 4 servings

Wheat germ adds a nutty flavor and texture to this simple yet delicious spaghetti dish.

- 2 tablespoons extra-virgin olive oil
- 1 medium onion (about 6 ounces), coarsely chopped
- 2 large cloves garlic, finely chopped
- ½ teaspoon dried oregano
- ¼ cup low-sodium vegetable broth
- ½ teaspoon coarse salt, plus additional, to taste
- Freshly ground black pepper, to taste
- 8 ounces spaghetti or linguine, cooked according to package directions until al dente, well drained
- 2 tablespoons wheat germ
- Crushed red pepper flakes (optional)

In a large nonstick skillet, heat the oil over medium heat. Add the onion and cook, stirring, until just beginning to brown, 5 to 7 minutes. Add the garlic and oregano and cook, stirring constantly, 1 minute. Reduce the heat to medium-low and add the broth, salt, and black pepper; cook, stirring, 1 minute. Add the pasta and toss until heated through, about 3 minutes. Remove from the heat and add the wheat germ, tossing well to evenly coat. Serve at once, with red pepper flakes (if using) and additional coarse salt passed separately, if desired.

Per serving: Calories 407 | Protein 13g | Total Fat 11g | Sat. Fat 2g | Cholesterol 0mg | Carbohydrate 65g | Dietary Fiber 4g | Sodium 364mg

Salad Bar Vegetable Lo Mein

Makes 4 servings

Ready-prepped salad bar vegetables are the hurried cook's best friends. If you purchase the exact amount you will need in the following recipe, they are surprisingly economical, as well. Feel free to substitute with your own salad bar favorites.

1 tablespoon peanut oil
1 tablespoon toasted (dark) sesame oil
1 cup sliced onion
1 cup sliced green bell pepper
2 large cloves garlic, finely chopped
2 cups sliced fresh mushrooms
1 cup shredded carrots
1 cup snow peas
1½ recipes Chow Sauce (page 79)
8 ounces lo mein noodles or other thin Asian pasta, cooked according to package directions until just al dente, drained and rinsed briefly under cold running water
Freshly ground black pepper, to taste
Low-sodium soy sauce or tamari, to taste (optional)

In a wok or large deep-sided skillet, heat the peanut oil and ½ tablespoon sesame oil over medium-high heat. Add the onion, bell pepper, and garlic and cook, stirring constantly, 1 minute. Add the mushrooms and carrots and cook, stirring constantly, 2 minutes. Add the snow peas and cook, stirring constantly, 1 minute. Reduce the heat to medium and add the Chow Sauce and remaining ½ tablespoon of sesame oil, stirring quickly to combine. Add the noodles and black pepper and cook, tossing and stirring constantly, until heated through, 2 to 3 minutes. Serve at once, with the soy sauce passed separately (if using).

Per serving: Calories 335 | Protein 11g | Total Fat 8g | Sat. Fat 1g | Cholesterol 0mg | Carbohydrate 58g | Dietary Fiber 3g | Sodium 913mg

Roman Beans and Orzo

Makes 4 servings

Kidney beans can replace the Roman beans, also known as cranberry beans, if desired.

1 tablespoon extra-virgin olive oil
½ cup chopped onion
¼ cup chopped green bell pepper
2 large cloves garlic, finely chopped
1 (15.5-ounce) can Roman (cranberry) beans, rinsed and drained
¾ cup low-sodium vegetable broth or water
2/3 cup prepared pizza sauce
½ teaspoon salt, or to taste
¼ teaspoon dried oregano
Freshly ground black pepper, to taste
½ pound orzo pasta, cooked according to package directions, drained

In a large deep-sided nonstick skillet, heat the oil over medium heat. Add the onion and bell pepper and cook, stirring, until softened, about 3 minutes. Add the garlic and cook, stirring constantly, 1 minute. Add the beans, broth, pizza sauce, salt, oregano, and black pepper; bring to a brisk simmer over high heat. Reduce the heat to medium-low and simmer, uncovered, stirring occasionally, about 10 minutes, until slightly reduced. Add the orzo and stir well to combine. Serve at once.

Per serving: Calories 380 | Protein 17g | Total Fat 6g | Sat. Fat 1g | Cholesterol 0mg | Carbohydrate 66g | Dietary Fiber 6g | Sodium 631mg

Seashell Casserole with Mushrooms, Peas, and Pearl Onions

Makes 4 servings

If you are looking for a comforting casserole like the one your grandmother used to make, try this tasty one-dish supper. Though optional, crushed potato chips lend a nostalgic touch.

4 ounces small shell pasta or elbow
    macaroni
¼ cup extra-virgin olive oil
1 cup chopped celery
¼ cup chopped onion
¼ cup all-purpose flour
2 tablespoons Dijon mustard
1 tablespoon fresh thyme leaves or about
    1 teaspoon dried thyme
2 cups low-sodium vegetable broth
¼ teaspoon salt
Freshly ground black pepper, to taste
1½ cups frozen peas and pearl onions, thawed
1 (4-ounce) jar mushrooms, drained
½ cup crushed potato chips or 2 tablespoons
    wheat germ (optional)

Preheat oven to 375F (190C). Lightly oil a 1½-quart baking dish and set aside.

In a medium stockpot, cook pasta according to package directions until just al dente. Drain and return to the pot. Set aside.

Meanwhile, in a medium saucepan, heat the oil over medium heat. Add the celery and onion and cook, stirring, until softened, about 3 minutes. Add the flour, mustard, and thyme; cook, stirring constantly, 1 minute. Gradually whisk in the broth and let come to a gentle boil, whisking often and adding the salt and pepper. Boil, stirring constantly, 1 min-ute. Stir in the peas and pearl onions and mushrooms and remove from heat.

Add the pea mixture to the cooked pasta, tossing well to thoroughly combine. Transfer to the prepared baking dish and sprinkle evenly with the potato chips (if using). Bake, covered, 25 minutes. Remove the cover and bake an additional 5 minutes, until lightly browned and bubbly. Let stand 5 minutes before serving.

Per serving: Calories 334 | Protein 13g | Total Fat 15g | Sat. Fat 2g | Cholesterol 0mg | Carbohydrate 39g | Dietary Fiber 6g | Sodium 677mg

Southwestern-Style Penne with Chilies, Corn, and Cilantro

Makes 4 servings

For a hotter dish, add up to one chopped jalapeño chili along with the bell pepper. For more fiber and protein, include the optional beans.

2 tablespoons extra-virgin olive oil
1 cup chopped onion
1 cup chopped green bell pepper
2 large cloves garlic, finely chopped
1 cup cooked fresh or frozen yellow corn
1 cup rinsed, drained canned red kidney or
    black beans (optional)
2 tablespoons drained chopped mild green
    chilies
1 teaspoon ground cumin
½ teaspoon salt, or to taste
Freshly ground black pepper, to taste
8 ounces penne or other short tubular pasta,
    preferably whole wheat, cooked according
    to package directions until al dente

4 scallions, white and green parts, thinly
    sliced
½ cup chopped fresh cilantro
Cherry or grape tomatoes, for garnish
    (optional)

In a large nonstick skillet, heat the oil over medium heat. Add the onion and bell pepper and cook, stirring, 2 minutes. Add the garlic and cook, stirring constantly, 1 minute. Add the corn, beans (if using), chilies, cumin, salt, and black pepper; cook, stirring, 1 minute. Add the pasta and scallions and cook, stirring, 2 more minutes. Remove from the heat and add the cilantro, tossing well to combine. Serve warm, garnished with the tomatoes (if using).

Per serving: Calories 338 | Protein 10g | Total Fat 8g | Sat. Fat 1g | Cholesterol 0mg | Carbohydrate 57g | Dietary Fiber 4g | Sodium 283mg

Main-Dish Vegetable, Grain, and Legume Combos

Conventional supermarkets are carrying more and more unconventional grains these days as more and more health-savvy shoppers ask for them. Wholesome barley, nutty bulgur, fluffy couscous (technically pasta), hearty polenta, earthy quinoa, and a wide array of rice—creamy arborio, fragrant basmati, rustic brown, and delicate jasmine—are all there. High in fiber, iron, and other nutrients, particularly in their whole form, these important complex carbohydrates add flavor and texture to countless vegetable combinations. Moreover, when combined with legumes (beans, lentils, peas), they are part of the complete protein plan necessary to sustain a nutritionally sound plant-based diet—just another delicious example of Mother Nature keeping it real.

Stuffed Acorn Squash with Long Grain and Wild Rice, Pecans, and Cranberries

Makes 4 main-dish servings

The stuffing for this festive fall and winter dish can be made a day ahead for easy entertaining.

2 medium acorn squash (about 1½ pounds each), halved, seeds and membranes removed

1 tablespoon extra-virgin oil

½ cup chopped onion

2 tablespoons dry sherry or cooking sherry

1 large clove garlic, finely chopped

2⅓ cups low-sodium vegetable broth

1 (6-ounce) package long-grain white and wild rice (¾ cup), seasoning packet excluded

½ cup dried cranberries

¼ cup pecan pieces, slivered almonds, or walnut pieces

2 tablespoons chopped fresh sage

½ teaspoon salt, or to taste

Freshly ground black pepper, to taste

Preheat oven to 425F (220C).

Cut a very thin parallel slice on the uncut sides of the squash to help them sit upright without wobbling. Place the squash, cut sides down, in a shallow baking dish just large enough to hold them in a single layer. Add about ½ inch of water to the pan. Cover and bake 45 minutes, until flesh is fork-tender. Remove from oven, pour off water, and turn the squash cut sides up; set aside. Reduce oven temperature to 350F (175C).

Meanwhile, in a medium saucepan, heat the oil over medium heat. Add the onion and cook, stirring, until softened, about 3 minutes. Add the sherry and garlic and increase the heat to high; cook, stir-ring constantly, until the sherry has evaporated, about 1 minute. Add the broth, rice mixture, cranberries, pecans, sage, salt, and pepper; bring to a boil. Reduce heat to between low and medium-low, cover, and simmer until the liquid has been absorbed, but the mixture is still quite moist, 25 to 30 minutes. Remove from the heat and let stand, covered, 5 minutes. Uncover and fluff with a fork. (At this point, completely cooled mixture can be stored, covered, in refrigerator up to 24 hours before returning to room temperature and continuing with the recipe; however, add about 10 minutes to final baking time.)

Mound equal amounts of the rice mixture into the squash halves. Return to the oven and bake, uncovered, until heated through, about 10 minutes. Serve warm.

Per serving: Calories 350 | Protein 13g | Total Fat 9g | Sat. Fat 1g | Cholesterol 0mg | Carbohydrate 59g | Dietary Fiber 4g | Sodium 579mg

Greek Bulgur-Stuffed Peppers with Mint

Makes 6 servings

Bulgur, a precooked cracked wheat product popular in the eastern Mediterranean since ancient times, can be found in most major supermarkets. If you can't locate the fine-grain variety, medium-grain bulgur can be used, but increase the initial simmering time by several minutes and add additional water, as necessary.

4 tablespoons extra-virgin olive oil

½ cup chopped onion

1 cup fine-grain (fancy) bulgur

2 large cloves garlic, finely chopped

1 (14.5-ounce) can stewed tomatoes, juices included

1½ cups water, plus additional, if necessary

1 teaspoon salt, or to taste

Freshly ground black pepper, to taste

½ cup finely chopped fresh mint

¼ cup finely chopped fresh flat-leaf parsley

2 tablespoons chopped walnuts, whole pine nuts, or slivered almonds (optional)

6 large green bell peppers (about 8 ounces each), top parts cut off, seeds and membranes removed

Preheat oven to 375F (190C).

In a medium nonstick skillet, heat 2 tablespoons of the oil over medium heat. Add the onion and cook, stirring, until softened, about 3 minutes. Add the bulgur and garlic and cook, stirring, 1 minute. Add the tomatoes with juices, water, salt, and black pepper; bring to a boil over medium-high heat. Reduce the heat to medium-low and simmer, uncovered, about 10 minutes, until bulgur is tender and liquids are absorbed, stirring occasionally and breaking up the tomatoes with a large wooden spoon. Add the mint, parsley, nuts (if using), and remaining 2 tablespoons oil, stirring well to combine. Remove from the heat and let stand 5 minutes.

Lightly pack the bell peppers with equal amounts of the bulgur mixture. Place in a shallow baking dish just large enough to accommodate the peppers in a single layer. Add enough water to the dish to measure about ½ inch. Cover tightly and bake 35 to 40 minutes, until the peppers are softened and heated through the center. Serve warm or at room temperature.

Per serving: Calories 232 | Protein 6g | Total Fat 10g | Sat. Fat 1g | Cholesterol 0mg | Carbohydrate 35g | Dietary Fiber 10g | Sodium 541mg

Two-Bean Garden Goulash

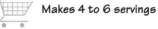 Makes 4 to 6 servings

Serve this tasty and satisfying vegetarian version of the Hungarian classic by itself in bowls, with lots of crusty bread, or over egg-free broad noodles (or broken egg-free fettuccine), mashed potatoes, potato gnocchi, couscous, or rice.

2 tablespoons extra-virgin olive oil

2 medium zucchini (about 6 ounces each), chopped

1 medium onion (about 6 ounces), chopped

2 tablespoons tomato paste

2 tablespoons sweet paprika

2 cloves garlic, finely chopped

1 (15-ounce) can red kidney beans, rinsed and drained

1 (15-ounce) can cannellini or other white beans, rinsed and drained

¾ pound plum tomatoes, seeded and chopped

1 (5.5-ounce) can tomato juice

¼ cup water

¾ teaspoon salt, or to taste

Freshly ground black pepper, to taste

In a large deep-sided nonstick skillet, heat the oil over medium heat. Add the zucchini and onion and cook, stirring, until softened, about 5 minutes. Add the tomato paste, paprika, and garlic; cook, stirring constantly, 2 minutes. Add the remaining ingredients and bring to a brisk simmer over medium-high heat, stirring occasionally. Reduce the heat to between low and medium-low and simmer gently, uncovered, stirring occasionally, until slightly thickened, about 15 minutes. Serve warm.

Per serving: Calories 307 | Protein 16g | Total Fat 8g | Sat. Fat 1g | Cholesterol 0mg | Carbohydrate 47g | Dietary Fiber 13g | Sodium 624mg

Barley Pilaf with Peas and Pearl Onions

 Makes 3 to 4 servings

This quick-cooking pilaf is as wholesome as it is delicious. Though optional, chopped pimento provides festive flecks of red.

1 tablespoon extra-virgin olive oil

1 cup quick-cooking barley

2 large cloves garlic, finely chopped

1 (14-ounce) can (1¾ cups) low-sodium vegetable broth

1½ cups frozen peas and pearl onions

2 tablespoons water

1 tablespoon chopped pimento (optional)

¼ teaspoon salt, or to taste

Freshly ground black pepper, to taste

¼ cup finely chopped fresh basil

In a large deep-sided nonstick skillet with a lid, heat the oil over medium heat. Add the barley and cook, stirring, 2 minutes. Add the garlic and cook, stirring constantly, 1 minute. Add the broth, frozen vegetables, water, pimento (if using), salt, and pepper; bring to a brisk simmer over medium-high heat. Reduce the heat, cover, and simmer until the barley is tender and has absorbed most of the liquid, 12 to 15 minutes. Add the basil and stir to evenly distribute the ingredients. Serve at once.

Per serving: Calories 353 | Protein 16g | Total Fat 6g | Sat. Fat 1g | Cholesterol 0mg | Carbohydrate 62g | Dietary Fiber 15g | Sodium 542mg

Barley Risotto with Asparagus

 Makes 5 to 6 servings

High in soluble fiber, barley has been shown to lower cholesterol. Its natural creaminess makes it an excellent substitute for arborio rice in traditional risottos. Use regular pearl barley, not quick-cooking barley, in the following recipe, which takes about 50 minutes to complete from start to finish. Fresh asparagus, blanched in boiling water a few minutes until crisp-tender, can be used in lieu of the frozen, if desired.

2 tablespoons extra-virgin olive oil

1 medium onion (about 6 ounces), finely chopped

1 large clove garlic, finely chopped

1½ cups pearl barley

1 cup dry white wine or white cooking wine (optional)

5 cups low-sodium vegetable broth (6 cups, if not using wine), heated, plus additional heated broth or water, if necessary

½ teaspoon dried thyme

¼ teaspoon salt, or to taste

¼ teaspoon lemon-pepper seasoning

8 ounces frozen asparagus, cooked according to package directions until barely tender, drained, cut diagonally into 1-inch pieces

Freshly ground black pepper, to taste (optional)

¼ cup slivered almonds, toasted (optional) (see Cook's Tip, page 13)

In a large deep-sided nonstick skillet, heat the oil over medium heat. Add the onion and cook, stirring, until softened, about 3 minutes. Add the garlic and cook, stirring constantly, 30 seconds. Add the barley and cook, stirring constantly, 2 minutes. Add the wine (if using) or 1 cup broth, thyme, salt, and lemon-pepper seasoning; cook, stirring occasionally, until most of the liquid is absorbed, about 3 minutes. Add the remaining broth, ½ cup at a time, stirring occasionally and waiting until it is almost completely absorbed before adding more (do not allow mixture to dry out). Add the asparagus with the last ½ cup of broth and cook, stirring occasionally, until the barley is tender but still chewy and the mixture is creamy, adding additional broth or water by the ¼ cupfuls, if necessary. Season with additional salt and black pepper, if necessary. Serve at once, garnished with the almonds (if using).

Per serving (with the optional wine): Calories 366 | Protein 19g | Total Fat 6g | Sat. Fat 1g | Cholesterol 0mg | Carbohydrate 54g | Dietary Fiber 14g | Sodium 654mg

Yellow Basmati Rice with Chickpeas

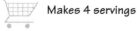 **Makes 3 to 4 servings**

You can omit the chickpeas or substitute them with black-eyed peas, if desired.

  1 tablespoon extra-virgin olive oil
  1 cup chopped onion
  2 large cloves garlic, finely chopped
  ½ teaspoon whole cumin seeds
  2 cups low-sodium vegetable broth
  ½ teaspoon salt
  ¼ to ½ teaspoon ground turmeric
  Freshly ground black pepper, to taste
  1 cup basmati or other long-grain white rice
  1 (15-ounce) can chickpeas, rinsed and drained
  ¼ cup slivered almonds (optional)
  ¼ cup chopped fresh cilantro or parsley
      (optional)

In a medium deep-sided skillet with a lid, heat the oil over medium heat. Add the onion and cook, stirring, until beginning to brown, about 5 minutes,

stirring occasionally. Add the garlic and cumin and cook, stirring constantly, 1 minute.

Add the broth, salt, turmeric, and pepper; bring to a boil over high heat. Stir in the rice and chickpeas and let come to a brisk simmer. Reduce the heat to low, cover, and simmer until all the liquid is absorbed, 17 to 20 minutes. Remove from the heat and stir in the almonds (if using) and cilantro (if using). Let stand, covered, 5 minutes. Fluff with a fork and serve at once.

Per serving: Calories 329 | Protein 16g | Total Fat 6g | Sat. Fat 1g | Cholesterol 0mg | Carbohydrate 54g | Dietary Fiber 5g | Sodium 562mg

Brown Rice and Lentils

Makes 4 servings

Straight from the pantry, this protein-packed recipe is a must-have in any basic vegan culinary repertoire. You can easily add your favorite vegetables as the dish simmers, and accent the flavor with herbs and spices such as curry powder, oregano, rosemary, or cumin, if desired.

  2 (14-ounce) cans (3½ cups) low-sodium
      vegetable broth
  ½ cup water
  ¾ cup dried lentils, rinsed and picked over
  ¾ cup brown rice
  2 tablespoons extra-virgin olive oil
  1 tablespoon onion powder
  ½ teaspoon garlic powder
  ¼ teaspoon salt, or to taste
  Freshly ground black pepper, to taste

In a medium stockpot, bring all the ingredients to a boil over high heat. Reduce the heat to between low and medium-low, cover, and simmer until lentils and rice are tender, stirring occasionally, about 45 minutes. Serve warm.

Per serving: Calories 361 | Protein 23g | Total Fat 8g | Sat. Fat 1g | Cholesterol 0mg | Carbohydrate 51g | Dietary Fiber 15g | Sodium 592mg

Per serving: Calories 323 | Protein 13g | Total Fat 8g | Sat. Fat 3g | Cholesterol 0mg | Carbohydrate 53g | Dietary Fiber 7g | Sodium 432mg

Jamaican-Style Black Bean and Coconut-Cornbread Bake

Makes 6 servings

The coconut milk–infused cornbread topping lends this delicious casserole a delightful taste of the tropics.

2 (15-ounce) cans black beans, rinsed and
    drained
1 (14.5-ounce) can diced tomatoes with mild
    green chilies, juices included
1½ cups frozen yellow corn, thawed
½ teaspoon jerk seasoning, or more, to taste
½ teaspoon salt
Freshly ground black pepper, to taste
½ cup all-purpose flour
½ cup yellow cornmeal
1 tablespoon sugar
1¼ teaspoons baking powder
²/₃ cup light coconut milk
2 tablespoons extra-virgin olive oil

Preheat oven to 350F (175C). Lightly oil an 8-inch-square baking dish and set aside.

In a medium bowl, stir together the beans, tomatoes and their juices, corn, jerk seasoning, ¼ teaspoon salt, and pepper until well combined. Transfer to the prepared baking dish.

In another medium bowl, whisk together the flour, cornmeal, sugar, baking powder, and remaining ¼ teaspoon salt. Add the coconut milk and oil, and stir well to combine. Spread evenly over the bean mixture. Bake, uncovered, about 30 minutes, until topping is lightly browned and a toothpick inserted in the center of the topping comes out clean. Let stand 5 minutes before serving.

Rosemary Lentils over Polenta

Makes 4 to 6 servings

These fragrant lentils can also be enjoyed over rice, tossed with pasta, or all alone, with lots of crusty bread to sop up the delicious sauce. To substitute regular polenta, or coarse-ground yellow cornmeal, for the instant variety, see Baked Broccoli and White Bean Polenta with Marinara Sauce (page 100) for the proper cooking method.

1½ tablespoons extra-virgin olive oil
1 cup chopped onion
4 large cloves garlic, finely chopped
4 cups low-sodium vegetable broth
3 cups water
1 cup dried brown lentils, rinsed and picked
    over
1 tablespoon chopped fresh rosemary or
    about 1 teaspoon dried rosemary
¼ teaspoon salt, plus additional, to taste
Freshly ground black pepper, to taste
1 large bay leaf, broken in half, or 2 small bay
    leaves
¼ cup chopped fresh flat-leaf parsley
1 cup instant polenta

In a medium deep-sided nonstick skillet with a lid, heat 1 tablespoon of the oil over medium heat. Add the onion and cook, stirring, until softened, about 3 minutes. Add half the garlic and cook, stirring constantly, 1 minute. Add 2 cups of the broth, 2 cups of the water, lentils, rosemary, ¼ teaspoon salt, pepper, and bay leaf; bring to a boil over high heat. Reduce the heat to between low and medium-low, cover, and simmer about 40 minutes, until lentils are tender. Uncover and increase heat to medium; cook, stirring occasionally, until mixture is reduced and slightly soupy (like chili), about 5 to 10 minutes. Stir in the parsley and remove from heat. Remove and discard the bay leaf halves. Cover and keep warm (mixture will thicken as it cools).

Meanwhile, lightly oil an 8-inch-square baking dish and set aside.

In a medium stockpot, bring the remaining 2 cups broth, 1 cup water, polenta, remaining ½ tablespoon oil, remaining garlic, salt, and pepper to a boil over high heat. Immediately reduce the heat to medium; cook, stirring often with a long-handled wooden spoon, 5 minutes. Immediately spoon the polenta into the prepared baking dish, pressing down with the back of a large spoon to form a smooth surface. Cover with foil and let stand about 15 minutes to become firm.

To serve, cut the polenta into desired number of squares and transfer to individual serving plates. Spoon equal amounts of the lentil mixture over the polenta and serve at once.

Per serving: Calories 424 | Protein 29g | Total Fat 6g | Sat. Fat 1g | Cholesterol 0mg | Carbohydrate 65g | Dietary Fiber 24g | Sodium 660mg

Southwestern-Style Black-Eyed Peas and Collard Greens with Rice

Makes 4 to 5 servings

Straight from the pantry, this tasty dish is proof that the possibilities for healthy eating are endless. Just about any bean or green that you have on the shelf can replace the black-eyed peas and collard greens, if desired. For a lower-carb meal to serve three, omit the rice.

1 (15.5-ounce) can black-eyed peas, rinsed and drained

1 (14.5-ounce) can diced tomatoes with jalapeño chilies, juices included

1 (14-ounce) can collard greens, rinsed and drained

½ cup water

3 tablespoons tomato paste

1 tablespoon extra-virgin olive oil

½ tablespoon ground cumin

½ tablespoon onion powder

1 teaspoon sugar, or to taste (optional)

½ teaspoon garlic powder

¼ teaspoon salt, or to taste

Freshly ground black pepper, to taste

1 small bay leaf or ½ large bay leaf

About 4 cups hot cooked white or brown rice (see Cook's Tip, page 100)

In a large saucepan, combine the black-eyed peas, tomatoes and their liquids, collard greens, water, tomato paste, oil, cumin, onion powder, sugar (if using), garlic powder, salt, pepper, and bay leaf; bring to a brisk simmer over medium-high heat, stirring occasionally. Reduce the heat to between low and medium-low and simmer, uncovered, stirring occasionally, until slightly reduced and thickened, about 15 minutes. Remove and discard the bay leaf. Serve warm, over the rice.

Per serving: Calories 405 | Protein 14g | Total Fat 5g | Sat. Fat 1g | Cholesterol 0mg | Carbohydrate 78g | Dietary Fiber 8g | Sodium 482mg

Cook's Tip: One-third cup of uncooked regular long-grain white rice, basmati rice, or jasmine rice will yield about 1 cup cooked. One-quarter cup of raw brown rice will yield about 1 cup cooked. To make 4 cups cooked long-grain white rice, combine 1⅓ cups white rice and 2⅔ cups salted water in a medium saucepan; bring to a boil over high heat. Reduce heat to low, cover, and simmer until all the water has been absorbed, 17 to 20 minutes.

Fluff with a fork and serve. To make 4 cups cooked brown rice, combine 1 cup brown rice and 2¼ cups salted water in a medium saucepan. Cook as directed for white rice, increasing cooking time to 35 to 40 minutes.

Broccoli Slaw and Red Pepper Stir-Fry with Peanuts

Makes 4 servings

This delicious low-carb stir-fry can be stretched to feed up to six if served over rice or tossed with Asian-style noodles. Shredded carrots can replace up to one-quarter of the broccoli slaw, if desired.

2 tablespoons reduced-sodium soy or tamari sauce, plus additional, to taste

2 tablespoons water

4 teaspoons black bean sauce

1 teaspoon cornstarch

2 tablespoons peanut oil

1 (12-ounce) package broccoli slaw

1 large red bell pepper (about 8 ounces), cored, seeded, and sliced into thin strips

2 to 4 scallions, thinly sliced, white and green parts separated

2 large cloves garlic, finely chopped

1 (5-ounce) can sliced bamboo shoots, drained (optional)

½ cup dry roasted peanuts

In a small bowl, whisk together the soy sauce, water, black bean sauce, and cornstarch until thoroughly blended. Set aside.

In a wok or large nonstick skillet, heat the oil over medium-high heat. Add the broccoli slaw, bell pepper, white parts of the scallions, and garlic; cook, tossing and stirring constantly, 2 minutes. Add the bamboo shoots (if using) and scallion greens; cook, stirring, 1 minute. Reduce the heat to medium and add the reserved soy sauce mixture; cook, stirring, 1 minute. Remove from the heat and add the peanuts, tossing well to combine. Serve at once, with additional soy sauce passed separately, if desired.

Per serving: Calories 215 | Protein 7g | Total Fat 16g | Sat. Fat 3g | Cholesterol 0mg | Carbohydrate 14g | Dietary Fiber 3g | Sodium 528mg

Baked Broccoli and White Bean Polenta with Marinara Sauce

Makes 8 servings

This tasty, gluten-free casserole can also be made with cauliflower or asparagus. While you can prepare the dish using instant polenta, which typically becomes tender after stirring about 5 minutes over medium heat, you will need to pre-cook the broccoli.

3 (14-ounce) cans (5¼ cups) low-sodium vegetable broth

1¼ cups water

2 cups polenta or coarse-ground yellow cornmeal

3 cups chopped frozen broccoli, thawed

1 (15-ounce) can cannellini or other white
    beans, rinsed and drained

2 tablespoons extra-virgin olive oil

2 large cloves garlic, finely chopped

1 teaspoon dried rosemary

½ teaspoon salt

Freshly ground black pepper, to taste

1 cup prepared marinara sauce, plus
    additional, to serve

Lightly oil a 13 × 9-inch baking pan and set aside.

In a large stockpot, bring the broth and water to a boil over high heat. Slowly add the polenta, stirring constantly with a long-handled wooden spoon. Reduce heat to low and add the broccoli, beans, oil, garlic, rosemary, salt, and pepper, stirring well to combine. Cover and cook, stirring occasionally, until polenta is tender, about 15 minutes. Remove from heat and let stand, covered, 5 minutes.

Preheat oven to 350F (175C).

Spread the polenta mixture evenly in the prepared baking pan. Let stand 20 minutes or until firm. Spread evenly with the marinara sauce. Transfer to center rack of oven and bake 15 minutes, until just heated. Cut into wedges and serve warm, with additional marinara sauce passed separately.

Per serving: Calories 295 | Protein 16g | Total Fat 5g | Sat. Fat 1g | Cholesterol 0mg | Carbohydrate 48g | Dietary Fiber 12g | Sodium 689mg

Quick Black Beans and Brown Rice

Makes 4 servings

This also makes a hearty filling for burritos.

1 tablespoon extra-virgin olive oil

1 cup chopped onion

2 large cloves garlic, finely chopped

1 (15-ounce) can black beans, rinsed and
    drained

1 (14.5 ounce) can stewed tomatoes, juices
    included

1 cup quick-cooking brown rice

¼ cup water

1 teaspoon dried oregano

1 teaspoon ground cumin

¼ teaspoon salt, or to taste

Freshly ground black pepper, to taste

Cayenne pepper, to taste (optional)

In a large saucepan, heat the oil over medium heat. Add the onion and cook, stirring, until softened, about 3 minutes. Add the garlic and cook, stirring constantly, 1 minute. Add the remaining ingredients and bring to a boil over medium-high heat, breaking up the tomatoes with a large wooden spoon. Reduce the heat to between low and medium-low and simmer, covered, until rice is tender, about 10 minutes. Remove from heat and let stand, covered, 5 minutes. Serve at once.

Per serving: Calories 334 | Protein 11g | Total Fat 5g | Sat. Fat 1g | Cholesterol 0mg | Carbohydrate 63g | Dietary Fiber 6g | Sodium 399mg

Greek Chickpeas and Spinach with Rice

 Makes 4 servings

This is also wonderful served over couscous or tossed with pasta, such as penne or farfalle.

1 tablespoon extra-virgin olive oil

1 cup chopped red onion

2 large cloves garlic, finely chopped

1 (15-ounce) can chickpeas, rinsed and drained

2 tablespoons finely chopped fresh dill, or
   about ½ tablespoon dried dill

2 tablespoons fresh lemon juice

½ teaspoon salt, or to taste

Freshly ground black pepper, to taste

1 (10-ounce) bag fresh spinach, torn into bite-
   size pieces

3 cups hot cooked rice (see Cook's Tip,
   page 100)

In a large nonstick skillet with a lid, heat the oil over medium heat. Add the onion and cook, stirring, until softened, about 3 minutes. Add the garlic and cook, stirring constantly, 1 minute. Add the chickpeas and dill and cook, stirring often, 2 minutes. Add the lemon juice, salt, and pepper and stir to combine. Add half the spinach, tossing and stirring until it just begins to wilt, about 2 minutes. Add remaining spinach, cover, and cook until spinach is wilted but not shriveled, about 2 minutes, tossing and stirring once or twice. Stir well and serve at once, over the rice.

Per serving: Calories 346 | Protein 12g | Total Fat 6g | Sat. Fat 1g | Cholesterol 0mg | Carbohydrate 63g | Dietary Fiber 3g | Sodium 331mg

Portobello Mushrooms Stuffed with Sun-Dried Tomato Hummus on a Bed of Spinach

 Makes 4 main-dish or 8 first-course or appetizer servings

This is an easy yet elegant dish for entertaining as it can go right from oven to table. Jarred roasted red bell peppers, chopped, can replace the sun-dried tomatoes, if desired.

1½ tablespoons extra-virgin olive oil

1 (10-ounce) bag baby spinach leaves

½ cup drained oil-packed sun-dried tomatoes,
   chopped, ½ tablespoon marinade reserved

Coarse salt and freshly ground black pepper,
   to taste

1½ cups prepared hummus

8 large (about 2 ounces each) portobello
   mushroom caps

Preheat oven to 400F (205C).

Smear the bottom of a 13 × 9-inch casserole with 1 tablespoon of the olive oil, and then line with the spinach leaves. Drizzle evenly with the remaining olive oil, followed by the reserved sun-dried tomato marinade. Sprinkle lightly with salt and pepper.

In a small bowl, mix together the hummus and sun-dried tomatoes. Sprinkle the insides of each mushroom cap lightly with salt and pepper. Fill each mushroom cap with equal amounts (about 3½ tablespoons) of the hummus mixture. Transfer the filled mushrooms to the spinach-lined casserole. Cover with foil (lightly oil underside if it will touch filling) and bake about 30 minutes, until the mushrooms are tender through the center and have started to release their juices. Serve hot, directly from the casserole, using a wide spatula to transfer the mushrooms and spinach to serving plates.

Per 2 stuffed mushrooms and ¼ of the spinach mixture: Calories 290 | Protein 10g | Total Fat 17g | Sat. Fat 2g | Cholesterol 0mg | Carbohydrate 29g | Dietary Fiber 8g | Sodium 322mg

Tahini Brown Rice with Artichokes and Chickpeas

 Makes 4 to 5 servings

This tasty dish showcases the versatility of tahini, a Middle Eastern paste made from ground raw (sometimes roasted) sesame seeds.

1 (14-ounce) can (1¾ cups) low-sodium
    vegetable broth
¼ cup plus ⅔ cup water
1 cup brown rice
1 (6-ounce) jar marinated, quartered
    artichoke hearts, drained, 1 tablespoon
    marinade reserved
¾ teaspoon coarse salt
¼ cup sesame tahini
2 tablespoons fresh lemon juice, or to taste
3 to 4 large cloves garlic, finely chopped
Freshly ground black pepper, to taste
1 (15-ounce) can chickpeas, rinsed and drained
¼ cup finely chopped fresh flat-leaf parsley

In a medium deep-sided skillet with a lid, combine the broth, ¼ cup water, rice, reserved artichoke marinade, and ¼ teaspoon of the salt; bring to a boil over high heat. Reduce the heat to between low and medium-low, cover, and cook until the rice has absorbed most of the liquid and is almost tender, about 30 minutes.

Meanwhile, in a small bowl, whisk together the remaining ⅔ cup water, tahini, 1 tablespoon lemon juice, garlic, remaining ½ teaspoon salt, and pepper. Add to the partially cooked rice mixture, along with the artichoke hearts and chickpeas; stir well to combine. Bring to a brisk simmer over medium-high heat. Reduce the heat to between low and medium-low, cover, and cook until most of the liquid has been absorbed but the mixture is still creamy, about 10 minutes. Remove from the heat and add the parsley and remaining 1 tablespoon of lemon juice, stirring well to combine. Serve at once.

Per serving: Calories 425 | Protein 18g | Total Fat 12g | Sat. Fat 2g | Cholesterol 0mg | Carbohydrate 64g | Dietary Fiber 6g | Sodium 628mg

Cajun-Style Rice and Corn with Kidney Beans

Makes 4 servings

Any bean can replace the kidney variety, if desired.

2 cups low-sodium vegetable broth
1 tablespoon extra-virgin olive oil
1 teaspoon Cajun seasoning
½ teaspoon salt, or to taste
Freshly ground black pepper, to taste
1 cup long-grain white rice
1 (15-ounce) can red kidney beans, rinsed and
    drained
1½ cups frozen yellow corn, thawed

In a medium deep-sided skillet with a lid, bring the broth, oil, Cajun seasoning, salt, and pepper to a boil over high heat. Stir in the rice and beans and let come to a brisk simmer. Reduce the heat to low, cover, and simmer until all the liquid is absorbed, 17 to 20 minutes. Remove from heat and stir in the corn; let stand, covered, 10 minutes. Fluff with a fork and serve at once.

Per serving: Calories 364 | Protein 17g | Total Fat 5g | Sat. Fat 1g | Cholesterol 0mg | Carbohydrate 66g | Dietary Fiber 7g | Sodium 584mg

Variation: *To make Jamaican-Style Rice and Corn with Green Pigeon Peas, substitute the Cajun seasoning with jerk seasoning and the kidney beans with 1 (15-ounce) can green pigeon peas, rinsed and drained.*

Jasmine Rice with Peas, Mushrooms, Pecans, and Currants

Makes 4 servings

Almonds, cashews, or pistachios can replace the pecans, if desired.

1 tablespoon canola oil

½ cup chopped onion

1 cup thinly sliced cultivated white mushrooms

1 large clove garlic, finely chopped

1 cup jasmine rice or other long-grain white rice

¼ cup pecan pieces

1 (14-ounce) can (1¾ cups) low-sodium vegetable broth

¼ cup Zante currants, raisins, or dried cranberries

½ teaspoon salt, or to taste

Freshly ground black pepper, to taste

1 cup frozen peas, thawed

In a medium saucepan, heat the oil over medium heat. Add the onion and cook, stirring, until softened, about 3 minutes. Add the mushrooms and garlic and cook, stirring constantly, 2 minutes. Add the rice and pecans and cook, stirring constantly, 30 seconds. Add the broth, currants, salt, and pepper; bring to a boil over high heat. Reduce the heat to low, cover, and simmer until all the liquids are absorbed, 15 to 18 minutes. Remove from heat and add the peas, tossing gently to combine. Cover and let stand 5 minutes. Uncover, fluff with a fork, and serve at once.

Per serving: Calories 318 | Protein 12g | Total Fat 9g | Sat. Fat 1g | Cholesterol 0mg | Carbohydrate 48g | Dietary Fiber 5g | Sodium 566mg

Curried Cauliflower and Potatoes with Black-Eyed Peas

Makes 4 servings

Delicious all by itself, this fragrant curried dish can also be served over rice or couscous to serve up to six. Chickpeas can replace the black-eyed peas, if desired.

2 tablespoons canola oil

1 small red onion (about 4 ounces), cut into ½-inch pieces

2 large cloves garlic, finely chopped

1 tablespoon mild curry powder, or to taste

2 cups low-sodium vegetable broth or water

1 large head cauliflower (about 2 pounds), cut into bite-size florets

¾ pound boiling potatoes, preferably red-skinned, cut into ½-inch cubes

½ teaspoon salt, or to taste

Freshly ground black pepper, to taste

1 (15-ounce) can black-eyed peas, rinsed and drained

2 to 3 teaspoons fresh lemon juice

In a large deep-sided nonstick skillet with a lid, heat the oil over medium heat. Add the onion and cook, stirring, until softened, about 4 minutes. Add the garlic and curry powder and cook, stirring constantly, 1 minute. Add the broth, cauliflower, potatoes, salt, and pepper; bring to a brisk simmer over high heat. Reduce the heat to medium-low and simmer, covered, until potatoes are just tender, about 10 minutes. Add the black-eyed peas and lemon juice and bring to a brisk simmer over medium-high heat. Cook, uncovered, adjusting the heat to maintain a brisk simmer and stirring occasionally, until potatoes and cauliflower are tender, about 5 minutes. Remove the skillet from the heat and let stand, covered, about 5 minutes, until much of the liquid has been absorbed. Serve at once.

Per serving: Calories 291 | Protein 17g | Total Fat 8g | Sat. Fat 1g | Cholesterol 0mg | Carbohydrate 43g | Dietary Fiber 14g | Sodium 602mg

Zucchini and Two-Bean Tamale Casserole

 Makes 6 servings

Ready-cooked polenta, available in tubes in either the international aisle or refrigerated section of many major supermarkets, makes quick work of this tasty Tex-Mex casserole.

1 (14.5-ounce) can diced tomatoes with jalapeño chilies, juices included

2½ tablespoons extra-virgin olive oil

1 cup chopped onion

2 large cloves garlic, finely chopped

2 tablespoons all-purpose flour

1 (15-ounce) can pinto beans, rinsed and drained

1 (15-ounce) can black beans, rinsed and drained

2 medium zucchini (about 6 ounces each), preferably 1 green and 1 yellow, cut into 1-inch pieces

1 teaspoon ground cumin

½ teaspoon salt, or to taste

Freshly ground black pepper, to taste

¼ cup chopped fresh cilantro (optional)

1 (16-ounce) tube cooked polenta, cut crosswise into 12 (½-inch-thick) rounds

Preheat oven to 350F (175C). Lightly grease an 11 × 7-inch baking dish and set aside.

Drain the tomatoes, pouring the juices into a 2-cup measure. Add enough water to equal 1 cup. Set aside.

In a large nonstick skillet, heat 2 tablespoons of the oil over medium heat. Add the onion and cook, stirring, until softened, about 3 minutes. Add the garlic and cook, stirring constantly, 30 seconds. Add the flour and cook, stirring constantly, 1 minute. Add the reserved tomato juice-water mixture and cook, stirring constantly, until slightly thickened, about 3 minutes. Add the beans, zucchini, reserved tomatoes, cumin, salt, and pepper; bring to a brisk simmer over medium-high heat, stirring occasionally. Cook, stirring often, until zucchini is softened, about 2 minutes. Remove the skillet from the heat and add the cilantro (if using), stirring well to combine.

Transfer the vegetable-bean mixture to the prepared baking dish. Arrange the polenta slices evenly over the top. Brush the polenta evenly with the remaining ½ tablespoon oil. Bake, uncovered, 25 to 30 minutes, until polenta is lightly browned and mixture is bubbly. Let cool a few minutes before serving warm.

Per serving: Calories 305 | Protein 12g | Total Fat 7g | Sat. Fat 1g | Cholesterol 0mg | Carbohydrate 51g | Dietary Fiber 11g | Sodium 326mg

Coconut-Curried Portobello Mushrooms with Basmati Rice

 Makes 4 servings

Because the Madras variety of curry powder is hotter than regular curry powder, it's better to use the lesser amount if a milder dish is preferred.

1 cup basmati rice

2 cups water

¾ teaspoon salt, plus additional, to taste

1 cup light coconut milk

4 scallions, white and green parts, thinly sliced

½ cup finely chopped fresh cilantro

1 tablespoon fresh lime juice

Freshly ground black pepper, to taste

2 tablespoons extra-virgin olive oil

1 pound portobello mushrooms, cleaned and stemmed, cut into ½-inch-thick slices

1 tablespoon chopped fresh ginger

1 (15-ounce) can chickpeas, rinsed and drained

3 large cloves garlic, finely chopped

1 to 2 teaspoons Madras (spicy) or mild curry powder

In a medium saucepan, bring the rice, water, and ½ teaspoon of the salt to a boil over high heat. Reduce the heat to low and simmer, covered, until rice has absorbed all the liquid, about 15 minutes. Stir in ½ cup of the coconut milk, half the scallions, ¼ cup of the cilantro, lime juice, and pepper. Cover and keep warm.

In a large nonstick skillet, heat the oil over medium heat. Add the mushrooms and ginger and cook, stirring occasionally, until the mushrooms begin to release their liquids, about 5 minutes. Add the chickpeas, remaining scallions, garlic, and curry powder; cook, stirring, 2 minutes. Stir in the remaining ½ cup coconut milk, and remaining ¼ teaspoon salt; cook, stirring, until heated through, about 2 more minutes. Remove from heat and stir in the remaining ¼ cup of the cilantro. Season with additional salt and pepper, as necessary. Serve at once, over the rice mixture.

Per serving: Calories 407 | Protein 14g | Total Fat 14g | Sat. Fat 4g | Cholesterol 0mg | Carbohydrate 60g | Dietary Fiber 2g | Sodium 469mg

Chickpea and Zucchini Sauté with Couscous

Makes 4 servings

To reduce the sodium in this tasty dish to 416mg per serving, substitute water for all the vegetable broth.

1 (14-ounce) can (1¾ cups) low-sodium vegetable broth

2 tablespoons plus 1 teaspoon extra-virgin olive oil

¾ teaspoon salt

1 cup instant couscous, preferably whole wheat

1 cup chopped onion

2 cloves garlic, finely chopped

1 (15-ounce) can chickpeas, rinsed and drained

2 small zucchini (about 4 ounces each), halved lengthwise, thinly sliced crosswise

½ teaspoon dried oregano

Freshly ground black pepper, to taste

1 cup cherry or grape tomatoes, halved

¼ cup chopped fresh basil, mint, or flat-leaf parsley

In a medium saucepan, bring 1½ cups of the broth, 1 teaspoon oil, and ¼ teaspoon of the salt to a boil over high heat. Stir in the couscous, cover, and remove from heat. Let stand, covered, 7 minutes. Uncover and fluff with a fork.

Meanwhile, in a large nonstick skillet with a lid, heat the remaining 2 tablespoons oil over medium heat. Add the onion and cook, stirring, until softened, about 3 minutes. Add the garlic and cook, stirring constantly, 1 minute. Add the chickpeas, zucchini, remaining ¼ cup broth, oregano, remaining ½ teaspoon salt, and pepper; cook, stirring, 2 minutes, until zucchini is just softened. Cover the skillet and reduce the heat to medium-low; cook, stirring a few times, until zucchini is tender, about 5 minutes. Remove from heat and add the tomatoes and basil, tossing well to combine. Serve at once, over the couscous.

Per serving: Calories 393 | Protein 18g | Total Fat 10g | Sat. Fat 1g | Cholesterol 0mg | Carbohydrate 60g | Dietary Fiber 6g | Sodium 643mg

Microwave Risotto with Baby Le Sueur Peas

Makes 4 main-course or 6 side-dish servings

Among all the canned vegetables on the shelves, I have a special place in my heart for those teeny-tiny, ultra-sweet Le Sueur peas, which I used to eat straight from the can back in the day when I had no time—or inclination—to cook. The use of the microwave not only speeds up the cooking time of traditional risotto, but virtually eliminates the constant stirring. The following recipe is based on a 1,000-watt microwave oven, so you might need to vary the cooking time accordingly.

2 tablespoons extra-virgin olive oil

2 tablespoons finely chopped onion

1 cup arborio rice

⅓ cup dry white wine or white cooking wine

¼ teaspoon salt, plus additional as necessary

Freshly ground black pepper, to taste

3 cups low-sodium vegetable broth, plus additional as necessary

1 (15-ounce) can low-sodium plain Le Sueur peas or Le Sueur peas with mushrooms and pearl onions, well drained

In a 1½-quart microwave-safe casserole with a lid, combine the oil and onion. Microwave, covered, on high, 3 minutes. Remove cover and continue cooking uncovered. Stir in rice, wine, salt, and pepper. Cook 2 minutes on high. Stir in 1 cup of the broth and cook on high 5 minutes. Stir in another 1 cup of broth and cook on high for 10 minutes, stirring half way through cooking time. Stir in ½ cup of broth and cook on high 4 minutes. Stir in remaining ½ cup of broth and cook on high 2 minutes.

Gently stir in the peas, cover, and cook on high 1 minute. Let stand, covered, 2 minutes. Rice should be tender yet still chewy and slightly creamy. If rice is too hard, add additional broth in ¼-cup increments and continue cooking on high, covered, in 1-minute intervals until desired consistency is achieved. Season with additional salt and pepper, as necessary. Serve at once.

Per serving: Calories 325 | Protein 15g | Total Fat 7g | Sat. Fat 1g | Cholesterol 0mg | Carbohydrate 47g | Dietary Fiber 4g | Sodium 660mg

Southern-Style Wilted Spinach with Peanuts over Brown Rice

Makes 4 servings

From the state of Georgia, famous for its peanuts, this delicious dish represents American southern cooking at its finest. For a milder dish, omit the jalapeño chili.

¼ cup salted peanuts, chopped

1 tablespoon peanut oil

1 cup chopped onion

1 jalapeño chili, seeded and finely chopped

2 cloves garlic, finely chopped

⅓ cup low-sodium vegetable broth

1 teaspoon fresh lemon juice

½ teaspoon salt, or to taste

Freshly ground black pepper, to taste

1 (10-ounce) bag fresh spinach, coarsely
  chopped

1 cup cherry or grape tomatoes, halved
  (optional)

3 cups hot cooked brown rice (see Cook's Tip,
  page 100)

Heat a large nonstick skillet over medium heat. Add the peanuts and cook, stirring constantly, until lightly toasted and fragrant, 1 to 2 minutes. Immediately remove peanuts from the skillet and transfer to a small holding plate; set aside.

Add the oil, onion, and chili to the skillet; cook over medium heat, stirring, until the vegetables are softened, about 3 minutes. Add the garlic and cook, stirring constantly, 1 minute. Add the broth, lemon juice, salt, pepper, and half the spinach; cook, tossing often with a wide spatula, 1 minute. Add the remaining spinach and cook, tossing often, until spinach is just wilted, 1 to 2 more minutes. Remove from heat and add the cherry tomatoes (if using) and half the reserved peanuts, tossing well to combine. Serve at once, over the rice, sprinkled evenly with the remaining peanuts.

Per serving: Calories 299 | Protein 10g | Total Fat 10g | Sat. Fat 2g | Cholesterol 0mg | Carbohydrate 46g | Dietary Fiber 7g | Sodium 376mg

Variation: *To make Southern-Style Wilted Collard Greens with Peanuts over Brown Rice, replace the spinach with 1 pound collard greens, stemmed, ribbed, and coarsely chopped. Cook as otherwise directed in the recipe, adding about 2 minutes to the final cooking time.*

Quinoa Pilaf with Dried Cranberries and Toasted Almonds

Makes 3 to 4 servings

Dried cherries, raisins, or currants can replace the cranberries, if desired. For a drier pilaf, reduce the broth by ¼ cup and simmer a few minutes less.

1 tablespoon extra-virgin olive oil

4 scallions, white and green parts separated,
  thinly sliced

1 cup quinoa, rinsed well and drained

2 cups low-sodium vegetable broth

⅓ cup dried cranberries

¼ teaspoon salt, or to taste

Freshly ground black pepper, to taste

¼ cup slivered almonds, toasted (see Cook's
  Tip, page 13)

In a medium nonstick skillet with a lid, heat the oil over medium heat. Add the white parts of the scallions and cook, stirring constantly, 1 minute. Add the quinoa and cook, stirring constantly, 2 minutes, until dry. Carefully add the broth, cranberries, salt, and pepper; bring to a boil over high heat. Reduce the heat to medium-low, cover, and simmer until the quinoa has absorbed the liquid, about 20 minutes. Remove from heat and stir in the almonds and reserved scallion greens; cover and let stand 5 minutes. Uncover and toss well with a fork to evenly distribute the ingredients. Serve warm.

Per serving: Calories 350 | Protein 17g | Total Fat 13g | Sat. Fat 1g | Cholesterol 0mg | Carbohydrate 44g | Dietary Fiber 7g | Sodium 540mg

Chinese-Style Stir-Fried Vegetables and Tofu with Hoisin Sauce

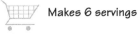 Makes 4 servings

This quick-cooking stir-fry can be stretched by serving over rice or tossed with any Asian-style noodle.

3 tablespoons hoisin sauce

3 tablespoons low-sodium soy sauce

1 tablespoon sugar

1 tablespoon toasted (dark) sesame oil

½ tablespoon peanut oil

1½ cups cubed, well-drained extra-firm tofu (see Buddhist-Style Kung Pao Tofu with Rice, page 111)

4 scallions, white and green parts, thinly sliced

1 medium red bell pepper (about 6 ounces), chopped

2 cups fresh broccoli florets, cut into bite-size pieces

2 large cloves garlic, finely chopped

In a small bowl, mix together the hoisin sauce, soy sauce, sugar, and ½ tablespoon of the sesame oil. Set aside.

In a wok or large nonstick skillet, heat the remaining ½ tablespoon sesame oil and peanut oil over medium-high heat. Add the tofu and cook, stirring often, until the tofu is lightly browned, about 5 minutes. Add the scallions, bell pepper, broccoli, and garlic; cook, stirring and tossing constantly, until broccoli is just softened, 2 to 3 minutes. Add the hoisin sauce mixture and cook, stirring often, until the broccoli is crisp-tender, 2 to 3 minutes. Serve at once.

Per serving: Calories 258 | Protein 18g | Total Fat 14g | Sat. Fat 2g | Cholesterol 0mg | Carbohydrate 20g | Dietary Fiber 4g | Sodium 667mg

Coconut-Curried Lentils with Basmati Rice

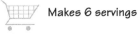 Makes 6 servings

The curried lentils are also delicious served over couscous, boiled potatoes, or all by themselves, accompanied with pita bread and a tossed green salad. Brown sugar can be substituted for the molasses, if desired.

1½ tablespoons extra-virgin olive oil

1 cup chopped onion

4 large cloves garlic, finely chopped

1 (14.5-ounce) can diced tomatoes, juices included

1 (14-ounce) can light coconut milk

1 cup dried lentils, rinsed and picked over

½ cup water

½ tablespoon molasses

1 to 1½ teaspoons mild curry powder, or to taste

½ teaspoon salt, or to taste

¼ teaspoon crushed red pepper flakes, or to taste (optional)

Freshly ground black pepper, to taste

½ cup chopped fresh cilantro

4½ to 6 cups hot cooked basmati rice (see Cook's Tip, page 100)

In a large deep-sided nonstick skillet with a lid, heat the oil over medium heat. Add the onion and cook, stirring, until softened, about 3 minutes. Add the garlic and cook, stirring constantly, 1 minute. Add the tomatoes and their juices, coconut milk, lentils, water, molasses, curry powder, salt, red pepper flakes (if using), and black pepper; bring to a boil over high heat. Reduce the heat to between low and medium-low and simmer, covered, until the lentils are tender but not falling apart, 40 to 45 minutes, stirring occasionally. Stir in the cilantro and remove from the heat. Serve warm, over the rice.

Per serving: Calories 414 | Protein 16g | Total Fat 9g | Sat. Fat 5g | Cholesterol 0mg | Carbohydrate 68g | Dietary Fiber 12g | Sodium 356mg

Mixed Asian Vegetables with Peanut Sauce over Rice

 Makes 4 servings

This is a quick and nutritious way to turn a bag of frozen mixed vegetables into a fabulous Asian-style meal. For extra protein, add some cubed extra-firm tofu to the skillet when you sauté the cooked vegetables.

½ cup water

2½ tablespoons creamy peanut butter

1 tablespoon low-sodium soy or tamari sauce

½ tablespoon cornstarch

2 large cloves garlic, finely chopped

1 teaspoon ground ginger

Pinch, or more, cayenne pepper (optional)

½ tablespoon peanut oil

½ tablespoon toasted (dark) sesame oil

1 (16-ounce) bag frozen Asian-style mixed
  vegetables, slightly under-cooked according
  to package directions, drained

3 cups hot cooked white or brown rice
  (see Cook's Tip, page 100)

In a small bowl, whisk together the water, peanut butter, soy sauce, cornstarch, garlic, ginger, and cayenne (if using) until thoroughly blended; set aside.

In a large nonstick skillet, heat both the oils over medium-high heat. Add the mixed vegetables and cook, stirring, 1 minute. Reduce the heat to medium-low and add the peanut butter mixture. Cook, stirring, until the sauce thickens, about 3 minutes. Serve at once, over the rice.

Per serving: Calories 352 | Protein 11g | Total Fat 9g | Sat. Fat 2g | Cholesterol 0mg | Carbohydrate 58g | Dietary Fiber 4g | Sodium 356mg

Greek-Style Roasted Potatoes, Peppers, Zucchini, and Chickpeas

 Makes 4 main-dish or 6 to 8 side-dish servings

This tasty meal also makes a great company side dish for six to eight people. To stretch it even further, serve over rice or orzo pasta.

1½ pounds small or medium red potatoes,
  quartered or cut into eights, depending on
  size

1 large green bell pepper (about 8 ounces),
  cored, seeded, and cut into ½-inch-thick
  strips

1 large onion (about 8 ounces), sliced into
  half-rounds

3 tablespoons extra-virgin olive oil

Juice of 1 lemon (about 3 tablespoons)

½ tablespoon dried oregano

¾ teaspoon garlic salt

Freshly ground black pepper, to taste

1 large zucchini (about 8 ounces), cut into
  1-inch pieces

1 (15-ounce) can chickpeas, rinsed and drained

1 cup cherry or grape tomatoes, halved

¼ cup pitted kalamata or other good-quality
  olives, halved (optional) (see Cook's Tip,
  page 16)

Preheat oven to 425F (220C).

On a large rimmed baking sheet, toss together the potatoes, bell pepper, onion, 2 tablespoons of the oil, half the lemon juice, oregano, garlic salt, and black pepper until thoroughly coated. Spread in a single layer and bake 15 minutes. Add the zucchini and toss well to combine. Spread in a single layer and bake an additional 15 minutes. Add the chickpeas and tomatoes and toss well to combine. Spread in a single layer and bake an additional 15 minutes, until potatoes are nicely browned and tender through the center. Transfer to a large serving bowl and toss with the remaining oil, lemon juice, and the olives (if using). Serve at once.

Per serving: Calories 350 | Protein 10g | Total Fat 12g | Sat. Fat 2g | Cholesterol 0mg | Carbohydrate 53g | Dietary Fiber 6g | Sodium 406mg

Curried Vegetables over Basmati Rice

Makes 4 to 5 servings

Use this recipe as a model and substitute with your own favorite vegetables—frozen asparagus, cut into 1½-inch lengths, are especially delicious. Instead of the rice, serve the vegetables over couscous, boiled potatoes, or alone, in small bowls, accompanied with pita bread to sop up the delicious coconut sauce.

1 tablespoon extra-virgin olive oil

1 cup chopped onion

1 tablespoon all-purpose flour

1 cup low-sodium vegetable broth

1 tablespoon curry powder

½ teaspoon salt, or to taste

Freshly ground black pepper, to taste

1 (16-ounce) bag frozen mixed broccoli and cauliflower florets, partially thawed

1 large red bell pepper (about 8 ounces), cored, seeded, and cut into thin 1½-inch-long strips

1 cup frozen peas, partially thawed

1 cup light coconut milk

3 to 4 cups hot cooked basmati rice (see Cook's Tip, page 100)

In a large deep-sided nonstick skillet with a lid, heat the oil over medium heat. Add the onion and cook, stirring, until softened, about 3 minutes. Add the flour and cook, stirring constantly, 1 minute. Add the broth, curry powder, salt, and black pepper; cook, stirring constantly, until slightly thickened, about 3 minutes. Add the broccoli and cauliflower mixture and the bell pepper, stirring well to combine. Cover the skillet, raise the heat to medium-high, and bring to a brisk simmer. Reduce the heat to between low and medium-low and simmer gently, covered, until the vegetables are just tender, about 10 minutes, stirring occasionally.

Add the peas and coconut milk to the skillet and bring to a simmer over medium-high heat, stirring occasionally. Reduce the heat to medium and cook, uncovered, stirring occasionally, until slightly thickened, 2 to 3 minutes. Serve at once, over the rice.

Per serving: Calories 372 | Protein 14g | Total Fat 8g | Sat. Fat 4g | Cholesterol 0mg | Carbohydrate 62g | Dietary Fiber 9g | Sodium 495mg

Buddhist-Style Kung Pao Tofu with Rice

Makes 4 servings

This is wonderful with Ginger Broccoli (page 118).

1 (14-ounce) package extra-firm tofu, drained

Salt and freshly ground black pepper, to taste

½ cup water

3 tablespoons low-sodium soy or tamari sauce

1 tablespoon light brown sugar

½ tablespoon cornstarch

1 to 1½ teaspoons Chinese hot chili oil

½ teaspoon ground ginger

1 tablespoon peanut oil

4 to 6 scallions, white and greens parts, cut into 1-inch lengths

3 large cloves garlic, finely chopped

¼ cup unsalted roasted peanuts

3 cups hot cooked white or brown rice

(see Cook's Tip, page 100)

Place the tofu on a deep-sided plate or shallow bowl. Top with a second plate and weight with a heavy can. Let stand a minimum of 15 minutes (preferably 1 hour). Drain excess water. Cut into ¾-inch cubes and season with salt and pepper.

In a small bowl, whisk together the water, soy sauce, sugar, cornstarch, hot oil, and ginger; set aside.

In a wok or large nonstick skillet, heat the peanut oil over medium-high heat. Add the tofu and cook, stirring often, until golden brown on all sides, 7 to 9 minutes. Transfer to a holding plate and set briefly aside.

Reduce the heat to medium and add the scallions; cook, stirring constantly, 30 seconds. Add the garlic and cook, stirring constantly, 1 minute. Add the reserved soy sauce mixture and let come to a simmer, stirring constantly. Reduce the heat to low and add the reserved tofu and peanuts; cook, stirring, until thickened and heated through, 1 to 2 minutes. Serve at once, over the rice.

Per serving: Calories 383 | Protein 15g | Total Fat 14g | Sat. Fat 2g | Cholesterol 0mg | Carbohydrate 51g | Dietary Fiber 3g | Sodium 465mg

Mexican-Style Zucchini-Rice Casserole with Pinto Beans

Makes 4 servings

This is a great recipe to make with a leftover half-pint of Chinese take-out white rice. Cooked brown rice can be substituted, if desired.

1 tablespoons extra-virgin olive oil

1½ pounds zucchini (about 4 medium), cut into ½-inch cubes

1 cup chopped onion

2 large cloves garlic, finely chopped

½ teaspoon salt, or to taste

½ teaspoon ground cumin

½ teaspoon dried oregano

⅛ teaspoon cayenne pepper, or to taste (optional)

Freshly ground black pepper, to taste

1 (15-ounce) can pinto or kidney beans, rinsed and drained

1¼ cups mild or medium salsa

1 cup cooked long-grain white rice (see Cook's Tip, page 100)

1 crushed taco shell, or crushed tortilla chips

Preheat the oven to 350F (175C). Lightly grease an 8-inch-square baking dish and set aside.

In a large nonstick skillet, heat the oil over medium heat. Add the zucchini and onion; cook, stirring, until tender, about 8 minutes, adding the garlic, salt, cumin, oregano, cayenne (if using), and black pepper the last few minutes of cooking. Add the remaining ingredients, except the crushed taco shell; cook, stirring, until heated through, about 3 minutes. Transfer to the prepared baking dish and cover with foil. Bake 20 minutes, until hot through the center. Uncover and sprinkle with the crushed taco shell; bake until lightly browned, about 5 minutes. Serve warm.

Per serving: Calories 251 | Protein 10g | Total Fat 5g | Sat. Fat 1g | Cholesterol 0mg | Carbohydrate 44g | Dietary Fiber 10g | Sodium 495mg

Cuban-Style Fried Rice with Black Beans and Pineapple

 Makes 3 main-dish servings or 4 to 5 side-dish servings

This is an economical and delicious way to use up a leftover pint container of Chinese take-out rice. If you cook the rice yourself, make sure the rice is completely dry before beginning the recipe and skip the first step, omitting 1 teaspoon of the oil.

- 4 teaspoons extra-virgin olive oil
- 2 cups cooked white rice (see Cook's Tip, page 100)
- 1 cup chopped red or green bell pepper
- 2 tablespoons chopped onion
- 2 large cloves garlic, finely chopped
- 1 (8-ounce) can pineapple chunks, drained, or 1 cup cubed fresh pineapple
- ¾ cup rinsed, drained canned black beans
- ½ teaspoon salt, or to taste
- Freshly ground black pepper, to taste
- Cayenne pepper, to taste (optional)
- 2 to 3 tablespoons finely chopped fresh cilantro
- Juice of ½ lime (about 1 tablespoon)

Mix 1 teaspoon of the oil with the rice, using your fingers to separate chunks; set briefly aside.

In a large nonstick skillet, heat remaining oil over medium-high heat. Add the bell pepper and onion; cook, stirring constantly, until softened and fragrant, 1 to 2 minutes. Add the garlic and cook, stirring constantly, 30 seconds. Add the rice, pineapple, beans,

salt, black pepper, and cayenne (if using); cook, stirring constantly, 2 to 3 minutes (or longer, if using freshly cooked rice), until rice begins to crackle and pop and is lightly browned. Remove from the heat and toss with the cilantro and lime juice. Serve at once.

Per serving: Calories 331 | Protein 8g | Total Fat 7g | Sat. Fat 1g | Cholesterol 0mg | Carbohydrate 61g | Dietary Fiber 4g | Sodium 360mg

Southwestern-Style Vegetable Casserole

 Makes 4 to 6 servings

This smoky-sweet casserole is delicious served with a batch of Southwestern-Style Cornbread (page 68).

- 2 tablespoons extra-virgin olive oil
- 1 cup chopped onion
- 1 cup chopped green bell pepper
- 1 cup frozen yellow corn, thawed
- 1 tablespoon ground cumin
- ¼ teaspoon salt, or to taste
- Freshly ground black pepper, to taste
- 1 (15-ounce) can cut sweet potatoes, well drained
- 1 (15-ounce) can black beans, rinsed and drained
- 1 (14.5-ounce) can diced tomatoes with green chilies, briefly drained
- ⅓ cup hickory-smoked barbecue sauce
- Cayenne pepper or hot sauce, to taste (optional)
- 1 crushed taco shell or crushed tortilla chips

Preheat oven to 350F (175C). Lightly grease a 2½-quart casserole with a lid and set aside.

In a large nonstick skillet, heat the oil over medium heat. Add the onion, bell pepper, and corn and cook, stirring, until just beginning to brown, about 7 minutes. Add the cumin, salt, and black pepper and cook, stirring, 1 minute. Add the remaining ingredients, except the crushed taco shell, stirring well to combine. Remove from heat and transfer to the prepared casserole. Bake, covered, 30 minutes. Remove cover and sprinkle with the crushed taco shell; bake an additional 5 minutes, until top is lightly browned. Serve warm.

Per serving: Calories 336 | Protein 10g | Total Fat 9g | Sat. Fat 1g | Cholesterol 0mg | Carbohydrate 57g | Dietary Fiber 9g | Sodium 559mg

Zucchini Stuffed with Refried Beans and Rice

Makes 3 main-dish or 6 side-dish servings

Canned vegetarian black beans can replace the standard pinto variety, if desired.

    3 large zucchini (about 8 ounces each),
        trimmed and halved lengthwise
    1 tablespoon extra-virgin olive oil
    ½ cup chopped onion
    2 large cloves garlic, finely chopped
    ¼ teaspoon salt, or to taste
    Freshly ground black pepper, to taste
    1 cup cooked white or brown rice (see Cook's
        Tip, page 100)
    1 cup vegetarian refried pinto beans
    ½ cup mild or medium salsa
    1 teaspoon ground cumin, or to taste

Preheat oven to 350F (175C). Lightly oil a baking sheet or shallow baking dish and set aside.

Scoop out the flesh of the zucchini, leaving a ⅜-inch-thick shell for each. Coarsely chop the pulp and set aside.

In a medium nonstick skillet, heat the oil over medium heat. Add the onion and cook, stirring, until softened, about 3 minutes. Add the garlic and cook, stirring constantly, 1 minute. Add the zucchini pulp, salt, and pepper; cook, stirring, until the zucchini is softened, 4 to 5 minutes. Remove the skillet from the heat and add the rice, refried beans, salsa, and cumin, stirring well to thoroughly combine.

Spoon the bean mixture into the zucchini shells. Transfer to the prepared baking sheet and bake about 30 minutes, until zucchini are fork-tender. Serve warm.

Per 2 stuffed zucchini halves: Calories 243 | Protein 9g | Total Fat 6g | Sat. Fat 1g | Cholesterol 0mg | Carbohydrate 40g | Dietary Fiber 8g | Sodium 626mg

Costa Rican–Style Spinach, Potatoes, and Black Beans

Makes 3 servings

Serve this rustic dish with lots of crusty bread to sop up the delicious juices.

    1 tablespoon extra-virgin olive oil
    1 cup chopped onion
    2 large cloves garlic, finely chopped
    1 (14.5-ounce) can no-salt-added diced
        tomatoes with jalapeño chilies, juices
        included
    1 (15-ounce) can sliced potatoes, rinsed and
        drained
    1 (15-ounce) can black beans, rinsed and
        drained
    ½ cup water
    1 tablespoon tomato paste
    1 teaspoon ground cumin
    Salt and freshly ground black pepper, to taste
    4 to 6 cups fresh baby spinach

¼ cup chopped fresh cilantro

Hot sauce, to taste (optional)

In a large deep-sided nonstick skillet, heat the oil over medium heat. Add the onion and cook, stirring, until softened, about 3 minutes. Add the garlic and cook, stirring constantly, 1 minute. Add the tomatoes and their juices, potatoes, beans, water, tomato paste, cumin, salt, and pepper; bring to a brisk simmer over medium-high heat, stirring occasionally. Reduce the heat to between low and medium-low and simmer gently, uncovered, until slightly thickened, about 10 minutes, stirring occasionally. Add the spinach and cilantro and cook, stirring occasionally, until spinach is just wilted, 3 to 5 minutes. Serve warm, with the hot sauce passed separately (if using).

Per serving: Calories 287 | Protein 14g | Total Fat 6g | Sat. Fat 1g | Cholesterol 0mg | Carbohydrate 48g | Dietary Fiber 11g | Sodium 575mg

Side Dishes and Slaws

Juicy red tomatoes, crunchy orange carrots, leafy green spinach, crisp purple cabbage, sweet yellow corn—fresh vegetables are bursting with flavor and color, vitamins and nutrients. The good news for cooks in a hurry is that many precut fresh and frozen veggies—and even some canned ones, too—can be pressed into service whenever a quick and easy side dish is in order. Best of all, when served over rice, pasta, polenta, or other grains, several of the following offerings are instantly transformed into delicious and nutritious real-deal meals.

Ginger Broccoli

 Makes 4 servings

This is one of my favorite ways to enjoy broccoli; cauliflower can be prepared in the same fashion, as well.

- ½ tablespoon peanut oil
- ½ tablespoon toasted (dark) sesame oil
- 3 large cloves garlic, finely chopped
- 4 teaspoons minced fresh ginger
- 1 pound broccoli crowns, trimmed and chopped
- 3 tablespoons water
- 1 tablespoon low-sodium soy or tamari sauce
- Salt and freshly ground black pepper, to taste
- 1 tablespoon plain rice vinegar

In a large nonstick skillet with a lid, heat the oils over medium-high heat. Add the garlic and ginger and cook, stirring constantly, until fragrant but not browned, 30 to 60 seconds. Add the broccoli and cook, stirring often, until the broccoli is bright green, about 2 minutes. Add the water, soy sauce, salt, and pepper, stirring well to combine. Reduce heat to medium, cover, and cook until the broccoli is just tender, about 3 minutes. Remove from the heat and stir in the vinegar. Serve at once.

Per serving: Calories 70 | Protein 4g | Total Fat 4g | Sat. Fat 1g | Cholesterol 0mg | Carbohydrate 8g | Dietary Fiber 4g | Sodium 170mg

Roasted Broccoli with Garlic and Lemon

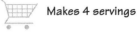 Makes 4 servings

The optional oregano lends this tasty broccoli dish a distinctively Italian accent.

- 1 pound fresh broccoli florets
- 2 tablespoons extra-virgin olive oil
- 1 large clove garlic, finely chopped
- ½ teaspoon dried oregano (optional)
- ½ teaspoon coarse salt
- Freshly ground black pepper, to taste
- Juice of ½ lemon (about 1½ tablespoons)

Preheat oven to 400F (205C).

In a large bowl, toss the broccoli, oil, garlic, oregano (if using), salt, and pepper until well combined. Arrange in a single layer on an ungreased baking sheet. Bake until stems are fork tender, about 15 minutes, turning once or twice. Transfer to a serving bowl and add the lemon juice, tossing well to combine. Serve warm or at room temperature.

Per serving: Calories 95 | Protein 4g | Total Fat 7g | Sat. Fat 1g | Cholesterol 0mg | Carbohydrate 7g | Dietary Fiber 4g | Sodium 254mg

Variations: *To make Roasted Sesame Broccoli with Garlic and Lemon, omit the optional oregano and replace the olive oil with 1 tablespoon peanut oil and 1 tablespoon toasted (dark) sesame oil. Toss with 1 tablespoon sesame seeds before roasting (optional).*

To make Roasted Cauliflower with Garlic, Lemon, and Capers, substitute cauliflower florets for the broccoli and toss the cooked dish with 1 to 2 tablespoons drained capers along with the lemon juice.

Indonesian-Style Marinated Broccoli and Cauliflower

Makes 4 servings

This is a great way to dress up a frozen bag of broccoli and cauliflower. Serve over rice and garnish with chopped peanuts for a complete meal. Madras curry powder has punch; use the regular variety for a milder dish.

1 tablespoon reduced-sodium soy or tamari sauce

1 tablespoon plain rice vinegar

1 tablespoon toasted (dark) sesame oil

1 tablespoon finely chopped fresh ginger

1 tablespoon creamy peanut butter

1 large clove garlic, finely chopped

1 teaspoon hot Madras curry powder, or to taste

¼ teaspoon salt

Freshly ground black pepper, to taste

1 (16-ounce) package frozen broccoli and cauliflower florets

In a large bowl, whisk together the soy sauce, vinegar, oil, ginger, peanut butter, garlic, curry powder, salt, and pepper until smooth. Set aside.

Meanwhile, cook the broccoli and cauliflower according to package directions. Drain well and immediately add to the soy sauce mixture; toss gently to combine. Let cool to room temperature, tossing a few times. Serve at room temperature. Alternatively, cover and refrigerate 2 hours or up to 1 day and serve chilled, or return to room temperature.

Per serving: Calories 91 | Protein 4g | Total Fat 6g | Sat. Fat 1g | Cholesterol 0mg | Carbohydrate 8g | Dietary Fiber 4g | Sodium 326mg

Roasted Butternut Squash with Sage and Cranberries

Makes 5 to 6 servings

Ready-cubed butternut squash, available in many major supermarkets in the produce section, particularly around the fall and winter holidays, makes easy work of this delicious side dish.

1¼ pounds cubed butternut squash

2 medium onions (about 6 ounces each), each cut into 8 to 10 chunks

3 tablespoons extra-virgin olive oil

Coarse salt, to taste

Freshly ground black pepper, to taste

¼ cup dried cranberries or cherries

4 large fresh sage leaves, finely chopped

Preheat oven to 375F (190C).

Place the squash and onions on a large ungreased baking sheet with sides; using a wide spatula, toss with the oil until thoroughly coated. Season with salt and pepper and toss well again. Spread in a single layer and bake about 30 minutes, turning once, until the vegetables are tender and lightly caramelized. Remove from the oven and add the cranberries and sage; toss well to combine. Return to the oven and bake 5 more minutes. Toss again and serve warm.

Per serving: Calories 143 | Protein 2g | Total Fat 8g | Sat. Fat 1g | Cholesterol 0mg | Carbohydrate 18g | Dietary Fiber 3g | Sodium 6mg

Asian-Style Cabbage Slaw with Cashews

 Makes 5 to 6 servings

Using a package of coleslaw mix means that this slaw can be ready in minutes. Chopped peanuts can easily replace the cashews, if desired.

- 1 (16-ounce) package coleslaw mix
- 4 scallions, white and green parts, thinly sliced
- 2½ tablespoons low-sodium soy or tamari sauce
- 2½ tablespoons canola oil
- 2 tablespoons cider vinegar
- Salt and freshly ground black pepper, to taste
- ⅓ cup unsalted cashew pieces

In a large bowl, toss all the ingredients, except the cashews, until thoroughly combined. Let stand about 10 minutes to allow the flavors to blend. Add the cashews and toss well to combine. Serve at room temperature. Alternatively, before adding the cashews, cover and refrigerate a minimum of 3 hours or up to 1 day and serve chilled or return to room temperature, tossing with the cashews just before serving.

Per serving: Calories 144 | Protein 4g | Total Fat 11g | Sat. Fat 1g | Cholesterol 0mg | Carbohydrate 10g | Dietary Fiber 3g | Sodium 320mg

Hot-and-Sour Carrots with Edamame

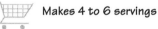 **Makes 4 to 5 servings**

Frozen baby lima beans can be substituted for the soybeans, if necessary.

- 2 tablespoons plain rice vinegar
- 2 tablespoons low-sodium soy or tamari sauce
- 1 tablespoon toasted (dark) sesame oil
- ½ tablespoon sugar
- ½ teaspoon Chinese chili paste, or to taste
- Salt and freshly ground black pepper, to taste
- 1 cup (about 6 ounces) frozen shelled edamame (green soybeans)
- 12 ounces shredded carrots

In a medium bowl, whisk together the vinegar, soy sauce, oil, sugar, chili paste, salt, and pepper. Set aside to let the flavors blend.

Meanwhile, in a large saucepan or medium stockpot, place the edamame in a steamer basket set over about 1 inch of water. Bring to a boil over high heat. Cover, reduce the heat to medium, and steam 5 minutes. Add the carrots and steam 2 to 3 minutes, until soybeans are cooked through and carrots are crisp-tender.

Carefully remove the steamer basket from the pan and add the hot edamame and carrots to the vinegar mixture; toss well to combine. Serve warm or at room temperature. Alternatively, cover and refrigerate completely cooled mixture a minimum of 2 hours or up to 2 days and serve chilled, or return to room temperature.

Per serving: Calories 149 | Protein 8g | Total Fat 7g | Sat. Fat 1g | Cholesterol 0mg | Carbohydrate 15g | Dietary Fiber 5g | Sodium 327mg

Maple-Glazed Carrots

Makes 4 to 6 servings

After one bite, you'll know why this simple yet delicious carrot dish has become an American classic.

- 1 (16-ounce) bag baby carrots
- 1½ tablespoons pure maple syrup
- 1 tablespoon canola oil

Salt and freshly ground black pepper, to taste

Pinch cinnamon

Pinch nutmeg

In a medium stockpot or large saucepan, place the carrots in a 9-inch steamer basket set over about 1 inch of water. Bring to a boil over high heat. Cover tightly, reduce the heat to medium, and steam carrots until just tender, about 5 to 10 minutes, depending on thickness. Drain well.

In a large nonstick skillet, heat the maple syrup and oil over medium heat. Add the salt, pepper, cinnamon, and nutmeg and stir well to combine. Add the carrots and raise the heat to medium-high; cook, stirring and tossing often, until hot and glazed, 2 to 3 minutes. Serve warm.

Per serving: Calories 93 | Protein 1g | Total Fat 4g | Sat. Fat 0g | Cholesterol 0mg | Carbohydrate 15g | Dietary Fiber 3g | Sodium 36mg

In a small bowl, stir together the barbecue sauce, lime juice, and hot sauce (if using). Set aside.

Meanwhile, bring a large stockpot filled with water to a boil over high heat. Add the corn and let return to a boil. Cover and immediately remove from the heat. Let stand, covered, 5 minutes.

Drain the corn in a colander and rinse under cold running water until cool enough to handle. Rub each ear of corn with ½ teaspoon of the oil. Season with salt and pepper. Grill or broil, turning often, until golden and lightly charred, 5 to 10 minutes, basting liberally with the reserved sauce during the last minute or so of cooking. Transfer the corn to a warmed serving platter. Sprinkle with the scallions and serve at once.

Per serving: Calories 169 | Protein 5g | Total Fat 5g | Sat. Fat 1g | Cholesterol 0mg | Carbohydrate 32g | Dietary Fiber 5g | Sodium 277mg

Barbecued Corn on the Cob

Makes 4 servings

Parboiling the corn insures that it will be grilled to perfection.

½ cup hickory smoke–flavored barbecue sauce

2 tablespoons fresh lime juice

Hot sauce, to taste (optional)

4 ears fresh corn, husked

2 teaspoons extra-virgin olive oil

Salt and freshly ground black pepper, to taste

2 scallions, white and green parts, finely chopped

Prepare a medium-hot charcoal or gas grill, or preheat a broiler. Position the grill rack or oven rack 4 to 6 inches from the heat source. If broiling, lightly oil a baking sheet with sides and set aside.

Coconut Creamed Corn

Makes 4 servings

Caribbean jerk seasoning or Cajun spice can replace the chili powder, if desired.

2 cups frozen yellow corn (unthawed)

1 cup light coconut milk

2 scallions, thinly sliced, white and green parts separated

¼ teaspoon mild chili powder

¼ teaspoon salt, or to taste

½ to 1 tablespoon fresh lime juice

Freshly ground black pepper, to taste

Pinch, or more, crushed red pepper flakes (optional)

Combine the corn, coconut milk, white parts of the scallions, chili powder, and salt in a medium saucepan. Bring to a boil over medium-high heat, stirring occasionally. Reduce the heat to between medium and medium-low and simmer briskly, stirring occasionally, until most of the coconut milk has evaporated, 12 to 15 minutes. Stir in the scallion greens, lime juice, black pepper, and red pepper flakes (if using). Serve warm.

Per serving: Calories 127 | Protein 5g | Total Fat 4g | Sat. Fat 3g | Cholesterol 0mg | Carbohydrate 21g | Dietary Fiber 2g | Sodium 165mg

South American–Style Corn Cakes

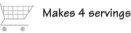 Makes 4 cakes

These South American favorites are the ideal accompaniment to chili or tacos.

    1 cup low-sodium vegetable broth
    2 tablespoons water
    1½ tablespoons canola or other mild vegetable
      oil
    ¼ teaspoon salt
    1 cup masa harina
    ½ teaspoon ground cumin
    ½ cup cooked fresh or frozen yellow or white
      corn

In a small saucepan, bring the broth, water, ½ tablespoon of the oil, and salt to a boil over high heat. In a medium bowl, whisk together the masa harina and cumin. Pour the boiling broth mixture over the masa mixture and stir well to combine (mixture will be thick). Add the corn, stirring until evenly distributed. Cover with a towel or plate and set aside at room temperature for 10 minutes.

Divide the dough into 4 equal pieces. Form each into a ball and then press into ½-inch-thick patties.

In a large nonstick skillet, preferably cast iron, heat the remaining 1 tablespoon oil over medium-high heat until hot. Cook the patties until slightly blackened, about 4 minutes per side. Serve at once.

Per serving (per cake): Calories 181 | Protein 6g | Total Fat 6g | Sat. Fat 1g | Cholesterol 0mg | Carbohydrate 27g | Dietary Fiber 3g | Sodium 265mg

Crimson Slaw with Cranberries

Makes 4 servings

Though not quite as colorful, yet equally as tasty, shredded green cabbage can be used in lieu of the red variety, if desired.

    2 tablespoons canola oil
    1 tablespoon cider vinegar
    1 tablespoon sugar
    ½ teaspoon salt
    Freshly ground black pepper, to taste
    1 (10-ounce) package shredded red cabbage
    ½ cup dried cranberries
    ¼ cup finely chopped red onion

In a large bowl, whisk together the oil, vinegar, sugar, salt, and pepper until thoroughly blended. Let stand a few minutes to allow the sugar to dissolve. Whisk again. Add the remaining ingredients and toss a few minutes until cabbage begins to soften. Let marinate at room temperature 20 minutes, tossing a few times. Serve at room temperature. Alternatively, cover and refrigerate a minimum of 1 hour or up to 2 days and serve chilled.

Per serving: Calories 96 | Protein 1g | Total Fat 7g | Sat. Fat 1g | Cholesterol 0mg | Carbohydrate 9g | Dietary Fiber 2g | Sodium 275mg

Maple Coleslaw

 Makes 6 servings

This delicious maple-sweetened slaw is ideal to serve with Pinto Bean Sloppy Joe Sandwiches (page 67) or Mushroom-Bean Burgers (page 71).

> ½ cup cider vinegar
> ¼ cup pure maple syrup
> ¼ cup canola oil or other mild vegetable oil
> 1 tablespoon sugar
> 1 tablespoon celery seed
> ½ teaspoon salt
> Freshly ground black pepper, to taste
> 1 (16-ounce) bag coleslaw mix (about 8 cups)

In a large bowl, whisk together the vinegar, syrup, oil, sugar, celery seed, salt, and pepper until thoroughly blended. Let stand a few minutes to allow the sugar to dissolve. Whisk again and add the coleslaw mix; toss until cabbage begins to soften. Cover and refrigerate a minimum of 3 hours or up to 2 days and serve chilled.

Per serving: Calories 148 | Protein 1g | Total Fat 10g | Sat. Fat 1g | Cholesterol 0mg | Carbohydrate 17g | Dietary Fiber 2g | Sodium 194mg

Hot-and-Sour Slaw

 Makes 4 servings

Chinese chili paste, a hot and garlicky condiment used to flavor countless Asian dishes, can be located in the international aisle of most major supermarkets.

> 3 tablespoons plain rice vinegar
> 1 tablespoon reduced-sodium soy sauce
> 1 tablespoon toasted (dark) sesame oil

> 1 teaspoon sugar
> ½ to 1 teaspoon Chinese chili paste, or
>   crushed red pepper flakes, to taste
> ¼ teaspoon ground ginger
> Salt and freshly ground black pepper, to taste
> 3 cups shredded green cabbage
> 1 cup shredded carrots
> 1 (5-ounce) can sliced bamboo shoots, drained
> 2 scallions, white and green parts, thinly
>   sliced

In a medium bowl, whisk together the vinegar, soy sauce, oil, sugar, chili paste, ginger, salt, and black pepper. Add the remaining ingredients, tossing until cabbage begins to soften. Serve at room temperature, or cover and refrigerate a minimum of 2 hours or up to 1 day and serve chilled, or return to room temperature.

Per serving: Calories 74 | Protein 2g | Total Fat 4g | Sat. Fat 1g | Cholesterol 0mg | Carbohydrate 10g | Dietary Fiber 3g | Sodium 174mg

Lemon-Walnut Green Beans

Makes 4 servings

Fresh asparagus can be prepared in the same manner, or see the Variation (page 124).

> 1 pound fresh green beans, trimmed
> 1 tablespoon extra-virgin olive oil
> 2 tablespoons fresh lemon juice
> 2 tablespoons chopped walnuts
> ½ teaspoon coarse salt, or to taste
> ¼ teaspoon dried rosemary
> ¼ teaspoon lemon-pepper seasoning
> 2 tablespoons chopped fresh chives or
>   scallion greens

In a large stockpot filled with boiling salted water, cook the beans until crisp-tender, 3 to 5 minutes. Prepare a large bowl of ice water. Drain the beans and immediately refresh in the ice-water bath for about 5 minutes. Drain well.

In a large nonstick skillet, heat the oil over medium-high heat. Add the green beans, lemon juice, walnuts, salt, rosemary, and lemon-pepper seasoning; cook, stirring constantly, until heated through, about 2 minutes. Remove from heat and add the chives, tossing well to combine. Serve warm.

Per serving: Calories 92 | Protein 3g | Total Fat 6g | Sat. Fat 1g | Cholesterol 0mg | Carbohydrate 9g | Dietary Fiber 4g | Sodium 263mg

Variation: *To make Orange-Almond Asparagus, substitute fresh pencil-thin or medium-thick asparagus, tough ends trimmed, for the green beans, slivered almonds for the walnuts, fresh orange juice for the lemon juice, dried thyme for the dried rosemary, and dried chopped orange peel for the lemon-pepper seasoning. Prepare as otherwise directed, seasoning the finished dish with freshly ground black pepper.*

Sesame Green Beans

Makes 4 servings

While fresh green beans are delicious here, the frozen variety is tasty, as well.

- ½ tablespoon peanut oil
- ½ tablespoon toasted (dark) sesame oil
- 1 tablespoon sesame seeds
- 1¼ pounds fresh green beans, trimmed, cut into 2-inch pieces, or 1 (16-ounce) package frozen cut green beans
- ¼ cup low-sodium vegetable broth
- ½ tablespoon low-sodium soy or tamari sauce, or to taste (optional)
- ¼ teaspoon salt, or to taste
- Freshly ground black pepper, to taste

In a large nonstick skillet with a lid, heat the oils over medium heat. Add sesame seeds and cook, stirring constantly, until fragrant and lightly browned, 2 to 3 minutes. Add the green beans and cook, stirring, until the beans are just softened (2 to 3 minutes for fresh, 5 to 6 minutes for frozen). Add the broth, soy sauce (if using), salt, and pepper and bring to a brisk simmer over high heat. Reduce the heat to medium, cover, and cook until the beans are crisp-tender, 3 to 5 minutes, stirring once or twice. Uncover and raise the heat to medium-high; cook, stirring constantly, until liquids are evaporated. Serve at once.

Per serving: Calories 81 | Protein 3g | Total Fat 5g | Sat. Fat 1g | Cholesterol 0mg | Carbohydrate 9g | Dietary Fiber 4g | Sodium 173mg

Portobello Mushrooms with Chipotle Mashed Sweet Potatoes

Makes 6 first-course or side-dish servings

Though the chipotle mashed sweet potatoes can be enjoyed alone, presenting them in succulent portobellos makes for a special side dish or first course.

- 1½ to 1¾ pounds sweet potatoes (about 3 medium), peeled and cut into chunks
- ½ cup light coconut milk
- 4 teaspoons extra-virgin olive oil
- ½ to 1 teaspoon finely chopped or pureed canned chipotle chili in adobo sauce
- ½ teaspoon garlic salt, or to taste
- Freshly ground black pepper, to taste
- 2 scallions, white and green parts, thinly sliced
- 6 large (about 2 ounces each) portobello mushroom caps

Preheat oven to 400F (205C). Lightly oil a baking sheet with sides or a shallow casserole and set aside.

In a large saucepan, place the sweet potatoes in enough salted water to cover by a few inches. Bring to a boil over high heat. Reduce the heat slightly and cook until very tender, about 20 minutes. Drain well and return to the saucepan; add the coconut milk, 3 teaspoons of the oil, chili, garlic salt, and pepper; mash until smooth but still slightly chunky. Add the scallions, stirring well to combine. Set aside to cool slightly.

Mound equal amounts of the sweet potato mixture on the gill side of each mushroom cap. Transfer the mushrooms to the prepared baking sheet and brush the tops evenly with the remaining 1 teaspoon oil. Bake in the lower third of the oven 10 to 15 minutes, until mushrooms begin to soften and release their liquids. Place on the center oven rack and bake 5 to 10 minutes, until the potatoes are lightly browned and mushrooms are tender when pieced with a knife. Serve at once.

Per stuffed mushroom: Calories 179 | Protein 4g | Total Fat 5g | Sat. Fat 2g | Cholesterol 0mg | Carbohydrate 32g | Dietary Fiber 4g | Sodium 198mg

Hawaiian-Style Sweet-and-Sour Roasted Pineapple and Bell Peppers

Makes 4 to 6 servings

Toss with chopped macadamia nuts or slivered almonds for added crunch and protein, if desired. To transform this delicious tropical medley into a main dish for four, serve over hot cooked white or brown rice.

3 cups cubed fresh pineapple

1 medium red bell pepper (about 6 ounces), cubed

1 medium green bell pepper (about 6 ounces), cubed

1 medium red onion (about 6 ounces), cut into thin wedges

1 tablespoon toasted (dark) sesame oil

1 tablespoon peanut, plain sesame, or canola oil

1 tablespoon dark or light brown sugar

½ teaspoon salt, preferably the coarse variety

Freshly ground black pepper, to taste

1 tablespoon sweetened coconut flakes (optional)

Juice of ½ lime, or to taste

Preheat oven to 400F (205C).

Arrange the pineapple, bell peppers, and onion on an ungreased baking sheet with a rim. Drizzle with the oils and sprinkle with the sugar, salt, and black pepper; toss with a wide spatula to thoroughly combine. Roast on the center oven rack about 30 minutes, until lightly browned, turning once. Remove from the oven and sprinkle with the coconut (if using), and then drizzle with the lime juice; toss well to combine. Serve warm or at room temperature.

Per serving: Calories 161 | Protein 2g | Total Fat 7g | Sat. Fat 1g | Cholesterol 0mg | Carbohydrate 25g | Dietary Fiber 4g | Sodium 240mg

Garlic-Herbed Mashed Potatoes

Makes 6 servings

While any boiling potato will work well here, the Yukon gold variety lends these scrumptious mashed potatoes a decidedly buttery flavor.

2 pounds Yukon gold or red potatoes, peeled and cut into small chunks

½ small onion (about 2 ounces), quartered

4 to 6 large garlic cloves, peeled, halved

1 bay leaf

2 sprigs fresh thyme

1 cup low-sodium vegetable broth, plus additional, as necessary

¼ cup extra-virgin olive oil

½ teaspoon coarse salt, or to taste

Freshly ground black pepper, to taste

1 tablespoon finely chopped fresh sage and/or rosemary

1 tablespoon finely chopped fresh parsley

In a medium stockpot, place the potatoes, onion, garlic, bay leaf, and thyme sprigs in enough salted water to cover by 1 inch; bring to a boil over high heat. Reduce the heat to medium-high and boil until the potatoes are very tender, about 20 minutes. Drain and return to the pot; remove and discard bay leaf and thyme sprigs.

Add the broth, oil, salt, and pepper to the pot and bring to a simmer over medium-high heat, stirring often. Remove from heat and mash well with a potato masher or large fork, adding additional broth, if necessary, to achieve desired consistency. Stir in the sage and parsley and serve at once.

Per serving: Calories 186 | Protein 5g | Total Fat 9g | Sat. Fat 1g | Cholesterol 0mg | Carbohydrate 23g | Dietary Fiber 3g | Sodium 251mg

Scalloped Potatoes with Chives

Makes 5 to 6 servings

The green parts of scallions can replace the chives, if desired.

⅓ cup low-sodium vegetable broth

2 tablespoons canola oil

1 tablespoon Dijon mustard

½ teaspoon garlic salt, or to taste

Freshly ground black pepper, to taste

2 (15-ounce) cans sliced potatoes, rinsed and drained

2 tablespoons chopped fresh chives

Preheat oven to 425F (220C). Lightly grease a 10-inch pie plate or quiche dish and set aside.

In a small bowl, stir together the broth, oil, mustard, garlic salt, and pepper. Set aside.

Starting from the outside and working toward the middle, arrange the potatoes in overlapping concentric circles in the prepared pie plate. Pour the broth mixture evenly over the top. Sprinkle evenly with the chives.

Bake about 25 minutes, until the top is lightly browned. Cut into wedges and serve at once.

Per serving: Calories 127 | Protein 3g | Total Fat 6g | Sat. Fat 1g | Cholesterol 0mg | Carbohydrate 16g | Dietary Fiber 3g | Sodium 819mg

Orange-Maple Mashed Sweet Potatoes

Makes 6 servings

An ideal side dish for the fall and winter holidays, this delicious sweet potato recipe is easy enough to whip up any time of the year.

2 pounds sweet potatoes (about 4 medium), peeled, cut into large chunks

½ teaspoon salt, or to taste

Freshly ground black pepper, to taste

¼ cup pure maple syrup

2 tablespoons orange juice

1½ tablespoons canola oil

½ teaspoon fresh lemon juice

Pinch ground nutmeg (optional)

In a large saucepan, place the sweet potatoes in enough salted water to cover by a few inches. Bring to a boil over high heat. Reduce the heat slightly and cook until very tender, about 20 minutes. Drain and return to the pan. Add the salt and pepper and mash well with a potato masher. Set aside.

Meanwhile, in a small saucepan, bring the maple syrup, orange juice, oil, and lemon juice to a boil over medium heat; boil until reduced and syrupy, 2 to 3 minutes. Remove from the heat and add to the mashed sweet potatoes, stirring well to combine. Season with additional salt and pepper, if necessary, and the nutmeg (if using). Serve at once.

Per serving: Calories 226 | Protein 3g | Total Fat 4g | Sat. Fat 0g | Cholesterol 0mg | Carbohydrate 46g | Dietary Fiber 5g | Sodium 199mg

Sweet Potato and White Potato Oven Fries

Makes 5 to 6 servings

If you would like to incorporate more good-for-you sweet potatoes into your diet, but can't resist the white variety, this recipe is for you.

2 tablespoons extra-virgin olive oil

1 teaspoon sweet paprika

½ teaspoon mild chili powder

½ teaspoon garlic salt, plus additional, to taste

Freshly ground black pepper, to taste

1 extra-large sweet potato (10 to 12 ounces), peeled, halved crosswise, cut lengthwise into thin French fry–style strips

1 extra-large russet potato (10 to 12 ounces), peeled, halved crosswise, cut lengthwise into thin French fry–style strips

Preheat oven to 450F (230C). Line a baking sheet with aluminum foil and set aside.

In a large bowl, whisk together the oil, paprika, chili powder, garlic salt, and pepper until thoroughly blended. Add the potatoes and toss until thoroughly coated.

Arrange the potatoes in a single layer on the prepared baking sheet. Bake on the center oven rack about 20 minutes, until the potatoes are beginning to brown. Transfer the baking sheet to the upper rack and bake until potatoes are golden and crispy, 5 to 10 minutes longer, turning once. Season with additional garlic salt, as necessary. Serve at once.

Per serving: Calories 143 | Protein 2g | Total Fat 6g | Sat. Fat 1g | Cholesterol 0mg | Carbohydrate 22g | Dietary Fiber 3g | Sodium 218mg

Grilled Ratatouille

Makes 6 servings

Ratatouille is a traditional Provençal recipe of stewed summer vegetables. This tasty American-style rendition is fun to serve at summer holiday barbecues.

2 medium zucchini (about 6 ounces each), quartered lengthwise

1 Japanese or Italian eggplant (about 8 ounces), quartered lengthwise

1 medium red bell pepper (about 6 ounces), cored, seeded, and quartered lengthwise

1 medium green bell pepper (about 6 ounces), cored, seeded, and quartered lengthwise

1 medium red onion (about 6 ounces), peeled and quartered lengthwise

¼ cup extra-virgin olive oil

Salt and freshly ground black pepper, to taste

1 (14.5-ounce) can stewed tomatoes, juices included

½ cup chopped fresh basil

2 large cloves garlic, finely chopped

Preheat a charcoal grill with a lid or a gas grill to medium-high heat. Position the grill rack 4 to 6 inches from the heat source.

Place the zucchini, eggplant, bell peppers, and onion on a large baking sheet with sides and drizzle with the oil. Season generously with salt and black pepper. Toss with a spatula to combine. Place the vegetables on the grill and cook, uncovered, about 3 minutes on each side. Cover the grill and cook without turning until the vegetables are just tender, about 2 more minutes. Return the vegetables to the baking sheet as they finish cooking.

Transfer the vegetables to a cutting board and coarsely chop. Transfer to a medium stockpot and add the tomatoes and their liquids, ¼ cup basil, and the garlic. Bring to a simmer over medium-high heat, stirring often. Reduce the heat to medium-low and simmer, covered, 10 minutes. Uncover and cook another few minutes, stirring occasionally. Remove from the heat and toss with the remaining ¼ cup basil. Season with additional salt and black pepper, if necessary. Transfer to a serving bowl and serve warm or at room temperature.

Per serving: Calories 140 | Protein 3g | Total Fat 9g | Sat. Fat 1g | Cholesterol 0mg | Carbohydrate 14g | Dietary Fiber 4g | Sodium 179mg

Baked Five-Spice Rice

Makes 4 to 6 servings

To turn this aromatic rice dish into a delicious main course for three or four, add 1 cup thawed frozen peas along with the scallion greens and optional pimento.

1 tablespoon toasted (dark) sesame oil

½ tablespoon peanut oil

1 cup jasmine or long-grain white rice

4 scallions, thinly sliced, white and green parts separated

1¼ cups low-sodium vegetable broth or water

¼ cup dry sherry or cooking sherry

1 tablespoon finely chopped fresh ginger

½ tablespoon five-spice powder

¼ teaspoon salt, or to taste

Freshly ground black pepper, to taste

2 tablespoons drained chopped pimento (optional)

2 tablespoons low-sodium soy or tamari sauce

Preheat oven to 350F (175C).

In a medium ovenproof skillet with a lid, heat ½ tablespoon of the sesame oil and the peanut oil over medium-high heat. Add the rice and white parts of the scallions; cook, stirring constantly, 3 minutes. Stir in the broth, sherry, ginger, five-spice powder, salt, and pepper; bring to a brisk simmer over high heat. Working quickly, cover the skillet and place on the middle oven rack. Bake 30 minutes.

Remove the skillet from the oven and stir in the scallion greens, pimento (if using), soy sauce, and remaining ½ tablespoon sesame oil. Cover and let stand 5 minutes. Uncover, fluff with a fork, and serve at once.

Per serving: Calories 265 | Protein 8g | Total Fat 6g | Sat. Fat 1g | Cholesterol 0mg | Carbohydrate 42g | Dietary Fiber 2g | Sodium 602mg

Green Tea Rice with Almonds

Makes 4 servings

Green tea adds a delicate, slightly floral flavor to this simple yet delicious rice dish. Earl Grey or regular black tea can be used, as well. For a tasty main dish to serve three or four, stir in 1 cup thawed frozen peas when you add the scallions.

1 green tea bag
2 cups boiling water
¼ cup slivered almonds
2 teaspoons peanut oil
1 teaspoon toasted (dark) sesame oil
½ teaspoon salt
Freshly ground black pepper, to taste
1 cup jasmine or regular long-grain white rice
2 scallions, white and green parts, thinly sliced

Place the tea bag in the boiling water and let steep for 2 minutes. Remove and discard tea bag. Set the tea aside.

Place the almonds in a medium-size dry saucepan and turn the heat to medium. Cook, stirring constantly after 1 minute, until fragrant and lightly golden, about 3 minutes. Add the hot tea, the oils, salt, and pepper and bring to a boil over high heat. Stir in the rice, cover, reduce the heat to low, and simmer until all the liquid has been absorbed, 17 to 20 minutes. Remove from heat and stir in the scallions; let stand, covered, 5 minutes. Fluff with a fork and serve at once.

Per serving: Calories 244 | Protein 5g | Total Fat 8g | Sat. Fat 1g | Cholesterol 0mg | Carbohydrate 39g | Dietary Fiber 1g | Sodium 271mg

Italian-Style Kale with Garlic and Lemon

Makes 4 servings

Mature fresh spinach or Swiss chard, cooked a few minutes less, can also be prepared in this manner.

2 tablespoons extra-virgin olive oil
2 large cloves garlic, finely chopped
1 pound fresh kale, stems and thick ribs removed
Juice of ½ lemon
Salt and freshly ground black pepper, to taste

In a medium or large stockpot, heat the oil over medium heat. Add the garlic and cook, stirring constantly, until fragrant and slightly softened, 30 to 60 seconds. Add the kale (do not toss), cover, and reduce heat to medium-low; cook for 7 minutes without stirring. Remove from heat and add the lemon juice, salt, and pepper; toss until well combined and wilted. (For more tender kale, return to medium-low heat and toss for 1 to 2 additional minutes.) Serve at once.

Per serving: Calories 99 | Protein 3g | Total Fat 7g | Sat. Fat 1g | Cholesterol 0mg | Carbohydrate 8g | Dietary Fiber 1g | Sodium 31mg

Spinach Strudel with Pine Nuts and Raisins

Makes 6 side-dish or 12 appetizer servings

Serve this savory Florentine-style strudel as an elegant first course for six to eight or tasty appetizer for up to twelve. The leading brand of frozen puff pastry is dairy-free.

1 tablespoon extra-virgin olive oil

2 cloves garlic, finely chopped

1 (6-ounce) bag baby spinach

Salt and freshly ground black pepper, to taste

½ (about 17-ounce) package (1 sheet) frozen
    puff pastry, thawed according to package
    directions

2 tablespoons raisins

½ tablespoon pine nuts, toasted, (optional)
    (see Cook's Tip, page 13)

Preheat oven to 375F (190C).

In a large nonstick skillet, heat the oil over medium heat. Add the garlic and cook, stirring constantly, 1 minute. Add the spinach and cook, stirring, until wilted, 2 to 3 minutes. Remove from the heat and season with salt and pepper. Let cool slightly.

Unfold pastry onto an ungreased baking sheet. Line the middle third of the pastry with half of the spinach mixture. Sprinkle evenly with half the raisins and nuts. Fold the third of the pastry to your left over the filling; line with remaining spinach mixture, raisins, and nuts. Fold the third of the pastry to your right as far over to the other side as it will comfortably stretch, pressing the dough together where it meets to seal. (Do not seal the ends.) Cut about 6 (1-inch long) slits across the top. Bake in the center of the oven about 25 minutes, until golden. Cool on the baking sheet on a wire rack 15 minutes. Cut into desired number of slices and serve warm.

Per ⅙ of strudel: Calories 241 | Protein 4g | Total Fat 14g | Sat. Fat 3g | Cholesterol 0mg | Carbohydrate 27g | Dietary Fiber 4g | Sodium 158mg

Smoky Succotash

 Makes 6 servings

If you don't have a smoky barbecue sauce on hand, use a plain variety and add about ¼ teaspoon liquid smoke to the recipe.

1 tablespoon extra-virgin olive oil

3 cups frozen yellow corn, thawed

1 cup chopped onion

1 (15-ounce) can baby lima beans, rinsed and
    drained

Salt and freshly ground black pepper, to taste

½ cup prepared hickory-smoked barbecue
    sauce

In a medium nonstick skillet, heat the oil over medium heat. Add the corn and onion and cook, stirring, until lightly browned, 7 to 10 minutes. Add the beans, salt, and pepper; cook, stirring, until beans are heated through, about 3 minutes. Add the barbecue sauce and cook, stirring, until sauce is heated through, about 1 minute. Serve warm.

Per serving: Calories 172 | Protein 7g | Total Fat 4g | Sat. Fat 1g | Cholesterol 0mg | Carbohydrate 32g | Dietary Fiber 6g | Sodium 174mg

Grilled Balsamic Summer Vegetables

Makes 6 to 8 servings

If this recipe looks appealing but you only need a vegetable side dish for three or four people, no problem. Use the extra half to make the Pasta Salad with Grilled Balsamic Summer Vegetables (page 51) and presto—dinner is covered for the next day.

1 large eggplant (about 1 pound), cut into
  ½-inch-thick rounds, sprinkled with salt,
  and set in a colander to drain for 30
  minutes (Do not skip this step; see Cook's
  Tip, opposite)
½ cup balsamic vinaigrette
2 tablespoons pure maple syrup
2 to 4 large cloves garlic, finely chopped
½ teaspoon salt
¼ teaspoon freshly ground black pepper
1 medium green bell pepper (about 6 ounces),
  cored, seeded, and cut lengthwise into
  eighths
1 medium red bell pepper (about 6 ounces),
  cored, seeded, and cut lengthwise into
  eighths
2 small zucchini (about 4 ounces each), cut
  into ½-inch-thick rounds
4 small plum tomatoes (about 2 ounces
  each), cored and cut lengthwise into
  quarters
1 medium red onion (about 6 ounces), cut into
  ½-inch-thick rounds
Dried oregano, to taste (optional)

Rinse the eggplant slices under cold running water and drain. In a small bowl, whisk together the balsamic vinaigrette, maple syrup, garlic, salt, and black pepper until well blended; set aside.

Divide the eggplant, bell peppers, zucchini, tomatoes, and onion among 2 self-sealing plastic bags; add equal amounts of the balsamic vinaigrette mixture to each bag and seal. Turn each bag several times to thoroughly combine. Let marinate 30 minutes at room temperature, or refrigerate 1 hour or overnight, turning bags occasionally.

Meanwhile, prepare a medium-hot charcoal or gas grill, or preheat a broiler. Position the grill rack or oven rack 4 to 6 inches from the heat source. If grilling, lightly oil a vegetable grid and set aside. If broiling, lightly oil a large baking sheet and set aside. Alternatively, place a stovetop grilling pan with grids over medium-high heat.

Remove vegetables from bags; reserve marinade. Grill or broil the vegetables until browned and tender, working in batches as necessary. As a general rule, cook the bell pepper about 4 minutes per side, and the eggplant, zucchini and onion about 3 minutes per side. Grill or broil the tomatoes about 2 minutes, cut sides up only. Place the vegetables on a large baking sheet (a second one, if broiling) as they finish cooking.

When all the vegetables are done, drizzle with the reserved marinade and sprinkle with oregano, if using. Season with additional salt and black pepper, to taste. Toss gently with a large spatula to combine. If desired, cut vegetables into bite-size pieces or smaller strips before tossing again and serving warm or at room temperature.

Per serving: Calories 164 | Protein 2g | Total Fat 10g | Sat. Fat 2g | Cholesterol 0mg | Carbohydrate 19g | Dietary Fiber 4g | Sodium 341mg

Cook's Tip: *Salting the eggplant before grilling is highly recommended. The rapid cooking over high heat tends to concentrate the eggplant's natural bitterness in its surface; salting will draw out much of this acerbity. For another method that is longer but won't tie up your kitchen sink, place the liberally salted eggplant slices in a bowl and add water to cover. Set a plate inside the bowl and weight with a large can of tomatoes to hold all the eggplant slices under the water. Set aside for 1 to 2 hours before draining and drying well between paper towels.*

Oven-Roasted Winter Vegetables Marsala

 Makes 6 to 8 servings

Marsala cooking wine is available in the condiment and seasoning aisle of typical supermarkets. It lends a nutty, slightly sweet taste to this colorful cornucopia of roasted vegetables. This is ideal to serve at a Thanksgiving or winter holiday gathering.

½ cup medium-dry Marsala wine or Marsala cooking wine

2 tablespoons low-sodium soy sauce

2 tablespoons extra-virgin olive oil

1 tablespoon chopped fresh thyme or about 1 teaspoon dried thyme

½ teaspoon salt, preferably the coarse variety, or to taste

Freshly ground black pepper, to taste

10 to 12 ounces (about 3 cups) fresh Brussels sprouts, trimmed and halved

8 ounces carrots, sliced into ⅜-inch thick rounds

8 ounces fresh parsnips, sliced into ⅜-inch thick rounds

1 medium red onion (about 6 ounces), cut into 12 wedges

Preheat oven to 450F (230C).

In a small bowl, stir together the wine, soy sauce, oil, thyme, salt, and pepper. Place the remaining ingredients on a large ungreased baking sheet with sides and pour the wine mixture over all; toss with a spatula to evenly coat. Cover with foil (lightly oil the underside, if desired, to avoid sticking) and bake 30 minutes. Remove the foil and stir and turn the vegetables. Bake an additional 15 minutes, until vegetables are lightly browned and tender, stirring and turning after 8 minutes. Serve warm

Per serving: Calories 131 | Protein 3g | Total Fat 5g | Sat. Fat 1g | Cholesterol 0mg | Carbohydrate 18g | Dietary Fiber 5g | Sodium 386mg

Zucchini and Fresh Corn with Tomatoes

 Makes 5 to 6 servings

You can enjoy this delicious dish in the winter with thawed frozen corn and canned tomatoes. For a complete meal for four, add 1 (15-ounce) can of rinsed and drained black or pinto beans the last few minutes of simmering, and serve over rice. If using canned tomatoes, you may want to decrease the salt by about half.

1 tablespoon extra-virgin olive oil

1 cup chopped onion

2 large cloves garlic, finely chopped

1 pound zucchini, cut into ½-inch cubes

2 pounds ripe plum tomatoes, peeled, seeded, and coarsely chopped (see Cook's Tip, opposite page), or 1 (28-ounce) can whole peeled plum tomatoes, drained, seeded, and coarsely chopped

1½ cups fresh corn kernels or frozen yellow corn, partially thawed

1 cup low-sodium vegetable broth

1 tablespoon tomato paste

1 teaspoon dried oregano

1 teaspoon sugar (optional)

½ teaspoon ground cumin

½ teaspoon salt, or to taste

Freshly ground black pepper, to taste

Cayenne pepper, to taste (optional)

In a large nonstick skillet, heat the oil over medium heat. Add the onion and cook, stirring, until softened, about 3 minutes. Add the garlic and cook, stirring constantly, 1 minute. Add the zucchini and cook, stirring, until just softened, about 2 minutes.

Add the tomatoes, corn, broth, tomato paste, oregano, sugar (if using), cumin, salt, black pepper, and cayenne (if using); bring to a simmer over medium-high heat, stirring often. Reduce the heat to medium-low and simmer, uncovered, until vegetables are tender and a sauce has formed, about 15 minutes, stirring occasionally. Serve warm.

Per serving: Calories 143 | Protein 7g | Total Fat 4g | Sat. Fat 1g | Cholesterol 0mg | Carbohydrate 25g | Dietary Fiber 6g | Sodium 363mg

Cook's Tip: *To peel the tomatoes, bring a medium stockpot filled with water to a boil over high heat; drop in the tomatoes and boil 20 seconds. Drain and rinse under cold-running water. Peel off the skins.*

Desserts

Almost everyone indulges their sweet tooth now and then, whether after dinner, at mid-morning snack, afternoon tea, or special occasions—not to mention when the midnight munchies strike. Whatever the excuse for splurging, here you will find shortcuts to classic favorites and many other delightful treats that will satisfy your cravings in less the usual time. Fruit cobblers, compotes, cookies, pies, strudel, turnovers—they are all here. Take your pick and enjoy!

Apple-Almond Caramel Bake

 Makes 8 servings

This is an awesome apple dessert you can pre-pare with dark brown sugar for an even richer caramel flavor. Pecans or walnuts can replace the almonds, if desired.

- ¾ cup all-purpose flour
- ½ cup granulated sugar
- 1 teaspoon baking powder
- 1 teaspoon ground cinnamon
- ¼ teaspoon salt
- 2 medium Golden Delicious apples (about 6 ounces each), peeled and coarsely chopped
- ½ cup slivered almonds
- ¾ cup plus ½ cup water
- ¾ cup packed light brown sugar
- ¼ cup canola oil

Preheat the oven to 375F (190C). Lightly grease an 8-inch-square glass baking dish and set aside.

In a large bowl, whisk together the flour, granulated sugar, baking powder, cinnamon, and salt. Add the apples and almonds and mix well to combine. Set aside.

In a small saucepan, bring the ¾ cup water to a boil. Remove from heat and quickly add the brown sugar and canola oil, stirring until well blended. Set briefly aside.

Add the remaining ½ cup water to the flour-apple mixture, stirring well to combine. Transfer the flour-apple batter to the prepared baking dish. Pour the brown sugar topping over the batter and bake 30 to 35 minutes, until golden and bubbly. Let cool about 20 minutes before serving. Serve warm or at room temperature.

Per serving: Calories 290 | Protein 3g | Total Fat 11g | Sat. Fat 1g | Cholesterol 0mg | Carbohydrate 48g | Dietary Fiber 2g | Sodium 123mg

Glazed Apple Tart

Makes 8 servings

Frozen puff pastry (the leading commercial brand is dairy-free) makes quick work of this luscious tart. Apricot jam can replace the apple jelly, if desired.

- ½ (about 17-ounce) package (1 sheet) frozen puff pastry, thawed according to package directions
- 2 tablespoons light or dark brown sugar
- 1 pound Golden Delicious apples (about 3 medium), cored and very thinly sliced
- ¼ cup apple jelly

Preheat oven to 425F (220C). Lightly grease an 8½- or 9-inch pie plate.

Unfold the pastry and press, free-form style, into the prepared pie plate, trimming off the corners, if desired. Prick pastry thoroughly with a fork along the bottom and sides. Bake on the center oven rack 7 minutes. Remove from oven and reduce temperature to 375F (190C).

Sprinkle the bottom of the pastry with 1 tablespoon sugar. Working from the outer edge, arrange the apples over the pastry in concentric circles. Sprinkle with the remaining sugar. Return to the oven and bake 15 to 20 minutes, until the apples are tender and the crust is golden (if edges are browning too quickly, cover the edges with foil or transfer tart to lower third of oven).

Meanwhile, in a small saucepan, heat the apple jelly over low heat until smooth and melted, stirring often. When the tart is finished baking, brush the melted jelly over the apples. Let tart cool until the jelly has set, about 30 minutes. Serve slightly warm or at room temperature. Completely cooled tart can be stored, covered, in the refrigerator up to 2 days; serve chilled or return to room temperature.

Per serving: Calories 213 | Protein 3g | Total Fat 8g | Sat. Fat 2g | Cholesterol 0mg | Carbohydrate 34g | Dietary Fiber 3g | Sodium 107mg

Blueberry-Peach Cobbler

Makes 8 servings

Made entirely from packaged frozen fruit, this outstanding cobbler can be enjoyed any time of the year. Feel free to use fresh blueberries and/or fresh peaches when in season.

- 1 (16-ounce) package frozen sliced peaches, thawed
- 2 cups frozen blueberries, preferably wild, thawed
- ⅓ cup granulated sugar
- 2 tablespoons fresh lemon juice
- 1 tablespoon cornstarch
- ⅔ cup all-purpose flour
- ½ cup old-fashioned rolled oats (not instant)
- 1½ teaspoons ground cinnamon
- ½ teaspoon salt
- ¾ cup packed light brown sugar
- 5 tablespoons vegetable shortening, cut into small pieces

Preheat oven to 375F (190C). Lightly grease an 11 × 7-inch baking dish and set aside.

In a large bowl, mix together the peaches, blueberries, granulated sugar, lemon juice, and cornstarch until well combined.

In a small bowl, stir together the flour, oats, cinnamon, and salt. Add the brown sugar, mixing well to combine. Add the shortening and, using your fingers, mix until mixture resembles coarse crumbs.

Spread the peach-blueberry mixture into the prepared baking dish. Sprinkle evenly with the flour-shortening mixture. Cover with foil and bake 30 minutes. Remove foil and bake 10 to 15 minutes longer, until golden brown and bubbly. Let cool 10 minutes before serving warm or at room temperature. Alternatively, completely cooled mixture can be stored, covered, in the refrigerator up to 2 days before serving cold or reheating in a low-temperature oven.

Per serving: Calories 317 | Protein 2g | Total Fat 9g | Sat. Fat 2g | Cholesterol 0mg | Carbohydrate 60g | Dietary Fiber 3g | Sodium 146mg

Mini Apple Turnovers

Makes 14 mini turnovers

These delicious little parcels are best enjoyed warm with a cup of coffee or tea.

- 1 (15-ounce) package lard-free frozen pie crusts
- 1 cup prepared apple pie filling, chopped
- Cinnamon sugar (optional)

Preheat oven to 400F (205C).

Carefully remove each frozen crust from foil dish and let stand at room temperature about 15 minutes to soften. Using your fingers, gently press out fold lines. Cut 7 (3½-inch) circles from each pie crust. Place about 1 scant tablespoon of the pie filling in the center of each circle (do not overfill). Fold circle in half over filling. Press edges with a fork or your finger to seal. Place on an ungreased baking sheet. Bake in the center of the oven 17 to 20 minutes, until lightly golden. Sprinkle with the cinnamon sugar (if using) and serve warm. Completely cooled turnovers can be stored, covered, in the refrigerator up to 3 days, or frozen up to 1 month; reheat in a low-temperature conventional oven.

Per turnover: Calories 112 | Protein 1g | Total Fat 6g | Sat. Fat 2g | Cholesterol 0mg | Carbohydrate 14g | Dietary Fiber 0g | Sodium 125mg

Apricot Baked Apples

Makes 4 servings

This homey, old-fashioned dessert is as healthful as it is delicious. Pineapple preserves can replace the apricot variety, if desired.

- 6 tablespoons apricot preserves
- 2 tablespoons raisins
- ½ teaspoon ground cinnamon
- ⅛ teaspoon ground ginger
- 4 medium tart baking apples (about 6 ounces each), preferably Granny Smith, unpeeled, cored with bases intact
- ½ cup water

Preheat oven to 375F (190C).

In a small bowl, mix together the preserves, raisins, cinnamon, and ginger until thoroughly combined. Fill the center of each apple with equal amounts of the apricot mixture. Transfer the apples to a baking dish just large enough to accommodate them in a single layer. Add the water along the sides of the dish and cover loosely with foil. Bake for 30 minutes. Uncover and baste the apples with the baking juices. Bake, uncovered, 10 to 15 minutes more, until fork tender. Serve warm, with the accumulated baking juices spooned over top.

Per serving: Calories 164 | Protein 1g | Total Fat 0g | Sat. Fat 0g | Cholesterol 0mg | Carbohydrate 43g | Dietary Fiber 4g | Sodium 16mg

Apple-Cranberry Compote

Makes 6 servings

Here is a fat-free fall or winter dessert that can be prepared up to two days in advance and enjoyed warm, cold, or at room temperature.

- 4 medium Granny Smith or other tart apples (about 6 ounces each), cored and coarsely chopped
- 1 (16-ounce) can whole cranberry sauce
- ¼ cup water
- 2 tablespoons light brown sugar
- 2 tablespoons fresh lemon juice
- 1 teaspoon ground ginger
- 1 teaspoon chopped dried orange peel
- ¼ teaspoon salt

In a large saucepan or medium stockpot, combine all ingredients and bring to a brisk simmer over medium heat, stirring often. Reduce the heat, cover, and simmer gently, stirring occasionally, until the apples are tender, about 15 minutes. Serve warm or at room temperature. Alternatively, completely cooled compote can be refrigerated, covered, up to 2 days and served chilled, returned to room temperature, or reheated over low heat.

Per serving: Calories 185 | Protein 1g | Total Fat 0g | Sat. Fat 0g | Cholesterol 0mg | Carbohydrate 48g | Dietary Fiber 3g | Sodium 115mg

Apple-Pumpkin Gratin

Makes 6 servings

The wonderful tastes and aromas of apple and pumpkin pie are all present in this delicious gluten-free dessert, perfect for easy entertaining during the fall and winter holidays.

- 1 cup canned pumpkin
- ¼ cup granulated sugar
- ¼ cup water
- 1 teaspoon pumpkin pie spice
- 1 pound Golden Delicious apples (about 3 medium), very thinly sliced, or coarsely chopped
- 2 tablespoons light or dark brown sugar

Preheat oven to 375F (190C). Lightly grease an 8½- or 9-inch glass or ceramic pie dish.

In a small bowl, mix together the pumpkin, granulated sugar, water, and pumpkin pie spice until thoroughly blended. If using sliced apples, work from the outer edge and arrange the apples in concentric circles in the prepared dish. If using chopped apples, spread in the prepared dish. Spread apples evenly with the pumpkin mixture. Sprinkle evenly with the brown sugar. Bake about 30 minutes, until lightly browned and bubbly. Serve warm.

Per serving: Calories 99 | Protein 1g | Total Fat 0g | Sat. Fat 0g | Cholesterol 0mg | Carbohydrate 25g | Dietary Fiber 3g | Sodium 6mg

Tahitian Bananas

 Makes 4 servings

Enjoy this simple banana sensation any time of the year. If desired, omit the rum extract and add 1 tablespoon of rum to the orange juice mixture before bringing to a simmer.

- ¾ cup orange juice
- ¼ cup frozen pineapple juice concentrate
- 1 tablespoon canola oil
- ½ teaspoon ground ginger
- ¼ teaspoon ground cinnamon
- ⅛ teaspoon ground nutmeg
- 2 teaspoons rum extract
- 4 ripe yet firm bananas, halved crosswise, then halved lengthwise
- Juice of 1 lime (about 2 tablespoons)
- 2 tablespoons light brown sugar

Preheat oven to 450F (230C). Lightly grease an 11 × 7-inch baking dish and set aside.

In a small saucepan, combine the orange juice, pineapple juice concentrate, oil, ginger, cinnamon, and nutmeg; bring to a boil over high heat. Reduce the heat to medium and simmer 1 minute. Remove

from heat and stir in the rum extract. Set aside to cool slightly.

Place the bananas, cut sides down, in the prepared baking dish. Brush with the lime juice. Pour the orange juice mixture over the bananas. Bake, uncovered, about 10 minutes, until bananas are just tender, basting a few times. Sprinkle evenly with the brown sugar and bake an additional 3 minutes, until sugar is melted. Serve at once.

Per serving: Calories 220 | Protein 2g | Total Fat 4g | Sat. Fat 1g | Cholesterol 0mg | Carbohydrate 47g | Dietary Fiber 3g | Sodium 5mg

Mixed Berries à la Orange

 Makes 4 to 6 servings

This is the ideal summertime dessert— light, lovely, and refreshing.

- ¼ cup orange juice, preferably freshly squeezed
- 1 tablespoon orange marmalade, at room temperature
- 1 tablespoon sugar
- 1 tablespoon Grand Marnier or other orange liqueur (optional)
- 2 pints (4 cups) fresh quartered strawberries, whole raspberries, whole blueberries, and/or whole blackberries
- 1 (11-ounce) can mandarin orange segments, drained

In a large bowl, combine the orange juice, marmalade, sugar, and liqueur (if using), stirring until the marmalade is dissolved. Add the remaining ingredients, tossing gently yet thoroughly to combine. Serve at once, or cover and refrigerate a minimum of 1 to 24 hours, and serve chilled.

Per serving: Calories 102 | Protein 2g | Total Fat 1g | Sat. Fat 0g | Cholesterol 0mg | Carbohydrate 25g | Dietary Fiber 4g | Sodium 8mg

Blackberry Crisp

 Makes 8 servings

Raspberries, strawberries, or blueberries can re-place all or part of the blackberries, if desired.

    2 pints (4 cups) fresh blackberries or frozen
        blackberries, thawed and drained
    ¼ cup granulated white sugar
    2 teaspoons cornstarch
    ¾ cup quick-cooking or old-fashioned rolled
        oats
    ½ cup all-purpose flour
    ½ cup packed light brown sugar
    ¼ cup slivered almonds
    2 tablespoons sunflower seeds
    1 teaspoon ground cinnamon
    ⅓ cup canola oil

Preheat the oven to 400F (205C). Lightly grease an 8-inch-square baking dish and set aside.

In a medium bowl, gently toss the blackberries, granulated sugar, and cornstarch until combined. Transfer to the prepared baking dish.

In another medium bowl, mix together the oats, flour, brown sugar, almonds, sunflower seeds, and cinnamon until well combined. Add the oil, stirring well to combine. Spoon evenly over the blackberry mixture. Bake on the center oven rack about 25 min-utes, until lightly browned and bubbly (if top is browning too quickly, cover loosely with foil or transfer to lower third of oven). Let cool about 15 minutes before serving warm or at room tempera-ture. Alternatively, cover and refrigerate completely cooled crisp up to 2 days and serve chilled, or reheat in a low-temperature oven.

Per serving: Calories 288 | Protein 4g | Total Fat 13g | Sat. Fat 1g | Cholesterol 0mg | Carbohydrate 42g | Dietary Fiber 5g | Sodium 6mg

Blueberry-Oatmeal Bars

 Makes about 2 dozen bars

Other fruit preserves or jams, such as raspberry, strawberry, pineapple, or apricot, can replace the blueberry variety, if desired.

    1 cup all-purpose flour
    ¼ teaspoon baking soda
    1 cup quick-cooking rolled oats
    ⅔ cup packed light brown sugar
    ½ cup vegetable shortening
    1 (10-ounce) jar blueberry preserves

Preheat oven to 350F (175C).

In a large bowl, whisk together the flour and bak-ing soda until thoroughly combined. Add the oats and sugar, stirring well to combine. Add the short-ening and, using your fingers, mix until mixture re-sembles coarse crumbs. Reserve ½ cup of the flour mixture.

Press the remaining flour mixture into an un-greased 11 × 7-inch baking dish. Spread evenly with the blueberry preserves. Sprinkle evenly with the reserved flour mixture. Bake on the center oven rack about 30 minutes, until top is lightly browned. Transfer to a wire rack and cool completely before cutting into about 24 bars.

Completely cooled bars can be stored at room temperature in an airtight container up to 3 days, refrigerated up to 1 week, or placed in a freezer bag and frozen up to 1 month. For best results, return to room temperature before serving.

Per bar: Calories 121 | Protein 1g | Total Fat 5g | Sat. Fat 1g | Cholesterol 0mg | Carbohydrate 20g | Dietary Fiber 1g | Sodium 20mg

Cherry-Berry Crisp

Makes 8 servings

You can make this incredibly quick and delicious dessert with just about any pie filling or berry.

- 2/3 cup packed light brown sugar
- 1/2 cup all-purpose flour
- 1/2 cup quick-cooking or old-fashioned rolled oats
- 2 tablespoons wheat germ (optional)
- 3/4 teaspoon ground cinnamon
- 1/4 teaspoon ground nutmeg
- 1/3 cup canola oil
- 1 (21-ounce) can cherry pie filling
- 1 pint (2 cups) fresh blueberries or frozen blueberries, thawed and drained

Preheat oven to 375F (190C). Lightly grease an 8-inch-square baking dish and set aside.

In a medium bowl, mix together the sugar, flour, oats, wheat germ (if using), cinnamon, and nutmeg. Add the oil, stirring with a fork to combine. Pour the pie filling into the prepared baking dish. Top with the blueberries, pressing down gently with the back of a spoon to immerse in the filling. Top evenly with the sugar-flour mixture.

Bake 20 to 25 minutes, until topping is lightly browned. Let cool 15 minutes before serving. Serve warm or at room temperature. Alternatively, cover and refrigerate completely cooled crisp up to 2 days and serve chilled, or reheat in a low-temperature oven.

Per serving: Calories 304 | Protein 2g | Total Fat 10g | Sat. Fat 1g | Cholesterol 0mg | Carbohydrate 54g | Dietary Fiber 2g | Sodium 16mg

Coconut Sorbet with Peanut Butter–Chocolate Sauce

Makes 6 servings

For a special presentation, serve this scrumptious dessert in Tortilla Sorbet Cups (page 147). The peanut butter–chocolate sauce also makes a delicious dip or fondue for fresh or dried fruit—in this instance, use less water for a thicker consistency.

- 1/2 cup chocolate syrup
- 1/4 cup smooth or chunky peanut butter, at room temperature
- 2 tablespoons water, or more, if necessary
- 3 cups coconut or chocolate sorbet
- Chopped peanuts, for garnish (optional)

In a small bowl or pouring container, stir together the syrup, peanut butter, and water until smooth, adding additional water as necessary to achieve a pourable consistency.

Divide the sorbet evenly among 6 serving bowls and top with equal amounts of sauce. Serve at once, garnished with the peanuts (if using).

Per serving: Calories 244 | Protein 6g | Total Fat 12g | Sat. Fat 6g | Cholesterol 0mg | Carbohydrate 33g | Dietary Fiber 1g | Sodium 123mg

Variation: *To make Chocolate-Almond Sauce, replace the peanut butter with almond butter and stir in 1/4 teaspoon pure almond extract, if desired.*

Mixed Fruit Salad with Maple Dressing

 Makes 4 to 6 servings

While you can peel the apples, if desired, the skins of the Red Delicious variety are not only a pretty contrast to the other fruits, but provide added fiber and important nutrients. Use this recipe as a model and substitute with other combinations of your favorite fruits.

¼ cup apple juice

¼ cup pure maple syrup

1 tablespoon fresh lemon juice

¼ cup raisins or Zante currants

2 medium Red Delicious apples (about 6 ounces each), cored and cubed

1 large ripe yet firm banana, thinly sliced

1 cup fresh blueberries

1 cup cubed fresh pineapple

1 cup cubed fresh cantaloupe or honeydew

In a large bowl, stir together the apple juice, maple syrup, and lemon juice. Add the raisins and let stand a few minutes to soften. Add the remaining ingredients and toss gently yet thoroughly to combine. Serve at once, or cover and refrigerate 1 hour or overnight and serve chilled.

Per serving: Calories 215 | Protein 2g | Total Fat 1g | Sat. Fat 0g | Cholesterol 0mg | Carbohydrate 55g | Dietary Fiber 5g | Sodium 10mg

Swedish Fruit Soup

 Makes 4 to 6 servings

Enjoy this virtually fat-free Swedish dessert prepared with any of your favorite dried fruit. Dried cranberries can replace half the raisins, if desired.

2 cups water

¾ cup mixed dried fruit, such as pitted dried prunes, apricots, dates, apples

¼ cup raisins

1 cinnamon stick

1 cup unsweetened pineapple juice

1 tablespoon quick-cooking tapioca

¼ cup currant or apple jelly

2 tablespoons light brown sugar

1 medium naval orange, peeled, thinly sliced, and quartered

In a medium saucepan, combine the water, mixed dried fruit, raisins, and cinnamon stick; bring to a boil over medium-high heat. Reduce the heat to low, cover, and simmer 10 minutes, stirring a few times.

Meanwhile, in a small bowl, combine the pineapple juice and tapioca; let stand 5 minutes. Stir into the cooked fruit mixture along with the currant jelly and brown sugar. Bring to a boil over medium-high heat. Reduce the heat to low, cover, and simmer 5 minutes, stirring occasionally. Remove cinnamon stick and gently stir in the orange segments. Serve warm or at room temperature. Alternatively, cover completely cooled mixture and refrigerate a minimum of 3 hours or up to 1 day, and serve chilled.

Per serving: Calories 220 | Protein 2g | Total Fat 0g | Sat. Fat 0g | Cholesterol 0mg | Carbohydrate 57g | Dietary Fiber 5g | Sodium 16mg

Mango Gratin with Brown Sugar and Lime

 Makes 4 servings

Here is a sweet ending to any spicy meal. Peeled and cubed fresh mango or papaya can be used interchangeably in the recipe.

1 (16-ounce) bag frozen cubed mango, thawed

1 tablespoon granulated sugar

2 tablespoons light brown sugar

Juice of 1 lime (about 2 tablespoons)

Preheat the oven to broil. Position rack in the upper third of the oven. Lightly oil an 8½- or 9-inch gratin or pie dish and set aside.

In a small bowl, toss the mango and granulated sugar until well combined. Transfer mango to the prepared dish. Sprinkle evenly with the brown sugar. Broil until lightly browned and caramelized in spots, 8 to 10 minutes, rotating the dish as necessary. Remove from the oven and drizzle evenly with the lime juice. Serve at once.

Per serving: Calories 91 | Protein 0g | Total Fat 0g | Sat. Fat 0g | Cholesterol 0mg | Carbohydrate 24g | Dietary Fiber 1g | Sodium 4mg

Baked Peaches with Pecans and Maple Syrup

Makes 4 servings

You can make this delicious dessert out of season using well-drained canned halved peaches, but decrease the baking time by about 5 minutes.

4 medium-size ripe peaches, peeled, sliced in half, pits removed (see Cook's Tip, below)

¼ cup pure maple syrup

¼ teaspoon ground ginger

¼ cup chopped pecans or walnuts

Preheat oven to 400F (205C). Lightly grease a shallow casserole large enough to hold the peach halves comfortably in a single layer and set aside.

In a small bowl, stir together the maple syrup and ginger until thoroughly blended. Add the pecans, stirring well to combine. Place the peach halves, cut sides up, in the prepared baking dish. Fill each peach half with about 1 tablespoon of the pecan mixture. Bake about 15 minutes, until peaches are tender. Serve warm or at room temperature.

Per serving: Calories 134 | Protein 1g | Total Fat 5g | Sat. Fat 0g | Cholesterol 0mg | Carbohydrate 24g | Dietary Fiber 2g | Sodium 2mg

Cook's Tip: *To peel the peaches, bring a medium stockpot filled with water to a boil over high heat; drop in the peaches and boil for 20 seconds. Drain and rinse under cold running water. Peel off the skins.*

Pineapple-Banana Fruit Cups with Coconut

Makes 4 servings

This ultra-simple, no-cook dessert is a refreshing conclusion to a warm-weather meal.

2 cups fresh pineapple chunks

2 large ripe yet firm bananas, peeled and sliced into ½-inch-thick rounds

¼ cup sweetened flaked coconut

Juice of 1 fresh lemon (see Cook's Tip, below)

In a medium bowl, toss all ingredients gently yet thoroughly to combine. Let stand about 10 minutes to allow the flavors to blend; toss gently again. Transfer to small dessert cups or bowls and serve at once.

Per serving: Calories 117 | Protein 1g | Total Fat 2g | Sat. Fat 1g | Cholesterol 0mg | Carbohydrate 27g | Dietary Fiber 3g | Sodium 14mg

Cook's Tip: *The juice of one medium-size lemon equals about 3 tablespoons.*

Pecan-Date Pie

 Makes 12 servings

This is the ultimate easy-bake holiday pie. Walnuts, almonds, hazelnuts, or macadamia nuts can replace half of the pecans, if desired.

1 (9-inch) deep-dish lard-free frozen piecrust, thawed 15 minutes

8 ounces (about 1¼ cups) finely chopped pitted dates

6 ounces (about 1½ cups) pecan halves or pieces

3 tablespoons pure maple syrup

3 tablespoons light corn syrup

1 tablespoon Grand Marnier or other orange-flavored liqueur (optional)

½ teaspoon pure vanilla extract

Preheat oven to 350F (175C).

Prick the bottom and sides of the pie crust with a fork and bake in the center of the oven about 10 minutes, until very lightly browned. Set aside to cool about 10 minutes.

In a large bowl, toss together the remaining ingredients until well combined. Transfer to the prebaked piecrust, pressing down on filling with the back of a spoon to evenly pack. Bake in the center of the oven about 25 to 30 minutes, until filling is lightly browned and crust is golden (if edges are browning too quickly, cover the edges with foil or transfer the pie to the lower third of the oven). Let cool about 10 minutes before serving warm or at room temperature. Completely cooled pie can be stored at room temperature in an airtight container up to 2 days, or refrigerated up to 5 days before returning to room temperature, or reheating in a low-temperature oven.

Per serving: Calories 354 | Protein 4g | Total Fat 21g | Sat. Fat 3g | Cholesterol 0mg | Carbohydrate 44g | Dietary Fiber 4g | Sodium 153mg

Pumpkin Strudel

 Makes 6 to 8 servings

This scrumptious pumpkin strudel is a holiday dessert to dream about.

1 tablespoon granulated sugar

½ teaspoon ground cinnamon

¾ cup canned pumpkin

¼ cup packed light brown sugar

⅛ teaspoon ground ginger

⅛ teaspoon ground nutmeg

½ (about 17-ounce) package (1 sheet) frozen puff pastry, thawed according to package directions

¼ cup chopped pecans or walnut pieces (optional)

Preheat oven to 375 F (190C).

In a small container, mix together the granulated sugar with ¼ teaspoon cinnamon; set aside. In a medium bowl, mix together the pumpkin, brown sugar, remaining ¼ teaspoon cinnamon, ginger, and nutmeg until thoroughly combined; set aside.

Unfold the pastry onto an ungreased baking sheet. Line the middle third of the pastry with half of the pumpkin mixture. Sprinkle with half the nuts (if using). Fold the third of the pastry to your left over the filling; line with remaining pumpkin mixture. Sprinkle with remaining nuts (if using.) Fold the third of the pastry to your right as far over to the other side as it will comfortably stretch, pressing the dough together where it meets to seal. (Do not seal the ends.) Cut about 6 (1-inch long) slits across the top. Sprinkle evenly with half the reserved cinnamon-sugar mixture.

Bake in the center of the oven about 25 minutes, until golden. Remove from oven and sprinkle with the remaining cinnamon-sugar mixture. Cool on baking sheet on a wire rack 20 minutes. Cut into 6 or 8 slices and serve warm or at room temperature. Completely cooled strudel can be stored, covered, in refrigerator up to 1 day. For best flavor, reheat in a low-temperature oven and serve slightly warm.

Per serving: Calories 254 | Protein 3g | Total Fat 11g | Sat. Fat 3g | Cholesterol 0mg | Carbohydrate 37g | Dietary Fiber 4g | Sodium 140mg

Peanut Butter–Coconut Granola Balls

Makes 20 balls

Some leading commercial brands of granola contain either dairy and/or honey, so check the label carefully. In a pinch, Grape-Nuts cereal can be substituted; however, the peanut butter balls will taste slightly less sweet.

½ cup granola

½ cup sweetened shredded coconut

¼ cup sunflower seeds

¼ cup raisins

2 tablespoons light or dark brown sugar

¾ cup creamy peanut butter

2 tablespoons wheat germ, or more, if necessary

In a small bowl, mix together the granola, ¼ cup of the coconut, sunflower seeds, raisins, and sugar.

Gradually stir in the peanut butter until thoroughly incorporated. Cover and refrigerate a minimum of 3 hours, or overnight.

Place the wheat germ in a small bowl. Form the chilled peanut butter mixture into 20 balls (about 1½ tablespoons each). Roll each ball lightly in the wheat germ to coat, using additional wheat germ, if needed. Serve chilled, garnished with the remaining coconut. (At this point, peanut butter balls can be stored, covered, in the refrigerator up to 5 days.)

Per ball: Calories 104 | Protein 4g | Total Fat 7g | Sat. Fat 2g | Cholesterol 0mg | Carbohydrate 8g | Dietary Fiber 1g | Sodium 52mg

Cranberry-Poached Pears

Makes 6 servings

For a festive holiday touch, garnish with dried cranberries and a fresh mint sprig.

4 large ripe yet firm Bosc pears, peeled, quartered, and cored

2 cups cranberry juice

1 cup water

2 tablespoons sugar

½ teaspoon dried chopped orange peel

½ teaspoon ground cinnamon

6 whole cloves

In a large saucepan or medium stockpot, bring all the ingredients to a brisk simmer over medium-high heat. Reduce the heat to between low and medium-low and simmer, covered, until the pears are tender, about 15 minutes, stirring and turning the pears occasionally. With a slotted spoon, transfer the pears to a serving platter or individual serving bowls.

Bring the poaching liquid to a boil over high heat; boil until reduced to about 1 cup, about 7 minutes. Strain the syrup evenly over the pears and serve warm or at room temperature. Alternatively, cover and refrigerate completely cooled pears up to 2 days and serve chilled, or return to room temperature.

Per serving: Calories 142 | Protein 1g | Total Fat 2g | Sat. Fat 0g | Cholesterol 0mg | Carbohydrate 35g | Dietary Fiber 5g | Sodium 18mg

Strawberry Cobbler

 Makes 6 to 8 servings

Serve this delicious dessert in bowls with spoons to capture all the scrumptious strawberry sauce.

- 6 cups fresh strawberries, stemmed, left whole if medium-size, halved if large
- ¾ cup (12 tablespoons) granulated sugar
- ½ cup plus 2 tablespoons all-purpose flour
- 1 tablespoon fresh lemon juice
- ⅛ teaspoon baking powder
- ⅛ teaspoon baking soda
- ⅛ teaspoon salt
- 3½ tablespoons vegetable shortening
- ⅓ cup water

Preheat oven to 375F (190C). Lightly grease an 11 × 7-inch pan and set aside.

In a medium bowl, toss together the strawberries, ½ cup plus 2 tablespoons of the sugar, 2 tablespoons of the flour, and the lemon juice. Transfer to the prepared baking dish.

In another medium bowl, whisk together the remaining ½ cup flour, the remaining 2 tablespoons sugar, baking powder, baking soda, and salt. Add the shortening, mixing well with a fork or your fingers until mixture is coarse and crumbly. Add the water and stir well to combine (mixture will be lumpy). Spread evenly over the strawberry mixture (some exposed fruit is okay). Bake on the center oven rack 20 to 30 minutes, until lightly browned and bubbly. Let stand about 10 minutes before serving warm or at room temperature. Alternatively, store completely cooled cobbler, covered, in the refrigerator up to 2 days before serving chilled or reheating in a low-temperature oven.

Per serving: Calories 257 | Protein 2g | Total Fat 8g | Sat. Fat 3g | Cholesterol 0mg | Carbohydrate 46g | Dietary Fiber 4g | Sodium 80mg

Raspberry Pinwheels

 Makes 20 pinwheels

While any cake and pastry fruit filling can replace the raspberry variety, do not use standard pie filling, as it is too bulky for the recipe. In a pinch, substitute with fruit jam.

- ½ (about 17-ounce) package (1 sheet) frozen puff pastry, thawed according to package directions
- ½ (10-ounce) can raspberry cake and pastry filling

Preheat oven to 400F (205C). Line a large baking sheet with parchment or waxed paper and set aside.

On a flat surface, unfold pastry sheet and spread evenly with the filling. Starting at short side closest to you, roll up like a jelly roll. Cut crosswise into 20 (½-inch-thick) slices. Transfer, cut sides down, to prepared baking sheet, spacing about 1 inch apart. Bake on the center oven rack 15 minutes, until puffed and golden.

Transfer pinwheels on the parchment paper to a wire rack to cool about 10 minutes, before serving warm or at room temperature. Completely cooled pinwheels can be stored in an airtight container at room temperature up to 1 day before using. Alternatively, pinwheels can be stored, covered, in refrigerator up to 3 days before returning to room temperature or reheating in a low-temperature oven.

Per pinwheel: Calories 77 | Protein 1g | Total Fat 3g | Sat. Fat 1g | Cholesterol 0mg | Carbohydrate 12g | Dietary Fiber 1g | Sodium 43mg

Crispy Peanut Butter Bars

 Makes 24 bars

These tasty, no-bake treats are easiest to cut with a pizza cutter, although any good sharp knife will do.

- ½ cup white sugar
- ½ cup packed light brown sugar
- ½ cup light corn syrup, preferably vanilla flavored
- ½ cup pure maple syrup
- 1 cup peanut butter, smooth or crunchy
- 6 cups crisp rice cereal

Lightly grease a 13 × 9-inch baking dish and set aside.

In a medium stockpot, bring the sugars and the syrups to a boil over high heat. Remove from heat and add the peanut butter, stirring well to thoroughly combine. Add the cereal, mixing to thoroughly coat. Transfer to the prepared baking dish, pressing down with a spatula. Transfer to a rack and let cool about 30 minutes before cutting into squares and serving at room temperature.

Completely cooled bars can be stored in an airtight container at room temperature up to 1 week, or stored in the refrigerator up to 2 weeks. For best results, return to room temperature before serving.

Per bar: Calories 161 | Protein 3g | Total Fat 5g | Sat. Fat 1g | Cholesterol 0mg | Carbohydrate 27g | Dietary Fiber 1g | Sodium 144mg

Variation: *To make Crispy Chocolate–Peanut Butter Bars, use chocolate crisp rice cereal in lieu of the plain variety.*

Tortilla Sorbet Cups

 Makes 6 servings

Use this recipe as a model and experiment with different sorbets and toppings. The leading brands of both strawberry and chocolate syrups are dairy-free.

- 6 (6-inch) fajita-size flour tortillas, at room temperature or slightly warmed to soften, if necessary
- 1 tablespoon canola oil
- 2 tablespoons sugar mixed with ½ teaspoon ground cinnamon
- 1 pint (2 cups) strawberry sorbet
- 6 tablespoons strawberry or chocolate syrup

Preheat oven to 375F (190C).

Make 4 evenly spaced 1½-inch cuts or tears from the rim toward the center of each tortilla. Brush tortillas evenly on both sides with the oil and sprinkle evenly on the top sides with the sugar-cinnamon mixture (about 1 teaspoon per tortilla). Gently push the tortillas into the wells of an ungreased 6-cup muffin pan, overlapping the cut edges to form cup shapes. Bake on the center oven rack about 10 minutes, until golden brown. Remove each tortilla cup from the muffin pan and transfer to a wire rack to cool completely. (At this point, tortilla cups can be stored in an airtight container up to 2 days before continuing with the recipe.)

To serve, place ⅓ cup of the sorbet in each tortilla cup and place in a small dessert bowl or custard cup (to prevent wobbling). Drizzle with 1 tablespoon of the strawberry syrup. Serve at once.

Per serving: Calories 227 | Protein 2g | Total Fat 4g | Sat. Fat 0g | Cholesterol 0mg | Carbohydrate 45g | Dietary Fiber 1g | Sodium 119mg

Raspberry Pinwheels with Lemon Sorbet

 Makes 5 servings

The pinwheels can be prepared a day ahead before assembling and serving this easy yet elegant dessert. Most commercial sorbets are dairy-free, but check the label carefully.

   2½ cups lemon sorbet
   ½ recipe (10 pieces) Raspberry Pinwheels
      (page 146), at room temperature
   Fresh raspberries, for garnish (optional)

Place ½ cup sorbet in each of 5 dessert bowls or goblets. Arrange 2 raspberry pinwheels attractively in each bowl and garnish with fresh raspberries (if using). Serve at once.

Per serving: Calories 246 | Protein 4g | Total Fat 10g | Sat. Fat 3g | Cholesterol 0mg | Carbohydrate 38g | Dietary Fiber 2g | Sodium 143mg

Metric Conversion Charts

Comparison to Metric Measure

When You Know	Symbol	Multiply By	To Find	Symbol
teaspoons	tsp	5.0	milliliters	ml
tablespoons	tbsp	15.0	milliliters	ml
fluid ounces	fl. oz.	30.0	milliliters	ml
cups	c	0.24	liters	l
pints	pt.	0.47	liters	l
quarts	qt.	0.95	liters	l
ounces	oz.	28.0	grams	g
pounds	lb.	0.45	kilograms	kg
Fahrenheit	F	⁵⁄₉ (after subtracting 32)	Celsius	C

Fahrenheit to Celsius

F	C
200–205	95
220–225	105
245–250	120
275	135
300–305	150
325–330	165
345–350	175
370–375	190
400–405	205
425–430	220
445–450	230
470–475	245
500	260

Liquid Measure to Liters

¼ cup	=	0.06 liters
½ cup	=	0.12 liters
¾ cup	=	0.18 liters
1 cup	=	0.24 liters
1¼ cups	=	0.30 liters
1½ cups	=	0.36 liters
2 cups	=	0.48 liters
2½ cups	=	0.60 liters
3 cups	=	0.72 liters
3½ cups	=	0.84 liters
4 cups	=	0.96 liters
4½ cups	=	1.08 liters
5 cups	=	1.20 liters
5½ cups	=	1.32 liters

Liquid Measure to Milliliters

¼ teaspoon	=	1.25 milliliters
½ teaspoon	=	2.50 milliliters
¾ teaspoon	=	3.75 milliliters
1 teaspoon	=	5.00 milliliters
1¼ teaspoons	=	6.25 milliliters
1½ teaspoons	=	7.50 milliliters
1¾ teaspoons	=	8.75 milliliters
2 teaspoons	=	10.0 milliliters
1 tablespoon	=	15.0 milliliters
2 tablespoons	=	30.0 milliliters

Index

About the Author

Donna Klein specializes in writing vegan cookbooks with a primary emphasis on authentic ingredients and minimal use of meat, dairy, and egg substitutes. She is also the author of *The Mediterranean Vegan Kitchen*, *The PDQ (Pretty Darn Quick) Vegetarian Cookbook*, *Vegan Italiano*, and *The Gluten-Free Vegetarian Kitchen*. Her food articles and recipes have appeared in the *Washington Post*, *The Yoga Journal*, *Body and Soul Magazine*, *Vegetarian Gourmet*, *Veggie Life*, *The Herb Companion*, *VegNews*, and *Victorian Decorating and Life Style*.

Ms. Klein studied at Le Cordon Bleu in Paris, and is a popular vegetarian cooking and food writing instructor in Montgomery County, Maryland, where she lives with her daughter Sarah and adopted dog, Trevor.